Praise fo

"*Just Do It* almost makes the reader feel part of a threesome."
— *New York Times*

"hilarious, romantic book"
— FoxNews.com

"I laughed so hard tears came to my eyes. And when I finished the book, although I haven't smoked in over a decade, I wanted a cigarette. Doug has hit the mark and done it in a way that appeals to both sexes and many generations. The only problem will be putting down the book long enough to 'Just Do It' with the one you love."

— BARTON GOLDSMITH, Ph.D., MFT, author of *Emotional Fitness for Couples*

"For their inspired every-day-for-100-days performance, Doug and Annie Brown have earned a place in the Harried Married Parents' Hall of Fame!"

— STACIE COCKRELL, Cathy O'Neill, and Julia Stone, authors of *Babyproofing Your Marriage*

"If you're one of the millions of couples saying, 'Gee, how come we aren't making love so often anymore,' you *have* to read this book. Many of us have thought of taking this journey, but only Doug and Annie have had the guts to do it and the grace to write about it."

— MIRA KIRSHENBAUM, author of *Too Good to Leave, Too Bad to Stay* and *When Good People Have Affairs*

"*Just Do It* is an exciting and hilarious story about a busy couple taking the time to put the passion back into their marriage. It's a fantastic read—very funny, and a touching story. I hope this inspires everyone to rediscover the intimacy in their relationships, even if they don't go to these extraordinary means!"

> —HARRY FISCH, M.D., coauthor of *Size Matters* and author of *The Male Biological Clock*

"101 straight days of sex between any two people is an impressive feat, but add the elements of encroaching middle age, fourteen years of togetherness, a couple of demanding jobs, and two small and willful children, and that feat becomes something extraordinary. Here, Doug Brown faithfully chronicles the happy consequences of this kind of radical pact, which turn out to be less about reaching sexual heights and more about the power of consistent intimacy to cement all that's good between two people.

> —LAUREN DOCKETT, coauthor of *Facing 30* and *Sex Talk*

JUST *DO IT*

How One Couple Turned Off the TV and

Turned On Their Sex Lives for 101 Days

(No Excuses!)

DOUGLAS BROWN

THREE RIVERS PRESS • NEW YORK

Published in the United States by Three Rivers Press, an imprint of the
Crown Publishing Group, a division of Random House, Inc., New York.
www.crownpublishing.com

THREE RIVERS PRESS and the Tugboat design are registered trademarks of
Random House, Inc.

Originally published in hardcover in the United States by Crown Publishers,
an imprint of the Crown Publishing Group, a division of Random House, Inc.,
in 2008.

Library of Congress Cataloging-in-Publication Data

Brown, Douglas J., 1965–
    Just do it: how one couple turned off the TV and turned on their sex lives for
101 days (no excuses!)/Douglas Brown.—1st ed.

    1. Sex in marriage.   2. Sex.   I. Title.

    HQ734.B8566 2008
    646.7'80973—dc22

                                                                        2008009177

ISBN 978-0-307-40717-7

Printed in the United States of America

Design Lauren Dong

10   9   8   7   6   5   4   3   2   1

First Paperback Edition

To Annie

Contents

JUST *DO IT*

Introduction

ike you, I've enjoyed my share of days I like to think of as "most excellent." The days my daughters were born, for example, are hard to beat. I recall a long spell at the Jersey shore in the early 1980s when the waves kept rolling in, glassy and lovely, and I surfed until it grew dark. There was a dawn-to-midnight rendezvous with my brother, when we hiked in alpine splendor and topped it off with green chile cheeseburgers, beer, and hammocks. And then there was the otherwise forgettable day the year I turned 40 on which my wife Annie said eight words that changed our life together in a most excellent way.

This smashing day began in Florida, where I had just finished a week-long conference dedicated to sex, popular culture, and the media. I am a reporter, and at the time sex—pornography, strippers, sex addiction, you name it—was one of my principal areas of coverage. A flight, which is never something I celebrate, devoured most of the afternoon, but things improved when Annie arrived to pick me up at the Denver airport. Her signature style, which she calls "messy sexy," was in full flower—thick auburn hair pinned loosely to the back of her head, with big strands falling to her shoulders; groovy patterned blouse exposing a hint of cleavage; tight jeans and her favorite Israeli sandals and red lipstick.

Her grin and sparkling eyes said "Welcome home, lovey!" And then I peered in the back of the minivan and there was Joni, nearly 7, and Ginger, approaching 3, their very beings quaking with "Daddy! Daddy! Daddy!"

That night, after we'd put the girls to bed, Annie and I, as usual, slipped into something comfortable: for Annie, threadbare pajamas emblazoned with faded roses; for me, blue sweatpants with five pockets that I'd been wearing for at least fifteen years. (I champion pockets whenever I get a chance; I have announced to Annie no less than 486 times since we began dating, "I love pockets!") Two front pockets held cotton handkerchiefs because I didn't go anywhere without cotton handkerchiefs (thus, perhaps, my obsession with pockets).

I believe I loosed a long "aaaaaah," a sound familiar to people who frequent hot tubs, as I slid my sweatpanted legs beneath the covers, pressed my back into the pillow with squat arms behind me, and prepared for an hour or two of reading before drifting into slumber. Soon, Annie squeezed her cute little body between the sheets too and, like me, propped herself up against a poofy, armed pillow. (These pillows are known as "husbands," for reasons that defy rigorous analysis, unless one concludes that husbands are things into which wives lean—a conviction that, I assure you, will be challenged by many, who will say, "If that's the reasoning, then they should be called 'wives.'")

And so we sat, side by side, cocooned in snug and reading quietly in our little house in a new subdivision on the prairie in Denver. At some point, I started talking about things I remembered about the conference, most of which survived like alien dreams in a relentlessly tropical setting. One solemn detail, however, remained crystalline.

"Get this," I said. "One guy from Denmark talked about how men who are involved in relationships but haven't had sex in a hundred or more days actually bond over their sad predicaments.

They form 'hundred-days clubs,' or something like that. At least that's what I thought he said. I had some trouble with his accent."

"The sexless marriage, it's a big Oprah thing," said Annie. "Two careers, kids, middle age, a bunch of years together. It can complicate the sex life."

Yes, I thought, *it can*.

We'd been together for about fourteen years, married for nearly eleven of them, with kids for almost seven. We both worked. Excellent sex had decorated the first half of our relationship, but the quality and quantity of sex had declined as we approached our mid-30s. Careers and age shifted our end-of-the-day enthusiasms from carnal athletics to pulling sheets to shoulders and whispering "good night." Two pregnancies and infancies had provided us acceptable rationales for begging off sex for longer and longer periods of time. We'd never abstained for one hundred days, but in those sex-challenged zones between the third trimester and infanthood, we'd probably gone six weeks without doing it. Now, more than three years after the birth of our second daughter, we did it about once a week, if we were lucky.

Our union was not suffering. We rarely fought, and we were attracted to similar things: cooking, hiking, playing games. We could talk together for hours without growing bored. Our children, the stars of our lives, drew us close. But I cannot paint over the fissures and rough patches, what the real-estate people call "wear and tear," that had crept into the house of Doug and Annie. Sex, for example, had turned into a mere adequacy, an activity relying on recitation and rote rather than free-form play. The panting excitement that had electrified the early days of our relationship had developed into something else: not a snore or a sigh but maybe a hum, a sound suggesting contentment and harmony. And you know, there's a lot to be said for contentment and harmony, but I think you will agree with me here: Zest, sparkle, and freewheeling passion have their moments, too.

Money, or the lack thereof, long ago had introduced tensions in our marriage, most notably after Annie stopped working during her third trimester with Joni. Between that exit from the working world and the genesis of Annie's hundred-days idea, we moved five times and Annie gave birth to two daughters, four years apart. One modest salary, as a result, was stretched awfully thin between bills, saving for house down payments and our growing family. Only a pittance was left for things like dinner dates and vacations, and it led to most of the sharpest exchanges between Annie and me.

Our latest move, from Baltimore to Denver, also contributed to the wear and tear. I'm close to my extended family, most of which lives in southeastern Pennsylvania. When we lived in Baltimore, we routinely spent time with my parents and my brother, with a sister-in-law and nephews and cousins and uncles and aunts. Annie and I had moved so many times that I thought another move would come easy, but it was not to be. Homesickness plagued me in Denver, and never had I been so curdled with guilt. The move had physically estranged Joni and Ginger from routine contact with my family's warmth and love, an outcome that flooded me with heartache: By accepting the gig in Denver, I'd hurt my kids and I'd hurt my parents. The move upended Annie, too, removing her from a happy nest of friends and the lovely house in Baltimore that we had bought for a pittance. At the same time, though, it brought her back to the West, a region she adored, and shortly after moving to the Mile High City, Annie scored her first real job in seven years. While I talked incessantly about returning to the East, Annie resisted. Here was another crack in our foundation.

Finally, the previous seven years or so had witnessed our turn from carefree-couple-without-kids to something altogether different: parents. Our children, for good reason, commandeered the center of our life together. This was not something to lament, but it was something we should have examined with greater care. Things had changed, some not for the better. A little recognition and attention might have helped.

In short, although the house of Doug and Annie remained sturdy, it needed a little updating, some renovation, a ration of what a certain kind of Realtor might call "pizzazz."

"It's a big problem for a lot of people, I think," said Annie, knitting a purple hat with a green top, a cap meant to look like an eggplant. "A challenge. How do you squeeze in sex?"

I returned to my magazine for a few moments, and then Annie turned toward me, grinning.

"I've got an idea," she said. "Why don't we start our own club, only we'll reverse it? Instead of not having sex for one hundred days"—here come those delicious eight words—"let's have sex for one hundred consecutive days."

I waited a few beats, studying Annie. I could tell she was serious.

What a most excellent day! I thought.

And then: *That's insane.*

1

What Will Help Us Cross the Finish Line?

Needless to say, I love my wife.

We were in our mid-20s when we met, both working in Philadelphia for a publisher of scientific and medical publications. A few months after I'd started toiling there, I stepped into the break room, and there stood Annie. It was her first day on the job. I gasped. She literally—and I mean it—took my breath away; I instantly felt winded, as if I'd just returned from an eight-mile run through Center City. The luxurious hair, the happy eyes, the startlingly mischievous smile, a grin that dazzled me with such force I swooned, a sensation followed immediately by nervousness. I was in the midst of an unsuccessful relationship, and upon encountering Annie I knew instantly I'd drop everything for her, if she'd have me.

Two long years later, both of us were free of relationship entanglements. The decks finally were clear. We lounged around the brick patio of her tiny row house, ate dinner at a place serving true Spanish tapas, and then visited a club for some music but left quickly because of the noise. The night was going well. We wanted to talk, not stare at a stage and listen to exceptionally loud music. When we arrived back at her house, she unveiled an array of cheeses, crackers, grapes, and a bottle of wine. We inhaled the eats, and we talked and talked and talked. And laughed a lot. By the next morning I was dreamily lost, joyfully adrift, blissfully intoxicated.

Fourteen years later, I still was, but the mystery of Annie had evolved into an anchored love, an appreciative understanding of her world. I suspected our erotic lives, however, still contained worlds unknown. We talked endlessly about where to live. We held confab after confab about how to raise our daughters. We routinely engaged in long discussions about our jobs and our dreams. But sex? We did not spend time mutually examining this activity that propelled our union beyond the realm of friendship. The reason, I think it's safe to say, is that although we liked chatting about cooking and food and we relished a good, gossipy gab about, for example, the parents of our girls' schoolmates, we never really "took" to holding forth about our sex lives because we found the subject embarrassing.

But now, after Annie's surprising brainstorm—allow me to revisit: My *wife* suggested we have sex, together, for *one hundred days in a row*—the topic collared more of my attention. Surely, I thought, the pattern of pettings and gropings that defined our bedroom romps had room for variation, contained the potential to be something more profound than an occasional release combined with a dab of relationship glue. Could sex command a more central role in our lives? And if it did, would it color the rest of our relationship? Would doing it for a hundred days change anything?

One Saturday night soon after I returned from the Florida trip we lost ourselves to an especially erotic round of lovemaking, an energetic game of dueling orgasms. "Wow, DJ," said Annie, who has called me DJ—for Douglas Jeffrey—since early in our courtship. "Let's keep doing it like *that*."

I was still gasping, collapsed spread-eagle on the bed. It felt as if my blood had effervesced, as if I'd enjoyed a champagne transfusion.

I considered Annie's suggestion, in light of our intention to launch into a three-month erotic odyssey. *Let's keep doing it like that.* And I thought: *Easier said than done.*

Some sessions, I was certain, would tumble into ecstasy. But others? Session number 46, a Tuesday night after a long day of work and child rearing? Would number 24, or 59, or 86 glide into rapture or just putz along, a sequence of strokes and grunts culminating in something mildly satisfying, like a Hershey's Kiss after lunch?

Was the quest even possible?

Annie, who is exceptionally competitive, led our evening strategy chats. One night, stretched out in a cute nightie while I sat up in bed reading, she tapped my leg with her foot. "DJ," she said in a singsong voice. "Planning session."

Down went the magazine.

"We need to think about fashion," she suggested.

"Clothes?" I said. "I thought we were going to talk about sex."

"Clothes are all about sex!" she said. "Or at least they should be. Let's pledge to dress up for each other more. I'll ditch the baggy-sweatshirt look. I'll wear makeup more regularly."

I thought about my wardrobe, which consisted largely of blue jeans, T-shirts, sweaters, and button-down shirts. What would I change? I couldn't think of anything.

"I'll shave more often?" I offered.

She glanced down at my blue sweatpants with five pockets.

"Seriously?" I whispered.

Annie shrugged. "You could lose 'em," she said, "if only for the marathon."

Or not, I thought. But after a few moments of internal debate, I relented. The tipping point was the realization that if Annie wore them every day, I'd fantasize about burning them in a ceremonial bonfire, complete with chants directed toward some omnipotent fashion god who would beatify me, and consider showering me with rewards, for ridding the planet of such hideousness. In addition, given the nature of the upcoming adventure, their retirement would be a small price to pay.

"Your turn," Annie said. "If we're going to try to have sex for one hundred straight days, what will help us cross the finish line?"

"Stockings," I blurted out. "Sexy stockings. The kind that stop at the thigh."

Annie raised her eyebrows.

"They're hot," I said. "There's a reason women in those stockings are plastered all over men's magazines."

She gave the request a few beats.

"Deal," she said. "Never really thought about them much."

This excited me. Feeling suddenly liberated—like a man who has sworn off booze for years, then decides one sizzling day to down a cold, lime-saturated Corona, and instantaneously with the first sip understands he will order another—I recklessly forged ahead.

"Porno," I offered. "That could be fun."

Annie shot me a look steeped in incredulity and skepticism, a look that said *You must be kidding.*

"From fashion to porno, all in five minutes," she said. "Interesting."

"Honey, they say some porno—not all, by any means—is good for sex lives. You learn new positions and techniques. It helps get you primed for, you know, *doing it.* And if we're doing it day after day after exhausting day, we might need some . . . assistance."

"Assistance?" she said. "This sounds awfully suspicious. Very guy."

"Not every night," I said, thinking strategically. "Probably not every week, even. Just once, for starters. If we think it's lame, we bail."

I was not porno-crazed, but the idea of watching some with

her appealed to me. The sex project, I understood (ingeniously, I might add), offered the perfect rationale for convincing Annie that viewing porno together would be worth a shot. In the context of our sex experiment, we'd do it in the name of chemistry: Just add porno, and see what happens.

"OK," she said.

Score!

"You've got your porno. But now it's my turn. Sex toys."

"Dildos?" I said, my heart pounding. Dildos, I believed, were for people who cheerfully reported they were "swingers," for couples who were "into" genres and subgenres of the blanket category "sexuality": leather, S&M, orgies, and so on. Annie and I, of course, dwelled within the broad category, but we'd never attached ourselves to a genre or subgenre, unless doing it in bed with your spouse falls into a genre or subgenre.

"I've got to research it. But I'm always hearing about how women are using sex toys. There are sex-toy parties. It's on *Oprah*. It's supposed to be healthy. But I'm nearly forty, and I've never even touched one."

I nodded slowly, but my mind was racing.

What kind of Pandora's box have we opened?

Annie studied my face. "I know what you're thinking," she said. "You've got nothing to worry about. Like I said, sex toys are mainstream, but I know nothing about them. For all I know, I'll hate them. But I think I should at least give a toy or two a try."

The idea of sex toys didn't thrill me, although, given my job, I knew about sex-toy parties and understood that they, allegedly, had become mainstream. I did have thigh-high stockings and porno on the horizon, however. It was a fair deal.

"Well," I said. "As long as you don't fall in love with your sex toy, it's cool with me."

"We're making progress here!" she said. "This is fun!"

By the end of the conversation, we'd also decided to read books about sex, to splurge more often on babysitters, to experiment with herbal concoctions that are recommended for libido, to take more baths together, and to massage each other. And when Annie said that "housecleaner" was the sexiest word in the world, I conceded that during the sexathon hiring a professional to scrub and dust might be a good idea. Annie also talked about getting a "Brazilian," a wax treatment that would remove most of her pubic hair. Between the Brazilian, her intention to routinely don lingerie, and the lipstick she decided she would wear during our sessions, I thought things seemed a bit lopsided, as if Annie's contributions to the effort amounted to some sort of erotic hegemony, which I suspected she would be happy to dissolve.

"You're doing a lot," I said. "Doesn't seem exactly fair. You're thinking about having your pubic hair ripped out, and I'm gonna boldly ditch my sweatpants?"

"True," Annie said thoughtfully. "I'm not sure how things can be even, though. You're not going to wear lingerie. You're not getting a Brazilian. No makeup for you."

"I know," I said. "I'll start lifting weights again, in our room. Get my muscles more . . . muscular. Try to introduce a little ripple into the abs."

"There you go," said Annie.

"And I'll try my best to keep running, no matter how beat I am, to spare you the transformation of your husband from middleweight lad to tubby schlub. And I'll spend more time on grooming, including the generous use of products involving scent."

"Great," said Annie. "So we're trying to make ourselves sexy for each other."

NEEDING HELP to have sex might seem desperate, but you must consider our daily routine. A typical weekday for me went something like this: breakfast, driving a child to school, commuting, work, commuting, dinner, cleaning up, reading books and telling stories to Joni and Ginger. Making sure the girls have their stuffed friends and their sippy bottles full of cold water. Shuffling downstairs, shuffling upstairs—sweatpanted and slippered—constantly poised for the next yawn. Capping all of this with a rousing round between the sheets sounded great in theory, but in practice I tended to punctuate the daily march of labor with collapse.

Annie's standard day? On Mondays and Fridays, when Ginger did not attend preschool and stayed home, it was a complex and demanding procession of ministrations and entertainments. Otherwise, it was similar to mine, without the commuting. Annie worked from home.

The air of the heavy sigh cloaked most weekday evenings, but if we followed Annie's fancy, starting in January—just a few months away—all of that shuffling and sighing had to be vanquished. We'd invite sex back into our tired little party, sassier and wilder and more voluptuous than before. Sex would roar at the flaming heart of our relationship, transforming our shambling evenings into festivals of spirited ecstasy. It would be great! All of it!

That was the idea, at least.

ABOUT A month after Annie dropped the bomb, I heard about the Adult Entertainment Expo and persuaded a few editors at the *Post* that I should attend. The Expo is the porn industry's annual convention, and I argued that seeing such a concentration of the industry under one roof would benefit me, the sex writer, as well as the paper, because I'd harvest at least a few stories from the gathering. The event always takes place the first weekend in January, in Las Vegas. Annie and I had pledged to have sex every day until the middle of April, so we both had to attend.

As already established, pornography is not one of Annie's enthusiasms. Toss her a skein of yarn and some knitting needles, and

soon a hat will be born. Direct her to a porn website, though—
something I never had done before the marathon, but trust me on
this one—and little more than a yawn will enter the world anew.
I wasn't convinced she would take to the porn-show trip, but I knew
Vegas intrigued her.

"So, honey, guess what?" I said one night in bed after I had
posed the Vegas idea to my editors. "Looks like we're going to
Vegas in January. I've got a work trip."

"That's fabulous!" said Annie. "What's the trip for?"

"Big convention," I offered. "Huge one. The paper thinks it
will be good for my coverage. They would like some stories, too.
You will come too, because of the marathon."

"What's the convention?"

I waited a beat. "Porno. The sex industry. They have a big show
every January in Vegas. And this year, we're going."

Annie gave me a light push, a combination of "no way!" and
"wow!"

"You're joking!" she said. I wagged my head. "We're going to a
porn convention? That is so *not* me." She shoved me again and
started to laugh. "And I'm so psyched!"

I hoisted an eyebrow.

"Vegas, for one thing," she said. "And it will be a total *freak*
show! I may not want to look at what they do for a living, but
being around a bunch of them? Should be fun!"

A few days later, I received an e-mail from Annie with the subject
line "BRAINSTORM." We long have averaged about a dozen
e-mails a day, most of them about meals, the girls, weekend plans,
gossip, and so on. Now, though, the topic of sex was sashaying
into the e-mail stream. Before clicking on the message I understood that it would refer to our erotic lives, and that it could be a
biggie.

"I have an awesome idea," she wrote. "We're going to Vegas at the beginning of January, which got me to thinking we should balance that with something more healthy, or spiritual, at the end of the month. And then I started looking at the calendar and it occurred to me that we might need little trips and adventures sprinkled throughout the marathon, to keep everything interesting. Waddya think?"

What I thought was, *She's crafty, she's clever, and now she successfully has married a sex marathon with something entirely different: a bunch of trips.* I did smile at my desk, reading the e-mail. Annie lives for little excursions. I appreciated how she made it seem natural that the two things, sex and vacations, needed each other.

"Capital idea," I replied. "Let's start planning."

That night we sat in bed with laptops, yellow legal pads, and pens, for our "brainstorm."

"Your parents are coming to watch the girls during the Vegas trip, right?" she said.

"Check."

"Excellent. And of course for New Year's Eve, my parents and brother are renting rooms at the hotel in Boulder, and we're all celebrating New Year's at the hotel."

"Right," I said. "It probably would be better, all things being equal, if we didn't start the sex marathon during a weekend with your parents and brother. But these festivities were planned before the marathon. We'll manage."

"Correct," said Annie. "OK, here's something new. I noodled around on the Internet today and found a Hindu place in the mountains, an 'ashram.'"

"Ashram," I said. "Great word."

"It sounded cool. Meditation, vegetarian food, lectures by swamis."

"There's another great word," I said. "Swami."

"There's yoga, if you want. Some sort of ceremony in a temple.

You don't have to be a Hindu, and you don't have to take part in anything. You stay in these little cabins, and you can just hang out in the cabin if you want. Sounds very relaxing."

"I'm on board," I said without hesitating, envisioning not yoga or meditating or a robed swami but instead a mountain cabin.

By the time we left the topic, about an hour later, the marathon had also gathered around itself an evening in a swank hotel in downtown Denver to mark the halfway point, a visit to Wyoming, and a night in a cabin somewhere. When I interjected that some of these trips might prove difficult, given the presence of two children in our family, Annie said she was "already on top of that." The nanny of a friend of Annie's had agreed—with the consent of Annie's nanny-blessed friend—to watch the kids whenever we went away for a night.

"You are *so* on fire!" I said. "We've got a nanny!"

"Let's just hope the girls take to her," Annie said.

MOM FLEW in from Philadelphia to watch the kids while Annie and I drove a few hours south to a hundred-year-old log cabin in the mountains to celebrate our eleventh wedding anniversary. I, of course, did not have to reveal our upcoming sex campaign, but I've always told my mom nearly everything. Annie and I were yakking about it to our close friends, because we knew they would get a kick out of the sexpedition (and might have good ideas for us), and it didn't take me long to announce the adventure to my parents (though in this case, I wasn't gunning for any ideas).

"Honey, that's a classic," said my mom after she finished laughing during a phone call weeks earlier when I'd hit her with the news.

"Here," she said to Dad, handing him the phone. "You've got to listen to this one."

"That's awesome," he said after the punch line—*And so, Dad, we're going to have sex for one hundred consecutive days*—"Totally awesome."

I felt as though I'd just won the Heisman Trophy.

Weeks later, Mom began laughing as soon as she entered our minivan at the airport.

"I sat beside this elderly woman," she reported as we drove back to our white-picket-fenced house. "She asked why I was coming to Colorado. I told her to visit my son and daughter-in-law and my precious grandchildren. But eventually she began asking me exactly what we were doing, and for some reason I told her."

"Everything?" I asked.

"Yeah," said Mom. "Every last detail. And you know what? She actually asked me, you know, how do they define 'it'?"

The kids were in the car, so she had to speak in code, but by the lift in her eyebrows we knew "it" meant sex.

"What did you tell her?" I whispered, instantly uncomfortable with the direction the conversation was headed.

"I told her I didn't know," she said.

I just nodded.

WE'D PLANNED the trip to the cabin long before Annie's sexathon brainstorm, and Mom had booked her ticket months earlier. Now, though, with the prospect of such sexual excess suddenly sprawling before us, the anniversary trip took on additional significance: training.

"Let's go nuts for three days and three nights," said Annie a few weeks before the cabin excursion. "Let's be decadent. Sex, sex, sex."

This was the first time Annie ever had prefaced a trip with extensive and ambitious sex plans. This whole project, I thought, was headed in the right direction. The prospect of a sex-lavish weekend in a secluded cabin nurtured a sweet intimacy between

Annie and me. One Saturday afternoon in the kitchen, while I was monitoring the progress of a vegetable soup bubbling on the stove, I noticed her stroking my arm as she talked. She turned to tear some lettuce leaves for a salad, and I wrapped my arm around her waist, earning a twist of her head and a kiss on the lips that fell somewhere in that lovely and indeterminate zone between a peck and a sexy-messy French kiss. Spontaneous episodes like this flowered, and it almost felt like the days leading up to our wedding. We knew something important about our union was about to change.

By the conclusion of our cabin sojourn, we'd had sex six times in three days, including one outdoor episode on the side of a cliff. We probably had enjoyed such a volume of sex before—but not since—Annie first got pregnant, nearly a decade earlier. And our last outdoor session had been at least as long ago.

Among other things, those hours spent lounging around the cabin (and doing it) kindled helpful conversations about our sex life, the most thorough inventory and review of our between-the-sheets activities since we'd started dating.

"I do notice women," I told Annie at one point. "Cleavage. Legs. Butts. I get little jolts all day, just walking around."

"Obviously," said Annie. "I sometimes follow your eyes. Do you ever follow mine?"

"Never," I said, marveling at her interpretive skills. I fancied myself something of a kung-fu master at, for example, examining cleavage while pretending to observe the bark of a nearby tree. "Should I?"

"If you did, you'd find that I notice things, too," she said. "I know all about little jolts."

I am familiar with, and do not like, jealousy. Yet this most unwelcome of guests, this vulgar intruder, suddenly stomped into my head like a tattooed, angry skinhead crashing a hippie commune. Here I was, barefoot and in a headband, swanning through a grassy glade of incense and herbal tea and sex, and suddenly I had to deal with this leering, mocking, taunting goon intent on dismantling everything.

"So, uh, you look at guys," I said, trying to sound cool. I may even have shrugged. "That makes sense. You're human, after all! Nothing you would act on, obviously. Just checking things out."

Annie, diagnostic genius that she is, instantly figured out the skinhead had arrived. She smiled. "Yes, DJ, just like you, I notice stuff," she said. "And I chose you, thank God, over everyone else on earth. Forever."

The commune gypsies blew pot smoke after the retreating skinhead.

The little trip, too, cemented our approach to what, exactly, would count as sex during the marathon—the query the elderly lady on the plane posed to my mom. Did oral sex cover it? Was foreplay sufficient? Before the spell in the cabin, we weren't sure. But by its end, we were solidly in the Bill Clinton school of thought about the nature of sex. Oral, no. Intercourse, yes. That's what we did day after day in the cabin, and although we understood that oral activity fell into the "infidelity" category and might constitute sex, we also considered that mere kissing, at least for us, counts as "infidelity" but wasn't sex. In addition, we felt that trading oral pleasures—not to mention kissing—for one hundred days was not much of a stretch. Intercourse posed more of a challenge.

For me, intercourse meant daily performance. I couldn't just sit back with my fingers webbed behind my head and enjoy a lavishment, or simply mosey my lips down Annie's torso. I had to get it up; I had to try to pleasure Annie during intercourse; and I knew that I often would, in fact, mosey my lips down Annie's torso, too. All of this was work. Annie had to perform as well, but daily intercourse also would force her, simply, to just *do it* with more volume than she found comfortable. When I was around Annie in the evening, especially if I thought sex loomed (and during the marathon, it would loom over everything), arousal arrived like an intern on his first day at the firm: eager, earnest, attentive, and bouncy with vigor (accordingly, arousal also wore pressed suits and ties knotted firmly at the neck, and his hair had Mitt Romney impeccability). Annie, on the other hand, didn't have an intern. She depended on a motley crew of part-timers who had to be called, with schedules that demanded massaging.

To put it directly, I found it easier to crave sex on most nights than did Annie. I don't think it's fair to describe my sex drive as potent and Annie's as wan. Instead, our drives simply were different. Getting me in the mood, often, took no more than a glance at her cleavage. Coaxing a thirst for sex out of Annie required more toil. Once the appetite arrived, though, it clamored for quenching.

Did our varying sex drives contribute to a sex life that had turned merely placid and steady? I don't think so. It is true that my engines fired up with greater ease, but it also stands that the sparking of our desires tended to coincide. For example, on Saturday morning we both understood that sex would decorate the evening, and when night arrived, my intern showed up precisely on time, and after some phone calls and waiting, so did Annie's part-timers. And then we would have sex. But on, for example, a Monday night after a long day of work and child rearing and tidying the house? No intern, and no part-timers. Both of us tended to don our comfortable clothes, slide into bed, and meander toward sleep.

All of this is one way of saying that starting in January, either Annie would finally receive the blessings of an apple-cheeked and enthusiastic intern (after her body had grown accustomed to nightly sex), or she still would have to rely on these talented but willful part-timers. Either way, we planned on doing it every day.

• • •

WE ELONGATED the weekend, stopping in a small town called Buena Vista for sandwiches and cappuccinos, lingering over the weekend's teeming delights. And talking about the task before us.

"We pulled it off," said Annie, her hand on my thigh. "I'm thinking a hundred days might not be so tough."

I thought one hundred days of sex had great potential for pleasure, and I believed a season of it could change our relationship, maybe for a year, maybe for the rest of our lives. But easy? Doubts fluttered as we crossed the mountains, but I kept them to myself. My wife wanted to have sex with me on one hundred consecutive days. It was like winning the lottery, and not just some unremarkable $3,400 payout from some unheralded state game, but nailing a much-anticipated Powerball drawing, a multi-million-dollar payoff that involves press conferences and news coverage. In short, now was not the time to think about the taxes I'd have to pay.

WE ARRIVED home, the girls literally ran to us and jumped in our arms, and right then it was awfully good to be back. But soon our happy little household began taking a Lord of the Flies turn.

"Aaahhhhh!" yelled Ginger during dinner.

"What!" I said, panicked. Had she bit her lip? Burned herself on something?

"I dropped my napkin!"

This event sparked a lengthy episode of crying and wailing. Moments later Joni slipped from her chair to perform a mid-chew headstand on the floor.

"Check it out, Mommy! I can talk and chew and do a headstand at the same time. Want me to recite the Girl Scout pledge? Maybe I can even hold up my two fingers from my right hand while I say the pledge, because you know you're really supposed to have your fingers out while you say the pledge. . . ."

The night culminated in a chain of events that can be described, simply, as "Ginger, let's put on your diaper, then your sleeper."

"I don't WANT to wear my sleeper!"

"C'mon, Ginger, it's not a big deal. Then we can read bookies, whatever you want."

"I HATE my sleeper!"

Ginger's tantrums never failed to amuse my mom, who had to leave the table with a hand covering her mouth to hide her laughter. I understood this: Ginger could act like a maniacal and deranged elf but often seemed extremely cute at the same time, at least to spectators.

Joni, as usual, savored her sister's spirals into fury. Ginger kicked a wooden buffet, threw her cloth napkin from the dinner table, ran into the kitchen and then around the dining table, and finally curled herself into a ball on the couch, weeping and yelling. She'd stiffened into something like a brick, so Annie held down her hands as I diapered her grapefruit-size butt. Within a few moments her sleeper top was wet with tears. *Payback!!* she was saying. *You never should have left!* Joni, who'd already slipped into her sleeper, stared at her temporarily crazed sister. And she grinned.

It was widely understood, at this point, that it was time for me to take over. Early in Ginger's life, Annie had dubbed me the "Ginger Whisperer" because only I was able to calm her down. My method, indeed, involved much gentle whispering, along with the animating of various available stuffed animals. For example, Foxy the Fox says, "I may be a fox, but I don't live in a den. I like bedrooms," to which Philippe the Skunk, whom I quickly pick up, replies: "Bedrooms are stinky. Dens are stinkier. I live in a castle, Foxy." And so on. It was not out of line for me to turn my hand into a spider from Brooklyn who crawls up Ginger's belly, across her face, and parks on her scalp. "Yo, Ginguh, what's in dis thing, dis head or whateva. Chocolate? Buddascotch?" I might also sing a lullaby (sorry, guys).

After roughly fifteen minutes of Ginger Whispering, she was laughing, and forty-five minutes later both girls' doors were closed and the two of them—we hoped—were sleeping.

No sex that night, no lucky number 7 to cap the weekend. Even if my mom hadn't been in our miniature rental house, it might have been a stretch.

"I'm dreaming of just lying in bed and doing nothing," said Annie. "Or a movie. A movie would be nice."

We all—Annie, my mom, and I—propped ourselves up in bed and watched a Woody Allen movie. (We kept our only television in the bedroom.) A hundred straight days of sex hadn't seemed so daunting in the cabin. But back at home that first night, bullied (and of course sweetened and warmed and electrified) by children, devoid of solitude, marinated in exhaustion, and swaddled in suburbia, it seemed . . . impossible.

My mom left for Philadelphia the next day, and we continued with our quest for just one week of the deed. We succeeded, but although the procession of sex sprinkled us with delights, it wasn't exactly easy. The ground-floor living space in our house—living room, family room, dining room, kitchen, Annie's office, mud room—was a single room. You could open the front door and take in the whole thing in a glance. Upstairs we had three small bedrooms. The unfinished basement was full of boxes of our belongings, never unpacked after our move from Baltimore. Our yard was the width of a driveway and the length of a UPS truck.

It was hard to move around and not bump into another family member. One toy on the floor would transform the whole living area into a clutter fest. With work, school, kids' activities, breakfasts, dinners, and the rest of the dizzying catalogue that comprises family life, days sometimes seemed to spin out of control, and the house's cramped space magnified the instability and did nothing to ease our transition from Mom and Dad to lovers.

We had moved to the rental house nearly two years earlier, after selling our house in Baltimore. We knew nothing about Denver when we arrived there for my job at the *Denver Post,* and friends of friends urged us to find a house in Stapleton, a new community in Denver being developed on the former site of Stapleton International Airport. Stapleton was based on "New Urbanism" principles, meaning porches on the fronts of houses, garages and alleys in back, sidewalks for walking, and public space quilting the subdivision.

It sounded great, and the schools apparently were acceptable, which was a new concept for us, coming from Baltimore. So we moved from our creaky old pile of bricks in Baltimore to a brand-new house modeled after a turn-of-the-century farmhouse.

And we suffered.

Several times we put down money to build a house, and each time we backed out. At some point, our mugs probably were taped to the desk of every sales associate working out of Stapleton's many "model homes," an unusual example of cooperation among those fierce competitors: *We do not like one another, but subjecting even our enemies to this indecisive couple is a torment too far.*

Compared to our Baltimore place, the houses felt cheap, as if they would tumble across the prairie during a strong gust of wind. The builders spun the tiny lots as an advantage—*No yard work! Go out and play in the public spaces instead of toiling in your dirty gardens!*—but the idea never sank in. I loved gardening. I yearned for a decent yard, with trees and tomato plants and maybe even a hill. Soon after moving to Denver, I began to ache for our old life in Baltimore. Meanwhile, a happy reentry into the work world, after her nearly seven-year break due to pregnancies and child rearing, was something Annie was loath to give up. Another move, she knew, would once again detach her from a job she loved. This was a confusing time in our lives.

Where was home? The question hung over everything. By the end of our trial week of sex, we realized that the unacceptable house, our unhappiness with our neighborhood, our confusion about where to live, and our profound sense of aimlessness were fueling our determination to spin ourselves into a frenzy of sex in the new year. It was more than a relationship experiment. It also was a pursuit that could divert us from a day-to-day existence that left us increasingly disoriented and occasionally blue.

"We need to step back," Annie told me. "Take a breather. Stop spinning our wheels so much. For at least one hundred days, starting soon, we'll just live in the present."

"In the now," I said. "I've always wanted to live in the now."

As THE January kickoff approached and we grew increasingly serious about the adventure, all sorts of sex-related topics seized our attention. One of my first initiatives involved spending time at Macy's, hunting for something comfortable I could wear after work that would not corrode Annie's libido. Sweatpants, I think it goes without saying, were out. The question, for me, was what sort of evening wear for guys counts as "sexy," or at least "agnostic in the context of erotic attraction"? Women enjoyed entire stores, big corporate leviathans, in fact, with shareholders and boards of directors, revolving around the places where evening wear and lust meet. Guys have sweatpants. And pajamas. I roamed over to the pajamas area of the men's department and began flipping through racks of light cotton pants, most of them striped. And none of them, at least in my size, with pockets.

But I'm a pocket man, I thought.

I never before had shopped for pajamas, probably because I'd always depended on my trusty blue sweatpants with five pockets. This pajamas excursion took much more time than I had scheduled—I'd say a solid twenty-five minutes—but eventually a pair grabbed me, something violet with dark blue stripes and gathered at the waist not only with elastic but with a string designed to be tied into a bow.

We'll see, I thought as the checkout clerk dropped them into a bag. *At least they are soft.*

That night I slipped into them while Annie brushed her teeth in the bathroom. I sat on the bed, wondering if the new attire would fail to attract her attention. As if.

"Hey, DJ, great pajamas!" she said the instant she entered the bedroom, wearing a silk robe. "I love them!"

"Not repulsive?" I asked.

"No," said Annie. "Sexy."

"They don't have pockets."

"Pockets, schmockets," said Annie. "You won't miss them." She reached over, pinched the fabric between her fingers, and began sliding her hand up and down. "Oooh," she said. "Soft. I bet they're comfortable."

There was much more to the training period than light cotton evening wear for men, of course. Every time we ran across news stories about sex, we'd forward them to each other. Friends, too, were sending us blogs and articles. Disaster scenes often flickered in the corners of our brains. Sickness? Must have sex. An argument? Must have sex. Staggering boredom? Sore groins, gas pains? Must have sex. Is there such a thing as too much sex? Could a hundred days of fluid exchange somehow damage our health?

Annie decided we both should see our doctor, a woman she trusted immensely and admired and used as both her general doctor and her ob/gyn. The doc's advice to Annie: birth control, for one. We had resorted to condoms for the previous few years. I didn't quite trust the vasectomy idea, and Annie felt the same about birth control. For the marathon, though, Annie was eager to return to the pill, especially one the doctor mentioned that seemed to have a relatively gentle effect on the body and, more tantalizingly for Annie, would allow her to skip periods for up to four months at a time. In addition, the doctor urged Annie to eat acidophilus every day, either in yogurt or as a supplement. The substance, she said, should keep Annie's vagina in "balance." Pee immediately after sex. Drink lots of water all day to help keep everything moist. "And lube," she said. "Use lots and lots of lube."

"Lube?" asked Annie.

"Well," the doctor said, "you know how two scoops of ice cream are really good by themselves but with chocolate sauce and whipped cream and a cherry they're much better?"

"Yeah," said Annie.

"OK, now you understand lube. Oh, and one more thing," the doctor said. "Make sure the lock on your bedroom door works."

I visited the doctor myself.

"Eat citrus fruits and tomatoes," she said. Semen is "basic" and Annie's vagina is "acidic." Too much "basic" could affect Annie's vagina—and not for the better. "Oh, and go to a sex shop before you start," she offered. "You might need stuff to, you know, jazz it up every once in a while."

We had planned on trying different sex products, so I knew what she meant, but why was "jazzing it up" one of the doctor's first recommendations? Was it that obvious?

"Got it," I said, gazing at the floor.

"What about male 'vitality' herbs?" I said. "They're safe, right?"

"Probably," she said. "Go for it."

I followed her out of the room to the mazelike realm of medical assistants and clerks wearing pink and purple uniforms and white clogs.

"Oh, and how could I forget!" the doctor shouted. "Viagra! You must experiment with Viagra!" She entered a closet and emerged with a sack of the pills. "If the erection lasts longer than is comfortable, call the hospital."

I instantly envisioned myself in an emergency room agonizing over a violent boner, beside the kid with the busted arm and the girl with a cut on her knee that demands stitches, their parents swooping upon them and whisking them away from the bad man, the spooky man, the man who represents all that is curdled and sour in America today.

Cheered by the doctor's enthusiasm for the project, we plunged ahead. We bought "libido enhancing" herbal supplements for me, and Annie invested in aromatic oils for the baths we would take. We bought candles and incense for the bedroom, which we decided to transform into a "sex den." The master bedroom—beige walls, beige carpet, cheap blinds—lacked charm, but it did contain a large walk-in closet (a first for us) and a bathroom with the biggest tub we'd ever enjoyed. It also had a cathedral ceiling and a window high on a wall. It had potential.

"Check it out," said Annie after work one night. She led me upstairs to the bedroom. "Behold," she said.

I beheld.

"Note the lack of photographs," she said. "I removed them. No parents, no children, no grandmas or grandpas. We love 'em, but they've got nothing to do with, you know, our sanctuary."

I walked through the room, admiring her handiwork. The new bedspread contained wild Indian designs. The basket containing hand weights and other gym equipment was stowed under the bed. The books stood neat on their shelves. Hidden was the wild tangle of electronic cords. On the bureau was a new incense holder with a fresh selection of aromatic sticks and cones. Resting on our bedside tables were scented massage oils and body lotions.

A piece of colorful cloth draped the television screen.

"No TV?" I asked, an eyebrow raised.

"Just no looking at the contraption when we're not using it," said Annie. "It's not the most pleasant-looking thing in the world. I call this 'den shui.' Kind of like feng shui, only without the ancient wisdom part."

One brilliant Sunday afternoon after I returned from a run, Annie looked up from the cookie dough she was rolling out—Christmas was coming, and the whole family tends to go overboard with baking during the holiday season—and said "Exercise."

"Exercise," I said, perplexed. "Exercise good."

"Yes," she said. "Exercise is something we haven't talked about."

I studied her for a moment, not sure where she was taking this, a back-and-forth I'd grown accustomed to over the years: Annie says something mysterious, I study her, and I wonder where she's heading.

"Like I said, I'm going to keep running during the marathon, no doubt about it," I responded. "I might even up my running a bit, unless it takes too much out of me. And there's the weight lifting."

"Good plan," she said. "Yoga, too. You should do yoga."

"Yoga," I whispered, half to myself. An unappealing image of me barefoot, in shorts and a T-shirt, doing some pose with my butt in the air in a room full of women, rushed into my brain. This was not a welcome intrusion.

"I'm definitely doing yoga, I'm hoping a lot of it, when we start," said Annie. "The ashram we're going to in January has yoga, and I'm doing it. That yoga studio down the street? They pump the temperature up to 105 degrees. By the time you leave, you feel like a rubber band. And the heat feels amazing when it's so cold outside. I know you'll love it if you just try it. Will you?"

Her eyes? Puppy dog. I believe she even batted her eyelashes. Her voice? Honey. I am not what you would call a "stoic"—I am the sort of guy who might be summed up as "a gift to cunning as well as to merely competent salespeople."

"Yoga," I said. "What the hell. How embarrassing could it be?"

It wasn't just our bodies that demanded attention, though. We needed to condition our minds as well, so we began combing the Denver Public Library for appropriate titles. We found books about ancient Egyptian sexual positions and traditional Japanese approaches to romance and sex. I read them all. We checked out dozens of books, which made for interesting excursions. With each of my library visits—*every one*—an almost caricatured version of "little old lady" stood in line behind me, smelling of lilac, hair a white meringue, clutching a sensible handbag. There she'd stand, a few feet away, as I dragged bar codes beneath lasers and titles flashed on a screen: *The Yin Yang Butterfly: Ancient Chinese Sexual Secrets for Western Lovers*; *A Lover's Guide to the Kama Sutra*; *The Multiorgasmic Woman* (I'm always thinking of Annie). I would stuff my stack of books into a plastic bag and slink away from the little old lady and her wool skirt.

Yet despite all of the fresh focus on the carnal world, the volume of actual sex hadn't changed for us since our return from the cabin.

"Do you think it's a problem?" asked Annie one night during our "training" period. "We're not having any more sex than usual."

I slugged back a big gulp of India Pale Ale, a style of beer Annie and I drank for its almost saffron bitterness, a flavor we treasured.

"I don't know," I said. "Maybe."

I'd been 40 for nearly half a year. I'd celebrated the summer day I said good-bye to those blessed 30s, repeatedly telling people, "Hey, it's just some random date. I guess I'm forty now, though I still feel like I'm twenty-five!" But weeks later, undercurrents of melancholy appeared.

During the sex conference in Florida, I encountered a very young and exceptionally talented New York writer whose virility could fairly be described as "majestic." His octopus grasp of cool, and the way women watching him ran their fingers along the edges of their cocktail glasses, were intimidating.

Shortly after that conference, the newspaper sent me to New York City to write a profile of the Colorado-native editor of *US Weekly*. The age of 40 is about average—even a bit on the young side—in many big-city newspapers, but it registered as nearly prehistoric in the *US Weekly* offices, where there was nothing less than a parade of youth: a brassy 20-something reporter with magnetic cleavage and spiky heels and a boozy job full of publicists and nightclubs; a fabulous and urbane youngster whose command of his own presence was so accomplished and daunting he seemed destined for a life of increasingly wonderful fabulousness; and the editor in chief herself, a breathtakingly stylish, sexy, and smart 30-something. All this brought back the deflating hiss I'd experienced in the company of the very young New York writer.

But by the end of the Manhattan trip, just weeks after Annie had dreamed up the sex marathon, the hiss was gone and, not to brag, was replaced with the welcome sound of a swelling balloon. *I may be getting old*, I thought, *but soon I'm getting laid. A lot more than ever. More than you.* So there.

2

I'm Going to Like It

Our sex odyssey commenced in a hotel room next to Annie's parents' room. I'm sure I don't have to spell this out, but the location placed certain constraints on the kick-off. It was like holding Mardi Gras in Salt Lake City, with the Mormon Tabernacle Choir headlining the Fat Tuesday festivities. Just anticipating the situation put me in mind of a guy fresh out of jail, sitting down for his first restaurant meal and being scolded by someone about calories and arteries. *You're kidding me, right?* The in-laws slept with Ginger wedged between them, in a hotel suite with a thin door leading to our room, where Annie had spent the past several days battling diarrhea and where Ginger had hurled the night before.

"Gas and vomit," said Annie when I arrived at the hotel in Boulder, where the rest of the clan had been hanging out for a few days while I worked in Denver. "Not exactly the aphrodisiacs I was looking for."

New Year's Eve often involves fine clothing, no children, lots of dancing, booze, and a long kiss the moment the year turns, followed of course by wonderfully sloppy sex. Although we'd never achieved such a New Year's Eve, not in fourteen years of togetherness, this year's stood as the least saucy of all. The hotel used a family angle to sell its New Year's Eve weekend package, and we volunteered to participate in a buffet of planned activities. We had agreed to the New Year's festivities with the relatives well before we came up with the idea of the marathon. We felt obliged to keep the date, and we didn't want to emerge as the couple equivalent of a wet rag at the party. So instead of moping and lamenting the flawed sexathon launch, we plunged into the parade of activities, understanding that at some point we would ring in the New Year with something far more ravishing than a midnight kiss.

We built small structures of uncooked spaghetti and mini marshmallows and tested their "earthquake readiness" by shaking them. Our "team"—our family—competed with other teams, dropping eggs from a balcony into boxes padded with toilet paper, to determine which team had built the softest egg nest (Joni sobbed when our egg shattered dramatically upon impact). We erected a small shelter made entirely from newspapers and masking tape. Annie tried to keep a hula hoop spinning around her hips. We made crowns out of construction paper, staples, glue, and a lot of sparkly things.

These activities went on . . . and on and on and on.

They went on *after* midnight, the place reeling and unstable with sugar-fueled kids and adults hooting and splashing in the pool and gorging on potato chips and sour-cream-and-onion dip and cheap cookies.

We had planned to start immediately after the clock struck midnight, but where was Annie when the year turned? With her family and Joni, crowding around the pool. Where was I? In our hotel room with Ginger, screaming, kicking, furious about her advanced state of exhaustion, about being away from her routine and her inability to continue watching *Dora the Explorer* into perpetuity. My Ginger-Whisperer sorcery wasn't having much effect.

The whole bedraggled group eventually returned to our suite of rooms. A red-faced Annie carried a sleeping Ginger—who finally had collapsed into sleep in my arms—into her parents' room and returned to our bed for sex and slumber. We had imagined transforming the room into an erotic sanctuary for the kickoff of the marathon, but we didn't come close.

"I don't care if our room smells like a rotting, steaming compost heap and looks like a junkyard," said Annie. "I'm going to have sex. And you know what?"

"What?"

"I'm going to like it."

We popped a bottle of the brand of New Mexico champagne we had drunk at our wedding and sat in bed, sipping and rubbing our eyes. Annie wore a black bra and panties emblazoned with "100 Days" in rhinestones across the butt, a Christmas gift from my parents, who obviously were, shall we say, enthusiastic about the venture. I wore white boxers. I brought my fingertips to her arm and dragged them lightly up and down. She stroked my side, and quickly we pressed our bodies together under the sheets, then our lips. I brought one hand to her hips, and I cupped her breast with the other, and she reached beneath my waistband and grasped me and I rolled onto my hands and knees. I tickled her neck with my lips, then delivered gentle kisses and nibbles all the way down her stomach, and then I began maneuvering my body south, getting the angles right, and after about ten minutes Annie entered Orgasmworld. I quickly barged inside and offered a quick "hello" followed five minutes later with a wave good-bye as my own orgasm unfurled. We shared a quick peck, rolled over, and fell into sleep. It was nearly 2 a.m.

Day 1 done, a notch on our bedpost, the first step in a journey that we hoped would stretch across almost all of winter and into spring.

AND THEN it was morning, and the feeling was . . . familiar.

A little more than eleven years earlier, we'd gotten married in a museum in Santa Fe, spent the night in a hotel in town (in a room rigged with sex-gag gifts planted by Annie's brothers), and risen to a dining room full of breakfasting relatives who—nudge, nudge, wink, wink—thought they knew what we'd done in bed just hours before. And now here we were again: at breakfast in the West surrounded by nudging, winking relatives.

It had been easy for me to tell my parents about the project. You will remember the Heisman Trophy. As Annie pointed out, the subject of sex is less fraught for sons than for daughters.

"The first time a woman really reveals to her parents that she had sex with her husband is when she calls to say she's pregnant," said Annie during the training period after I had gleefully unveiled our sex marathon to my parents. The sexathon, to them (I thought), had great potential for serving as evidence of manliness. But Annie worried that her behavior would be deemed something other than evidence of femininity.

"I don't know how my parents are going to react," she said. "I don't have any girlfriends I can call and ask, 'Hey, how did your parents respond when you told them you were going to have sex for a hundred straight days?' "

Annie did end up revealing our sexy march to her mom and dad, through an e-mail, shortly before New Year's. By then the idea of the marathon had gained prominence in our little society of two, and as the kickoff approached, she found it increasingly difficult to hide it from her parents, with whom she talked several times a week.

"It's too big a deal for me," she reported the day she fired off the e-mail. "Keeping it from them feels dishonest."

To paraphrase their response: They didn't jump for joy, they didn't weep, and they essentially said, "Hey, it's your life. Have fun with it."

BECAUSE WE started the hundred-day sexcapade with 1 a.m. sex, the rest of the day was "free"—no pressure. Both of us remarked

in the morning how "relieved" we were that we had a night "off."
This, we concluded, was not a good sign. It was day 1, and already
we thrilled to the prospect of a sex-free evening.

"I guess it's all about pacing," said Annie as the kids played and
we loaded the car. "We've got to take advantage of every breather
we get. I know I'm going to be tired tonight, and now I don't have
to do anything. I can just . . . be tired."

"I wonder if our views will be different on day 75? It will be
cool to find out if daily sex makes us even hungrier for it," I said.
"Will the prospect of no sex be a bummer by day 75, instead of
being something to celebrate?"

"Day 75," said Annie. "Hard to imagine."

Annie's family left for a two-day drive to Missouri. We piled
into our own minivan and zipped back to our house, gliding on a
sex-adventure high until, while we were unpacking, Ginger freaked
out, because we didn't have any "shell noodles"—macaroni and
cheese. She flopped on her stomach and screamed for twenty minutes. Welcome home!

It was a rude return, but the evening softened. While Ginger
finally slept and I read Joni her last book of the evening, Annie
drew a hot bath—the water extravagant with salts and oils and
essences—lit Japanese sandalwood incense, and illuminated the
room with no less than ten fancy scented candles (most of which I
had bought at a boutique in Denver one afternoon while still in
training, spending more than $100 on scented columns of wax). I
brought a pair of India Pale Ales to the bath and slipped into the
big tub across from a smiling Annie.

"What we're doing is healthy," she said. "I wish we'd thought
of it before."

"It would have been a bit easier a decade ago," I said. "But
maybe it wouldn't have had the same impact."

We luxuriated in the sweltering sanctuary for half an hour, our
legs touching, trading anecdotes about the weekend and the girls,

dreaming together about where we could take our lives. Maybe we would move to Ireland, a favorite place—Annie had spent a year in Tullamore on a sheep farm in high school and had returned, to Dublin, in college—and raise our girls in a whitewashed cottage on the spectacular west coast. Or maybe we would open a charming bistro in a semirural idyll just outside my hallowed Philadelphia, with the girls growing up in the kitchen and sprawling gardens. Or maybe we would leave our 2003 Denver rental house for something nineteenth-century and whimsical in a historic part of Denver, a neighborhood with broad blue spruce trees and front-yard wildflower meadows and busy porches. Dreaming was something we did whenever we found ourselves alone together: I'd listen to Annie's reveries, she'd pay attention to mine, and together, like sculptors working on the same block of swirling and speckled granite, we'd shape something that was neither Annie nor Doug but Us.

Afterward, we slipped between clean sheets—to mark the hundred-days adventure, I'd washed them before the Boulder festivities (sadly, I wasn't sure I'd ever washed our sheets before), an act that made Annie swoon—kissed, and plummeted into sleep.

GINGER WOKE us up the following morning, a holiday Monday, and so we began what we thought would be a seminormal marathon day: a procession of activities followed, we assumed, by sex. Annie headed to the yoga studio, a small space in the bottom of an apartment building in our neighborhood, just five minutes away. She'd first visited it a few weeks earlier, and immediately copped discipleship, buying yoga pants and a mat, talking dreamily about the heat and the stretching, and proselytizing. As she bent and twisted her body for ninety minutes, I umpired the girls, and I understood, with some reluctance, that one day soon our roles would be reversed: I'd be attempting to fold my creaky joints in a room packed with limber young women, with my butt in the air, while Annie minded the children.

For now, though, my calcifying knees and leathery hamstrings had nothing to worry about. Recognizing a simmer between the girls that could easily boil over into shouts, tears, and slammed doors, I shepherded them into the minivan and drove to Bass Pro Shops, an enormous sportsman's cathedral about ten minutes from the house.

As a kid in semirural, semisuburban Pennsylvania, hunting and fishing had captured my imagination. I'd not held a gun since high school, and although I still fished occasionally, I did it more to please the girls than for my own enjoyment. Going to Bass Pro Shops was like revisiting a congenial slice of my adolescence. Fishing poles clustered in vast forests. In the sprawling firearms area, big-bellied, cowboy-hatted men pressed gun stocks to shoulders and squinted. Stuffed animals bared their teeth, spread their wings, and flapped their tails. Intimidated—I was wearing a black Irish cap that could be mistaken for a beret, and a jaunty tartan scarf knotted around my neck, neither of them exactly screaming "bowhunter"—I tried to demonstrate my wildlife expertise.

"Look, girls, a weasel!" I exclaimed, pointing at one of the taxidermied creatures. *Say, that fella knows his critters!* I imagined the men thinking. *He knows his squirrels from his weasels!*

I like to think I'm a macho guy; I just don't wear it on my sleeve. But certainly there was a chance, as I strolled around Bass Pro Shops in my jaunty scarf and impish little hat, that the guys all around understood instinctively that I don't spend much time watching sports on TV and that I am unfamiliar with my car's alternator, clueless about weaponry, and uncertain about the purpose, if not the mere description, of a roof truss. So increasingly, as the girls and I traversed the unfamiliar environment, full of men who probably were at ease in every aisle of The Home Depot and to whom V-8 surely meant more than a Bloody Mary ingredient, I felt fraudulent. I saw something behind these men's eyes, the words they were thinking: *Interloper! Pretender! Fancy lad!*

Maybe I should wear my machismo on my sleeve a bit more, I thought, ogling a cast-iron Dutch oven and imagining it full of chili and swinging over a crackling evening campfire (now cookery, *that* I understand). No such misgivings, of course, tattooed the girls' brains. They dug the whole scene from their seats in the shopping-cart chariot—Ginger in the high jumpseat, the constantly coughing Joni sitting lower in the carriage—especially the wall-size fish tank full of trout and enormous catfish, and the towering grizzly bears.

As we toured this massive temple to critters and the tools that dispatch them, it occurred to me, with great pleasure, that even though it was unlikely I'd ever go musket-hunting for elk or bear, I was beginning my own hunt of a sort. Only it was trophy sex I was after, not antelope. True, I'd "bagged" only one session so far, but no matter! I was a sharpshooter! More trophies were on the way!

On the drive back to the house, I could not contain myself: I had to tell Annie about our excursion, so I called, thinking she would be home from yoga.

"How was yoga?" I said.

"It rocked!" she said. "I can't wait for you to check it out."

"I'll be doing that soon enough, I'm sure," I said. "You're never going to believe where we were."

"Where?"

"Bass Pro Shops."

"Wow," said Annie. "Must have been, uh, something else."

"That it was. I'll fill you in when we get back."

"See you soon, honey," said Annie. "ILYSM."

"ILYSM."

You might think that this acronym—standing for "I Love You So Much"—represents sappy at its sappiest, and it would be unreasonable for me to quarrel with your assessment. Nevertheless, at some point during our marriage, I believe while we were living in South Florida, we began inventing acronyms and attaching them at the end of e-mails to each other. Annie would send "YW,YL,YBF," and it would be my responsibility to figure out "Your Wife, Your Lover, Your Best Friend." I would then send along some similar puzzle, maybe "H,L,SMFL" and she'd be tasked with figuring out "Husband, Lover, Soul Mate For Life." After a few weeks of the complicated word games, we both stuck with ILYSM, which quickly migrated from e-mails to conversations. Nearly a decade later, we still traded in ILYSMs on a daily, and sometimes hourly, basis.

THE GIRLS and I returned to our balsa-wood house just minutes after the traded ILYSMs, and Annie and I then began the long jaunt through a day at home: refereeing fights between sisters, cooking soup for the family, grilling chicken legs for Joni's week of lunches, while a neighbor played in front of our house with one of his kids.

As usual, the neighbor refused to acknowledge my presence. It may be, at least in part, the porch itself that evoked, to put it mildly, so little enthusiasm toward us from our neighbors. Their porches held expensive teak furniture and Buddhas and trellises laced with blossoms in the summer, and happy oak swings hung from their porch ceilings. Their porches looked like the covers of catalogues. Our porch looked like a photograph capturing something profound about poverty, with its toys and bikes and old chairs and my Big Green Egg—a hulking ceramic grill.

Living in our neighborhood, in fact, was the negative image of my experience in Bass Pro Shops. In both milieus, I was an interloper, an intruder. The key difference: At Bass Pro Shops I felt too urbane and soft-handed—a fancy lad—and in the 'hood I felt like a moonshine-swiggin', banjo-pickin' hillbilly. The plastic deer that stood sentinel in our front yard—a buck with a target on its side, its gaze perpetually fixed over the plastic white picket fence hemming in all of the houses on the block—only punched up this Beverly Hillbillies experience. Sly Annie had named it Ira, her rebellious response to the shoddy treatment we'd received from neighbors since the day we moved in. Fed up with the endless and inexplicable cold shoulders, Annie bought Ira in a sporting goods store one afternoon and parked him in the yard. "Happy eleventh anniversary," she told me.

Ira was the only piece of plastic animal yard art in Stapleton.

THAT NIGHT, we wrapped the girls in their sleepers and read them a blizzard of books.

"Whew," said Annie when she returned from Joni's room after tucking her in for the night at her 8 p.m. bedtime. "Exhausting. And this is a holiday."

"But we've got work to do now," I offered.

She shot me an eyebrow hoist that said: "Purrrr."

While Annie poked around on the Internet, I took a shower, something I rarely did in the evening. But with the prospect of a romp before me, I decided to get clean. I even rubbed my body afterward with a moisturizing bath bar picked up by Annie for the sake of the marathon and that, I hoped, would somehow make me sexier.

Annie then showered, and I filled the bedroom with candles in aromas of "vanilla jasmine tabac" and "champagne," and I lit patchouli incense. She appeared—graceful, smelling like spring—in gorgeous and expensive French lingerie I had bought her for Christmas, a gift inspired by the expedition.

We sat cross-legged on the bed for a few minutes. Then I shot Annie my signature "Wanna screw?" look—lifted eyebrows, a sideways half smile—and she scooted toward the pillows to give us room. I followed, bringing my lips to hers. And then . . . click.

The dreaded sound of a child's bedroom door opening.

Joni's cough had grown worse. I slipped into a vintage silk robe that had been presented to me as a gift by close friends ("It's so you!")—it looked like something Thurston Howell III would wear—and rummaged around for cough syrup. I administered it. But then Joni reported that when my mother, whom she calls "Lulu," has a cough "she props herself up in bed and does something, like coloring."

"That may be, my little friend," I responded. "But coloring isn't in your future for tonight. Good night."

I pirouetted from Caring Dad to Horny Husband the instant I returned to the bedroom, the moment I saw Annie on the bed. Her very presence breathed hubba-hubba.

"Everything OK?" she asked as I locked our bedroom door.

"It is now," I said.

OUTSIDE OF her family and close friends, Annie had not mentioned the sexathon to anybody, which probably was the best way to go, all things considered. I, however, had blathered on about the endeavor to anybody with ears. It was the whole Heisman Trophy thing.

On this, my first day back in the office after kicking off the sexpedition, my boss blushed when she saw me. Another boss reddened as well. Yet another beheld me, took a few steps back, and asked, "Uh, how's it going?" He actually circumnavigated me after I answered, as if I'd morphed into some hellion driven by fierce, feral loin power. Strangely—or maybe not—I fancied their reactions. I felt stronger. I felt suave. I felt—gasp—*Mediterranean*. I'd instantly become an objectified sexual being: *That man had sex last night! He's going to do it again tonight! Wow!*

A friend fired off an e-mail in the middle of the afternoon: "How hard has it been? You must be bushed. Go get yourself something at Hole Foods."

Ha ha.

Awash in erotic glory, and temporarily without a tight deadline, I spent the day clicking through websites, yakking on the phone, and occasionally fixing on the evening's bedroom demands. I savored the thought of another flesh romp. Then I started getting e-mails from a very tense Annie.

We'd sold our house in Baltimore a few years earlier for a splendid profit, had not bought a house in Denver, and now paid cheap rent. This unhinging from the fiscal bargain so many families enter into—*Thou shalt sink into house debt for the sake of permanence and stability*—had propelled us into a state that Annie described as "extremely spendy." And when it came to money, I was—and remain—clueless. Annie handled the taxes, the bills, the balancing of the books. My relationship to money was ridiculously simple: I earn money. I spend money. The end.

One of Annie's e-mails on this first day back at the office reported that I'd forgotten to deal with some complicated (not!) parking reimbursement program through work, which meant we suddenly owed $270. Doh! It gets worse: We also had received a nasty warning from a bill collector commanding us to pay a parking ticket (one that now was more than double the original amount). The ticket—surprise!—was mine. As Annie's e-mails, probably five or six, filled my inbox, I decided very consciously that my mission that night would be the delivery of a most splendid orgasm.

I arrived home, and a frazzled Annie—busy with getting dinner ready and offering details about the extent of our "spendyness" ("Do you know how much money we are spending every month at Target? Half the time, I don't have any recollection of what we're buying there. All I know is that every month Target shows up on our credit card bill.")—headed off to yoga again. It was my charge to feed the girls and tuck them in and make her reentry from Yogaworld seamless.

The evening began well enough. The girls and I sat around the round dining room table that owned the center of our tiny living space, eating lentil soup (I made it on New Year's Day) and spaghetti. Lentil soup was not high on either girl's list of faves, but they both treated spaghetti like treasure. They changed into their sleepers while I cleaned up, without incident. They played with little plastic dolls called Polly Pockets, which have a wardrobe of lots of rubbery clothes and can occupy the girls for hours. Eventually, we moved into story time. I read Ginger a load of books and slid her beneath the covers. Joni and I then embarked upon our nightly tour of *Harry Potter,* book five, in Annie's and my room because the bed was bigger and the light stronger. Suddenly the bedroom door creaked open and in stepped Ginger. This happened rarely. I wondered if she sensed something was up between Annie and me.

"Ginger," I said, "you must go to sleep, in your own room."

"Noooooooo!"

I carried her, shrieking and weeping, into her room, plopped her in bed, performed a little Ginger Whispering, shut the door behind me, and returned to Joni. Then I heard "Baa Baa Black Sheep," the roared version. Ginger, in her dark bedroom, was singing the nursery rhyme full volume at the ceiling. Joni and I listened, both of us grinning.

"She's a character," I murmured.

"A *crazy* character," added Joni.

We sat on my and Annie's bed while I read to Joni, trying to find a volume loud enough to cut through Ginger's nursery rhyme aria (she repeated the song over and over) but not so thunderous it would disturb Ginger and propel her, again, out of her bedroom. Just as I finished a chapter, the song faded, and I led Joni from our bedroom to her own, tucked her into bed, handed her the stuffed cartoon character Maisy—her close companion since she turned 1—and returned to our bedroom, which I wanted to straighten up before the night's festivities.

I'd just as soon bag the sex-den spiffying and, instead, bring a beer to bed, read for a while, and go to sleep. But things had changed. I returned the sex den to its former glory, putting away my dirty clothes, removing clutter that had gathered on bureaus and bookshelves since Annie first transformed the room, and lighting candles and incense. The candles decorated the room with a lively orange light, and the wand of Japanese incense sent out delicate tails of smoke. I fluffed the pillows and ran my palm over the brown-and-crimson East Indian coverlet, making it smooth. The room said: *I'm ready, baby.*

Annie arrived home, nearly glowing from her ninety minutes of yoga. Gone was all evidence of tension, anxiety, and worry about money. She showered. I read a book about Taoist approaches to conserving sexual energy. Then I showered, too, and came to the bed nude. Annie was wearing a nightie. She offered to massage my feet with a moisturizer that smelled like a forest, and I closed my eyes and sank into pleasure.

"I feel like a new woman," said Annie as she kneaded my soles. "Yoga is amazing."

Then she lay back, and I massaged her feet.

"Damn," she said. "That's made me so hot."

My thirst for sex suddenly felt urgent, a feeling I silently celebrated. Before the marathon, such a long day—that is to say, a normal day—would not have included sex-den neatening (in fact, there wouldn't have been a sex den). Neither of us would have showered, Annie would not have donned lingerie, and foot massages would have taken place only in our dreams. And dueling sex drives? Negative. We'd have enjoyed dueling sleep drives. But now we could not wait to satisfy our lust. So we did.

I fell asleep swaddled in comfort and well-being.

• • •

WHEN I opened my eyes in the morning, my joints ached. My head felt like a gargoyle had stuffed it with cotton. I'm a lad who gets ill. "Please," I whispered, staring at the ceiling. "I can't get sick now. Wait for a few months. Please?" *I'm just going to pretend everything is fine,* I thought.

This was to be Annie's first day alone at home since before Christmas. Annie was an independent contractor, toiling out of the house for a gourmet pasta company, although she did travel to the plant once a week for meetings. She spent much of her time trying to expand the farmers' market business, to find people in cities around the country who were willing to spend their weekends hawking the company's enormous selection of pastas at farmers' markets. She also wrote two newsletters about food—one for the pasta company and one for a local monthly newspaper—and she did a lot of recipe-testing for the pasta outfit.

While Annie worked out of the house, I sat in a downtown office on the second floor of a skyscraper across from a McDonald's and, of course, within an archipelago of Starbucks coffeehouses. My office was far from repellent. Newsrooms are electric places, with lots of desks massed close together, reporters engaged in lively phone conversations, televisions broadcasting news, and loads of sardonic wit and skepticism. But still, I'd rather work from home, as I had done for four years in Baltimore, in the attic of our Colonial brick house. I envied Annie's situation.

At some point during the day, while running a quick errand, I walked past the place where I get my hair cut. One very hip woman with a nose ring dangling from her septum and spiky hair smiled at me through the big window. *Wow!* I thought. *She actually knows who I am!* Then I remembered that a few weeks before I had told the hot hipster who cuts my hair about the sex marathon. She'd probably mentioned it to Nose Ring. So it wasn't my innate coolness that rigged me in her memory, but the sex-adventure thing. Which disappointed. I liked to think women look at me with at least a spritz of sexual interest. It's something I took for granted when I was younger, even though, let's face it, the presumption could easily fit into the category "hallucination." I had observed, however, that women increasingly were looking through me, not even registering my presence on the stage, as it were. With every wrinkle, I was fading deeper into the background, and camouflage isn't what I desired. I think it's fair to say that, with the possible exception of Carthusian monks who elect to spend the majority of their lives within a cell, most men would agree: We like to be noticed.

So here we were, at the very pith of the middle-aged man's complaint, the descent from vigorous male to wan wallflower, the transformation from brilliant sun to dim star, at least in the eyes of young women. Nose Ring, I concluded, never would have smiled if she hadn't known about the sex thing. Which made me think: *Maybe the sexpedition is like my red Corvette.* Either way, I sniffled and ached my way back to the office and through the day, toying with heading home and going to bed.

Annie, however, gently proposed something different.

"Why not try the yoga tonight?" she asked minutes after I walked in the door.

"You kidding?" I said. "I feel like crap."

"I'm telling you, the hot room could do you wonders. Even if you just sit in the heat and do a few stretches, I bet you'll feel better."

I was an old hand with brutal colds and the flu, and after fourteen years of it, Annie, bless her, had more experience dealing with another person's illnesses than is reasonable. She'd not bargained for a pro bono career in medicine when she married me. I'd tried every natural approach to vanquishing my miserable colds and flus over the years, from gigantic doses of vitamin C to zinc supplements to an ecosystem of herbs and spices. Nothing worked. As I considered Annie's suggestion, I thought maybe I *could* incinerate the bug spreading through my body. I did not relish heading out to the yoga studio, but I was more fearful of the cruddiness developing into something worse. How, I wondered, would I manage sex with a fever?

"I'm game," I said after a few minutes of puttering around the kitchen.

"*Seriously?*" said Annie. "I'm shocked. I'm also excited. I think it will work."

"Thanks, Doc."

As I drove through the frigid darkness to the studio, I imagined the scene. At least, I hoped, some hot hippie lass would lead the class. But the teacher, to my great disappointment, was a guy. Shirtless, rippled with muscle, movie-star handsome, Cheshire-cat grinning, he was an engine of enthusiasm, positively gushing with happiness, it appeared, at my arrival. *So this*, I thought, *explains Annie's passion for yoga.* I became aware of seeds of jealousy germinating in a brain that was supposed to be living for the moment— to, as you will recall, "live in the now." I found an open spot in the young-woman-crammed room, rolled out Annie's mat, and fell into the same relaxed pose as the rest of the class: on my knees (they cracked loudly) with my torso bent at the waist, thrusting my hands out in front of me and resting my forehead on the mat.

Dionysius eventually entered the room, and everyone rose. He talked briefly about compassion and love and then folded himself into the "down dog" position. Everyone followed his lead. And so, within the first minute of yoga practice, there I was with my butt in the air in a room full of women. Just maintaining the pose in the equatorial heat of the room caused sweat to gloss my body and drip from my forehead and nose. When Dionysius finally urged us up and into another pose, I realized my long-sleeved T-shirt not only was unwise but was intolerable. I felt as if I was being smothered. So I stripped off the shirt, tossed it beside my mat, and continued. My spare chest and arms and marshmallow waist (another casualty of middle age; until my late 30s, any correlation between food consumption and waist size had seemed merely theoretical) were on full display and, in fact, spotlighted thanks to my proximity to the Teacher with the Perfect Body.

I pressed forward, though, and soon forgot about my aging stomach and biceps. The seeds of jealousy withered away. I lost myself in the poses and in the all-consuming, hundred-degree heat, and soon my nagging ailments seemed to melt. Dionysius— Billy—knew how to teach and how to inspire. I coaxed my body into places it never before had visited. It hurt, but in a good way. Yoga most definitely would pump my libido, I concluded. If nothing else, I'd be able to go back home and join Annie for some good pretzel sex.

The practice ended, we all lay on our backs with our eyes closed, and I embraced the heat, my rubbery muscles, the Indian music. Then I gasped: My feet were in Billy's hands. Billy was massaging my feet.

He must do this with everybody, I thought, panic rattling my brain.

Only two people had ever massaged my feet: Annie and the woman who gave me my one and only professional massage. As Billy stroked my soles, I thought: *Wow, does this feel awkward.* I thought: *Wow, would a lot of guys have a major problem with this.* And as it went on: *Wow, the last time I had a foot massage—about twenty-two hours ago—it prefaced sex, so wow does this feel doubly awkward.*

When Billy left my feet, waves of relief flooded my entire being. I sneaked a peek to see if he rubbed anybody else's soles, but he was somewhere behind me and I wasn't sure it was acceptable, during this resting phase, to sit up and start looking around. So I stayed on my back, with my eyes closed, until he said some more words about love and compassion and left the room.

I came home, downed a beer, brewed a mug of some herbal detox tea—I thought of it as a yin-yang approach to illness—and retired to the sex den, where Annie awaited. She'd fed the kids, read them their stories, and tucked them into bed without too many emotional shenanigans. She sat in our king-size bed waiting for me, wearing lingerie and lipstick, looking gorgeous. But I could see fatigue in her eyes, the accumulation of the day: the work, the cooking, the cleanups, the myriad details of maintaining a family and a life.

"What did you think?"

"Amazing," I said, undressing and getting ready to pop into the shower. I was drenched in sweat. "I don't feel sick anymore. I feel great, in fact."

"I'm so excited you love yoga, DJ!" she said with an enthusiasm bordering on mania. "This will be *great* for—"

"But does Billy rub your feet when it's all over?"

"What?" said Annie. "He rubbed your feet?"

My mind racing: "Yes! Rubbed! Massaged!"

"That's strange," said Annie, looking pensive. "I've never seen him do that."

"What?"

"Kidding! He rubs everybody's feet at the end. And it's awesome."

I exhaled. "Good one."

After my shower we tried something brand-new: lube, bought the week before at Target, the corporation to which, apparently, we were contributing an alarming portion of our income. School supplies, leggings, hangers, picture frames, Polly Pockets, spatulas, a world of other things made in China . . . and now, lube.

This Target safari, like most of them, had involved the girls, which made for an especially interesting trip. Eagle-eyed Joni tended to note all of the contents of our cart. When she wasn't familiar with an item, she asked about it. If she'd asked about the lube, we could have lied—*It's shampoo, honey*—but this hadn't occurred to us. So Annie bought the lube separately while I pushed the girls around in the cart, and then we purchased everything else.

So, lube. I'd never considered it before, in part because I believed my powers of stimulation should be enough. But on doctor's orders—you know, *jazzing it up*—we decided to give lube a whirl.

"Oh my *God,* DJ," Annie said. "Wow."

I changed my mind about lube.

We'd gone *fourteen years* without lube. We're marginally intelligent people, we're adventurous, we appreciate debauchery, we drink. How on earth hadn't we blasted past our inhibitions and lathered up with lube? Why hadn't anybody told us about its sublime majesties? We had entered middle age entirely lubeless! We both realized immediately that we'd make up for this cheerless oversight. Thank you, Doc.

Science, not to mention the Almighty, may have produced something slipperier than lube, but I've never encountered it. That's the heart of the matter with lube: It's satiny and slick. Good lube does not permit friction—which you understand is a necessary condition for intercourse—to change its composition from slippery to sticky. This transformation is common in other substances—consider lotions or soap—but is not part of the equation with quality lube. Lust quickly commandeered our brains. And soon, Annie submitted to a splendid orgasm. And then I followed.

"TOMORROW'S THE big day," said Annie in the morning as we lay beside each other.

"Vegas," I said.

"Porno," replied Annie.

As the Vegas trip inched closer, our anticipation ripened. The prospect of a (nearly) complete, and in this case tactile, immersion in porno excited me, but so did Vegas, a special place for me because my grandparents lived there for part of my adolescence. My grandfather worked as a poker dealer at the MGM Grand in the 1970s and 1980s, then at Bally's, then at another casino or two. I grew up outside Philadelphia and had never experienced anything but rolling hills, steamy summers, primeval forests, and winter snow, until the day, at the age of 10 or 11, we landed in Las Vegas. The air felt so different, somehow more clear yet full of sparkle. The sun literally dazzled, and the casino lights at night lit a corner of my brain that remains bright and beguiled.

Much later, after Annie and I married, we'd drive from our home in Albuquerque to Vegas to visit Gramps, and we both took to the city, to the clang of coins pouring into metal trays and the sashaying cocktail girls balancing platters of sweating beer bottles above their shoulders and the placards on taxis advertising strip clubs. It's phony, it's wrong, it's twisted, and it understands this about itself.

After Gramps died in the mid-1990s, we returned only once, for Annie's 30th birthday, for a weekend of booze and high jinks, one of our last vacations before having children. We stayed in the hotel New York New York for a few nights, hit a royal flush playing video poker (it was a nickel machine; the winnings paid for the room), and had a good romp or two in the big hotel bed. Those were the days before pregnancies, child rearing, careers, and age taxed our time and nicked at our energy.

Now we were returning to Vegas for the pornography industry's annual sex circus, a three-day festival of flesh, including that world's own Oscars where women vied for awards in categories such as "Best New Starlet" and "Best Supporting Actress–Video" and guys prayed for victory in, say, the "Best Male Newcomer" category. Joni and Ginger, of course, were not joining us for the Carnival of Depravity. My parents were flying in from Philadelphia to watch them.

They arrived, and spears of guilt and remorse pierced me when we met at the airport, during the drive to our house, and for the rest of the day. I regretted leaving their orbit two years earlier for Colorado, hauling their precious granddaughters halfway across the country for the sake of a job. I missed them. I missed the Northeast. I missed my home. It pained me to simply drop them off at their hotel, but I had to go to a restaurant where I was interviewing a man who collected fedoras, like the kind Gramps wore, for a somewhat unusual story celebrating classy old hats and critical of the ubiquitous baseball cap.

As I waited for the fedora guy, I found myself staring at the legs of a woman sitting in a booth across from me. The sight of those legs rising from her tall boots and then ducking behind a short skirt transfixed me until the hat aficionado appeared. This was not unusual—random women often captured my imagination—but in light of our project, and of the discussion Annie and I had had in the cabin about how we both "notice" attractive members of the opposite sex, I considered the degree to which sex routinely consumed my thoughts. We're animals, sniffing everywhere, looking, looking, looking, thrilling to the little jolts of raunch that charge our brains throughout the day. I never regaled Annie with my daily catalogues of lust chestnuts, but now I understood that she, too, maintained her own cache of them.

I wonder if she's checked out any guys today? I thought.

Several carnal jolts later, I was back in the office, and at the tail end of the day I was e-mailing with an old buddy about the marathon. He wrote: "You know what I like best about this whole thing? That it was Annie's idea. I'm going to have to use that little tidbit on Zoe. Maybe she'll counter with 200 straight days."

"Good luck."

Then I rushed home to be with Mom and Dad for dinner at our house. Eventually, they left for their hotel with Joni. Ginger, we feared, might not adjust well to sleeping in a hotel room without her mom and dad. But she would freak if she saw Joni leave with her grandparents. So we pretended that both girls would sleep in our house for the night, but while I eased Ginger into bed with a story and talk about how much fun she would have with her grandparents, my parents and Joni drove off to the hotel.

By then, the hour was late, and Annie and I were rising early the following morning to fly to Vegas. We showered, Annie slipped into some lingerie, I wore those "sexy" pajama bottoms, and we sat on the bed together.

"Let's just do it tonight," Annie said, rolling over to her bedside table and squirting lube into her hands. "Not much foreplay."

Given the day's stresses and our attendant exhaustion, this was a welcome idea. At the same time, though, I wondered whether we should be shrugging our shoulders and submitting to a quickie simply to satisfy the requirements of the marathon. We began lazily pecking at each other's lips and caressing the places that gave us shivers. Soon, appetite lassoed both of us, and we joined, rocking together, holding each other as we moved until I orgasmed. Annie, however, did not, and I asked her if it mattered.

"My orgasms take more work. I'm fine with orgasm-free sex. Sometimes."

The sex for both of us was routine and perfunctory, but sex it was, on the fifth day of the marathon, marking one of our longer strings of consecutive days of doing it since before Joni was born.

"Short and sweet," said Annie as we curled ourselves into croissants under the covers.

WE WONDERED if Ginger would notice the absence of Joni as we drove the five minutes from our house to my parents' hotel. But it was 6 a.m., she was barely awake, and she sat silently in her car seat as we piloted the minivan. My groggy dad opened the hotel door into a dark room where I could hear Joni's heavy sleep-breathing.

"Hi, honey, put the little girl right here," said Mom. She pulled up the covers. I slid Ginger into the nest.

"Here," I said, placing a bag on the floor beside the bed. "We've got presents for the girls when they wake up."

Dad slid into his bed—my parents knew they would have at least one of the kids for the night, so they had requested two beds—and I crept back to the door.

"Thanks so much, you guys," I whispered. "I love you."

"Love you," they both whispered.

And then it was like Dorothy opening that door leading from the Kansas farmhouse to Oz. We had three days in Vegas before us: no kids, few responsibilities, a free hotel, and sex, sex, sex. Jolly good fun!

SURELY, WE thought in the airport, some of the other people flying from Denver to Las Vegas were also attending the porno show. When any woman in the airport betrayed even the tiniest nod to the salacious—excessively tight jeans, bared midriff—we'd glance at each other and raise our eyebrows.

She a porn star?

After about the fifth eyebrow signal, while observing a passenger across the aisle on the plane, Annie grabbed my thigh and squeezed.

"I love you, DJ," she said. "I love that we play games. We have *fun*."

An attractive bleached blonde wearing a low-cut sheer blouse and a denim jacket walked down the aisle toward us. Her breasts swayed with each step. I could see her nipples. Annie and I whipped our heads around and traded eyebrow liftings, grinning wide.

"No doubt," I said.

I sat next to the window on the plane and gazed down on the pageant of western space below: white peaks and black crevasses and dark pine trees; level red expanses pimpled with flat-topped buttes and ribboned with canyons; brown desert like fields of sandpaper. And then we landed. Soon we were at the Flamingo, a classic Strip hotel and casino opened by mobster Benjamin "Bugsy" Siegel on New Year's Eve 1946, almost exactly sixty years prior to our visit. I clearly remembered the Flamingo from my adolescent visits, but much of the Strip had changed, even since our 1990s trips.

One of the many odd things about Vegas is that the destruction of so many first-generation casinos doesn't stab at the heart with the ferocity that might accompany the leveling of historic buildings in other cities. Vegas never pretends to be anything but a shape-shifting fantasy. Even Disney banks on Magic Kingdom nostalgia and shared communion with "ancient" touchstones— the classic rides and attractions may get face-lifts but rarely encounter wrecking balls. Vegas's permanence rests not with the buildings and the urban grid but with the town's perpetual and compulsive reinvention of itself. Change is the constant. In twenty years, when I'm pushing senior-citizenhood, Vegas will have mutated again, several times over. And if it hasn't, I'll be bored with it all.

That said, I'd hate to see the Flamingo come down. What's not to love about giant pink flamingos?

We got a big room with a view of the Strip. The bed hovered like an aircraft carrier on an ocean of blue shag, where we dropped our bags, zipped them open, and began retrieving clothes. What, we'd both wondered earlier, does one wear to a porn convention?

Spiky pumps for Annie? Leather pants for me? I went with jeans, a white button-down shirt, and a charcoal pin-striped sport coat, a look I'd never tried before but one I'd seen in magazines. It seemed hip, it seemed young, and given the environment, I was ready to shoot for both. However, when I combined the pin-striped jacket with the jeans, I did not immediately feel hip or younger; instead, I felt like somebody trying to look hip and younger, a feeling that, to be fair, did correspond with reality. Annie wore a combination she'd gone with several times before: a short corduroy skirt, maroon boots, and a pair of wild leggings covered with different-colored swirls and shapes that compel people to ask her if the collage is an especially ambitious tattoo project.

Then we joined the plodding phalanx of ogling Middle America conventioneers like us, the couples looking for a few days of packaged license, the ball-capped yahoos wearing "What Happens In Vegas, Stays In Vegas" T-shirts, out for a weekend of heavy drinking, wallet thinning, and excitable notions of erotic fireworks.

We entered the Venetian, the site of the show, and immediately I encountered a category of woman I had never actually seen in person: porn stars dressed as porn stars (of course, previously and unwittingly I may have encountered hundreds of porn stars in real life, only instead of dressing like porn stars they were wearing sweat suits). Their outfits were tight and tiny, their heels towering, their breasts . . . just . . . gigantic. Disembodied, engorged, taut udders, missiles, a monstrous throng of them bouncing through the casino, catching the eyes of men and women everywhere in Hawaiian shirts and turquoise blouses, clutching cigars and lukewarm bottles of Miller. Heads swiveled, mouths opened, and jaws did actually drop.

Oh my GOD.

And that was just on the casino floor.

Then there was the show itself, where Annie wandered wearing the first press pass ever to dangle from her neck. She was there to take pictures. The *Post* didn't send a photographer to accompany me, and Annie's no professional photographer, but we thought a picture might come in handy, if not for the paper then at least as something I could stick on the *Post*'s website. The laminated pass thrilled her like few things I'd ever witnessed. Our press passes gave us nimble access to the upstairs explosion of porn stars and to the downstairs horizon of sex-toy vendors and symposium speakers and porno technology geeks and their online businesses.

Everywhere we walked, hard-core sex played on gigantic flat-screen televisions. And beneath the televisions? The actual women in the videos—the stars of the scenes that were playing above—signed autographs, posed for pictures with their fans, and licked their lips with great suggestive power.

"Check out that rack!" shouted a guy wearing sweatpants and a Raiders sweatshirt and hat, pointing toward a woman in fishnet, thigh-high stockings, a thong, and a top barely larger than a butterfly. It was some rack. Watching this sad sack inspired several thoughts, including: *All things considered, sweatpants really don't have much going for them.* He got in line as he high-fived his buddy, another Raiders-clad and sweatpanted young fellow.

"Hey, hottie," said another porn star, wearing ethereal pink wings on her back—she looked like some sort of sex pixie—and wrapping her arm around a chubby guy in a flannel shirt. On the screen above her, she shouted, "Yes! Yes! Oh yeah, baby! Right there! Yeah!" She pulled the flannel guy closer, and they posed for a camera and grinned.

A pair of hand-in-hand female porn stars, their faces glinting with glitter, passed me as I stood and watched, taking notes.

"I need a drink," said one of them lowly.

"Like, three," said her friend.

"Party!" screamed an enormous man with a shaved head and a fine suit and eyes red-rimmed already, from what—booze? drugs? both? "Woo-hoo!" He pointed at a woman in a thong and steep pumps who was bent over at her waist and grabbing her ankles for the sake of a photograph. "I'm gettin' me some of *that!*"

Despite the volume of unfortunate but by no means surprising frat-boy high fives and what might best be described as "hollers," I must admit there was something positively erotic for me, at least for a bit, about being in the company of women who would do just about anything sexual. I brushed against them in the crammed halls as I wandered with Annie, scribbling in my notebook, and I encountered them at their booths and immediately imagined them naked (it didn't take much imagination). At the same time it crossed my mind that these women had done everything, things unimaginable, with male porn stars, men whose résumés hinge on the length and breadth of their . . . manhood. Would anything less than a giraffe's neck satisfy these nymphs? And if sex equals work in their world, doesn't that equation have great potential to make sex drudgery?

It wasn't only strutting female porn stars and their male fans filling the convention space, however. Female spectators—most there with their boyfriends or husbands, some just into porno—competed in "best anal orgasm sounds" contests, where they moaned "Oh! Oh! Oh! Yes, baby, harder! Yes!" into microphones. Women—both porn fans and actors—got tied to tables in S&M demonstrations. Asian displays in the sex-shop portion of the show highlighted amazing toys, including a wheezing, whirring Willy Wonka–esque contraption that jerks off men.

It was dizzying, amazing. Annie and I gawked at the latex-sheathed fetish queens and their gay counterparts, the guys Swiss-cheesed with studs and rings and swaddled in black leather. We could not believe the breasts. We could not believe the blow-up dolls, or the "pocket vaginas"—rubbery, flesh-colored sleeves—that men buy and have "sex" with. We could not believe the dildos like butternut squash and anacondas and Pringles cans.

"Oh my God," Annie said when we arrived at our first dildo display. "Is that supposed to be a penis?"

"Maybe in some alien universe," I offered sheepishly.

Annie started talking up the sex-toy vendors, which made me slightly uncomfortable. I shot around nervous glances as she chatted, as if we were in a public park and Annie, for some reason, had decided to cop a few rocks of crack from a wandering dealer.

"You want something called Two Fingers and a Thumb," said one vendor, a young women who could have passed for an Iowa sorority girl and who confirmed, for me, Annie's earlier contention that sex toys had gone mainstream. She directed Annie to an aisle in the sex-toy area where the item was on sale. We steered through the crowds, and suddenly there it was: purple, shaped sort of like a saguaro cactus. Behold: Two Fingers and a Thumb.

Annie didn't hesitate, handing the vendor $25, dropping Two Fingers into our sack of convention swag (and what swag it was!) and marching back into the flesh spectacle. It was her first sex toy. *So that's my competition*, I thought, eyeing it as a chess master sizes up a new opponent. *Piece of plastic with a battery inside. Looks like a weird fork.* The mere prospect of a sex toy jangled my nerves a bit, but the reality of the thing bleached away some of the worry. If I couldn't outperform a plastic fork, then I simply wasn't worthy.

My brother Mike called as I stood before a display of "clown porn" performers—people who dress up like clowns and have sex.

"Hey, Slug," he said when I answered my cell phone. "How's the big show?"

"You've got to get here some year, man," I said. "It's crazy. In a good way."

"How's Annie handling it?" he asked. Mike knew Annie didn't exactly fit the "porn fanatic" profile.

I smiled at her ogling the clowns wearing thongs, pasties, glittery pumps . . . and red-ball noses that matched red Afros.

"She's digging it," I said. "It's hard not to."

Annie and I lost ourselves in the show, this cavalcade of decadence. We paced down the aisles, our eyes wide, past porn stars licking penis lollipops and posing for pictures, past Jenna Jameson high on a display signing autographs, worshipful men lined up to get a picture of themselves with the High Priestess of Porno. The experience drove us both into something like a trance, a condition we both found quite agreeable. But we were having dinner with an old friend of mine that evening, and we had to complete number 6 before the night's end. So we returned to our room, parted the heavy curtains, and let in the lights of the Strip. We showered and then flopped onto the big bed.

"Whaddya' say, straight to the chase?" said Annie.

"That's two quickies in a row," I said warily.

"We've got, what, ninety-something lovemaking sessions to go?" said Annie as we embraced on the bed. "And most of them will be in our bedroom in Denver. But we're in Vegas now, we're going out to dinner, and we've got to move!"

I dragged my palm across her hip and kissed her.

"You're talking sense," I said. I stroked her for a few minutes before she invited me inside. Then for the first time in a while—probably since a summer beach vacation more than a year earlier—we did it at an elevation lower than a mile in the sky. Vegas sits at about twenty-one hundred feet.

"Sex is good closer to sea level," said Annie after we'd finished, both of us lost in a post-sex high, propped up in bed.

"It is," I said. "Sex is good at sea level, too. And way up high in Denver."

"We've done it in places higher than Denver," said Annie.

"Definitely," I said, quickly reviewing our history of sexual encounters. "Although I can't think of where they were."

"Aspen, for one," said Annie.

Another one came to me. "And Taos."

We compiled a list of our high-elevation sexual encounters, a discussion that would not have taken place if sex had remained on the periphery of our lives, and we spooned with each other not in bright desert moonlight but in the low glow of Vegas's neon night. Then we got dressed and walked through the glow to an Indian restaurant.

I woke up to a triple cappuccino from Starbucks.

Annie lives for the presentation of sunny surprises. After fourteen years together, I'd still occasionally come home from work to a plate of olives, feta cheese, and bread, or to a hot wedge of homemade socca—an Annie specialty—a Provençal flatbread made from chickpea flour, olive oil, and salt. All of this, mind you, after a day of dealing with work and the kids. I'd mention in the morning that I wanted to build our music collection, and what would await me in the evening? A $25 gift certificate from iTunes. How did Annie spend her first commission check from her pasta-selling job? She bought me a new laptop.

Among other things, Annie's genius for gifting reflects her deep desire to please others, to ripple happiness outward. The morning cappuccino was a tiny installment in a vast and dense history of laboring for cheer. It was work, this pleasing others, and Annie was an artisan. I, on the other hand, remained a greenhorn, a struggling student. Over the years, on many occasions, I'd pledged to sharpen my skills, but I hadn't made much progress. And there, in Vegas, after nearly a week of sex, I once again committed myself to a more rigorous effort to please Annie.

"This makes my day," I said to her, cradling the hot paper cup in my hands.

"I think I can make it even better," she said, flashing me a crafty look.

"Of that, I'm certain," I said, feeling the first carnal throb of the day.

We downed our caffeine concoctions, and then we were out the door, back to the Venetian for another day of porno. Even more people packed the labyrinthine space than the day before. I scurried around grabbing people to interview for stories—about cell-phone and video iPod porn, dating software, and herbal sex stimulants. Annie and my high school buddy, nicknamed Shave, who was in town on business and had been our previous night's dinner companion, wandered around without me. When I saw them again, Annie had stopped at a table where Randy West, seemingly the only straight male porn star in the place, was signing autographs. She talked with him for a bit, I saw him wield a pen, and then Annie returned, grinning, her face red, holding out the photograph. There he was, leaning against a fireplace mantel, standing on a furry beige rug. And there it gleamed, ascending from his waist: the Leaning Tower of Pringles.

Talk about competition.

"What? You got his autograph?" I stammered, looking at her picture of Man and Anaconda emblazoned with a personal note: "Annie, hard at work for you!"

"I'm getting one, too!" I said, feeling not a shred of jealousy but, instead, a bubbly excitement. Annie had opened the door. Now I could pose with a porn star of my choosing and feel not even a gentle pang of guilt. I passed a few female stars, none of them autograph-worthy. And then I saw her, Smoking Mary Jane, bedecked in subtle dominatrix garb. Her bright red lips lifted in a smile as I approached.

"Can I get your autograph?" I asked, feeling foolish and 14.

"Of course, baby," she said. She signed and then beckoned me beside her. I followed obediently. She wrapped her arm around my waist and smiled at Annie's camera. I reached my arm around her corseted torso. Her canyon cleavage pulled my eyes down. I lost myself in the flesh vortex. Click.

Annie, Shave, and I retreated to a sleek bar in the casino, a place of low couches and low tables, dim lights, and expensive liquor—the kind of bar we had not entered since having children. We drank beer and relaxed and remained vigilant for porn-star sightings, although the expiration date of their novelty was swiftly arriving. It would have been fun to hang out in that bar for hours. But it was not to be.

"Shave," I said. "I hate to be blunt, but Annie and I have to have sex, so we've got to split. We'll see you for dinner."

He laughed. He was aware of our marathon. "I get it, Slug," he said.

And then Annie and I were back in our bed on the sixth floor, giddy about the new silicone lube that she scored at the show: teardrop-shaped bottles of a product poised to hit the market later in the year. "Best lube in the world," one sales rep, a smiling woman with a highly exposed rack, assured Annie. "You'll see." During the show, vendors also hawked herbal supplements aimed at boosting "stamina" or "arousal," and I'd grabbed a bunch of them. While drinking at the bar with Shave, I'd secretly—I didn't want Shave to think we already were hunting for ways to "jazz it up"—popped one packed with Chinese herbs, and by the time we got to the room I felt myself throbbing.

"These Chinese herbs rock," I told Annie.

There was the possibility, too, that two days spent gawking at barely dressed porn stars had amplified my sex drive.

Annie showered while I sipped a beer in the room, and when she returned to the bed, wet and warm, her face flushed, the throbbing grew more urgent. We began kissing immediately, our hands grabbing at each other. I didn't want to rocket her to an or-gasm, so I teased her, drawing her close, then pulling her back, near again, but not quite. And then I let her go, and she jumped, and without hesitation I slid inside.

"Yeah," she said quietly through a smile, sounding nothing like a frenzied porn star but instead just like Annie. She sounded real.

"I feel all loosey-goosey," said Annie as we got dressed for dinner. "I'm ready for a cocktail or two and a meal. In a casino."

AFTER A big dinner and a margarita, I split for the awards ceremony. The show's organizers gave only me, the reporter, a free pass. Annie would need a real ticket, and they were selling for close to $500. Needless to say, Annie, our secretary of the treasury, did not consider for a moment the idea of dropping that kind of dough on a ticket to an awards show for an industry she did not hug close to her heart. The James Beard Awards? She might have coughed up big bucks.

"Have fun, honey," she said. "Spoon with me when you slip into bed tonight, OK?"

We kissed good-bye, Shave left for his hotel, and I followed a long red carpet stretching several hundred yards past blackjack tables and roulette wheels and slot machines before arriving at the enormous banquet room where the ceremony was being held. Camera-wielding men lined the sides of the rug with such closeness and mass—such impenetrability—that it looked like a winding canyon. Flashes erupted in staccato. Men clutching video cameras begged porn stars to stop and vamp, and many did. Nobody pleaded with me to bend over, but I was greeted with obvious awe and jealousy by the walls of yahoos. They thought I was in the industry! *This is awesome,* I thought. *They think I'm in porno!*

The show still stands as one of the strangest and most depraved events I've ever witnessed. The "starlets" and, for the most part, their male benefactors—the producers and directors of the videos—paraded through a press gaggle jammed with media from around the world. They posed, they answered reporters' questions, and they vamped.

"Belladonna!" cried one guy from an Italian publication. "Are there any lines you wouldn't cross?"

Punk Belladonna, with her tattoos and her apparent lack of breast implants, answered: "I did a gang bang once, and I didn't like it much. It was twelve guys." She also reported that she was "not into" women who had turned into men, and that she "probably" wouldn't engage in bestiality.

A tuxedoed guy with slicked-back dark hair and a puffy face, who looked like a particularly curdled mobster—the kind of "bad" gangster Tony Soprano himself would end up slaughtering—sauntered into the press crush with a smattering of porn stars. He introduced them as "my girls."

"I'm beautiful and nasty," said a redhead with curly hair who later received the coveted "Best Starlet" award.

Porn legend Ron Jeremy—he of cheesy mustache, fat torso, squat stature, and elephantine penis—stood with the gigantic, cue-ball-bald owner of the Bunny Ranch brothel in Nevada and reported that his penis was "still active."

"It hasn't got any cobwebs yet," he said. "Jenna may catch up someday, but not yet."

When asked where she got her dress—just like at the Oscars!—"actress" Britney Foster gave a little curtsey, smiled, and replied, "From Neiman's."

Well, not so Oscars.

A girl in a silver dress with glitter-plastered eyelids told the press, "I am nominated for 'Best Anal.' "

Jenna Jameson came wrapped in pink, her breasts pleading to break free. A pair of giggling porn stars in stiletto heels chased each other down the carpet. A big man with an elaborate cane and a dramatic pimp outfit walked slowly, answering questions with single words. Party favors from Larry Flynt for every guest decorated the banquet hall's big round tables. Among the gifts? Rubbery "portable pussies."

A porn star who won a big award yelled to her costar: "I love your cock!" Another woman pumped her fists in the air when her name was announced for "Best Actress Video"; then she approached the podium and took a deep breath.

"OK," she said. "I'm going to soak this up a little bit. This feels good. Thank you so much. This feels so good to me."

A presenter announced that "the woman I'm with" has "agreed to marry me," and people all around the room cheered and clapped. A veteran porn director won an award and said without a whisper of irony, "It's the acting, the acting, that gets it year after year." A producer launched into an obscenity-peppered rant about the government and then told everyone, "I will never, ever, cop a plea, take a deal, or sell this industry out." He also apologized, repeatedly, to the many people he said he'd "shit on" during his career.

Savannah Sampson won for "Best Actress Film" and told the audience, "My family is ashamed of what I do, so thanks for the support."

Then the manic emcee said, "If you've got a little coke left, do it now. We're almost there." He called one guy in the audience a douche bag, he persuaded a guest to take off her shirt, and he berated a man for failing to whip out his penis. The ceremony wrapped up at 12:30, and it was obvious that for many members of the audience a big night of partying was just getting started. Sex? Probably more sex happened in Las Vegas that night, per capita, than anywhere else on earth.

I'd already contributed to the day's quotient.

The awards ceremony wallowed in sex like nothing I'd ever encountered, and I appreciated the players' almost innocent enthusiasm. They believed that they were stars and that their awards were shining achievements. Most of them radiated pride as they cradled their trophies onstage and accepted kisses and accolades from their colleagues. I felt no compulsion to demonize them—in fact, I rather liked them—but by the conclusion of the event any enthusiasm I'd had for pornography had turned a bit limp.

Real sex, I knew, had nothing to do with deals, studio pimps, starlets, or money. I fantasized about Annie's and my big bed, and of Annie lost in slumber. I dreamed of slipping between the sheets, not of sex. It was late, the meal and booze had diffused my vigor, and the earlier, stirring round of wanton intimacy had bathed me with contentedness.

I'm beat, I thought as I walked back to Annie through the chilly desert air. *But damn, do I feel strong.*

3

Don't Wait for Chemistry

t had been a week of firsts: my first yoga, Annie's first purchase of a sex toy, our first encounter with porn stars, my first herbal aphrodisiac. Our first lube.

I found myself reaching toward Annie more instinctively than ever, or at least since early in our courtship. During many walks through casinos, we held hands, a pretty basic form of touch that had receded over the years: We were more arm-in-arm types. Earlier in the week, when we sat side by side in our king-size bed reading after work, we rested against each other rather than migrating to our respective edges of the bed. As the week progressed, the sex, too, improved. It wasn't just that we were trying new things, that we were "jazzing it up." When we did it now, everything seemed a dash less restrained, a few degrees hotter.

I loved how Annie soldiered through the porn show. She's not the porn type—no tattoos, no love of rock-and-roll lifestyles or drugs, of late-night partying or flashy cars, of Hollywood or belly-button piercings. Even *Sex and the City* bored her after the first season. Annie is wholesome. Few things make her happier than spending a day in the kitchen. She loves exercise, being in nature, and taking the kids to museums and libraries. She knits. But she's also exceedingly adventurous. She takes huge chances.

We had been dating for only three months when Annie decided to say good-bye to all of her Philadelphia friends and move with me to Minneapolis, where I was attending graduate school. We loved Minneapolis but grew tired of the long winters. Annie's solution? Moving to sunny New Mexico, without jobs, a place to live, or friends. We rolled into town with our stuff crammed into garbage bags, lived for a bit in an edgy motel, and eventually scored work and an apartment.

We remained in the Land of Enchantment—or as locals call it, bittersweetly, the "Land of Entrapment"—for more than five years, until a job for me yanked us away to South Florida. With Annie entering her second trimester with Joni, I moved to Florida first and lived alone for a few months in a sleazy, prostitute-approved motel on Route 1 in a town called Boynton Beach. Annie and I racked up a $700 phone bill in one month. Then I lived in a dumpy apartment swarming with lizards, where a highly pregnant Annie visited, tears streaming down her face when I met her at the airport because, she told me, "I love you so much."

That was before she encountered the swarming reptiles.

At last we moved together to a townhouse complex in Delray Beach, with a parking lot full of flashy sports cars. People in the complex might not be able to afford a home, but they didn't hesitate to lease a new Porsche, an approach to life that is the rough opposite of what you encounter in New Mexico—in Annie's beloved New Mexico. I grew up going to beaches in southern New Jersey. Almost everything about the ocean pleases me. So I found things to like about South Florida—the sugar-sand beaches, the turquoise water, the salty breezes, and sea life. Annie lacks any affinity for beaches and the ocean, and she loathes steamy heat, flat landscapes, and swamps. The flying, defiant cockroaches that looked prehistoric, the poisonous frogs, the lizards skittering across our bed—none of it worked to Florida's advantage.

One day weeks after Joni was born, Annie squinted her eyes as she sat on the couch in our cheap rental townhouse. She pointed at the opposite wall.

"Why is the wall moving?" she asked.

She rose, took a few steps, and screamed.

"Ticks!" she said, almost hurling herself back onto the couch.

A horde of ticks had assembled on the wall, and they were marching down to the floor, to the rest of the house. That was about six months into our Sunshine State sojourn. Months later, we elected not to do the sensible thing—staying put, buying a house, clocking four or five years of work experience under our belts before moving on. Instead, we hauled ourselves out of Florida to Washington, D.C., for yet another job of mine, piling our stuff and our year-old daughter into a cramped apartment for about a year and a half. The place was so pint-sized that Annie and I slept on an enclosed porch—sweltering in summer, freezing in winter—that provided incomparable views of the empire of rats thriving behind our building.

Now, several moves later, we stood in the serpentine airport security line, just hours after starting our second week of sex with a morning session on the splendid Flamingo bed. As the queue inched along, I studied the list of forbidden objects. Swag from the Expo filled our bags—maybe thirty pounds of lube samples, porno DVDs, herbal aphrodisiacs, T-shirts, bags, and so on.

"Do I have a lighter in there?" I mused aloud to Annie.

"I think you do," she said.

I contemplated pawing through my bag to find it as we inched ahead in line, but doing that would have meant revealing to everybody around me the stash of triple-X-rated souvenirs inside my bag.

"I'll take my chances," I said.

Trying to convey a sense of wholesomeness to the Transportation Security Administration employees clustered around the metal-detecting machines—"Golly, ya'll, I'm just a dad!"—I placed my shoes, belt, and the stuff in my pockets into one of those gray plastic bins, followed by my bags larded with pornographic swag. Then I smiled with all the innocence and humility I could muster and walked—rather amiably, I thought—through the metal detector.

The woman working the conveyor belt kept my bag inside the detector for longer than usual.

"OK, sir, step aside. Come down here with me," she said. "We need to go through your bag."

I nervously tossed out another Gomer Pyle "golly" grin and waited as she publicly emptied the sack-full-o'-sex until she found the lighter.

"Here it is," she bellowed, holding up a black lighter emblazoned in pink with the word "Pussy." "You're good to go, sir."

"Sorry," I whispered, feeling the eyes of the airport boring into me.

WE ARRIVED home beat, desiring nothing but quick and soft landings into our own bed, but first there was some child rearing to accomplish. Where Vegas was an extreme variation on a theme of our young lives together—if it were a game, think "quarters"— the return to our tiny house packed with kids and my parents seemed like chess. Fun, yes; if you like chess, and I do, fun figures into its attraction. We picked up our precious little girls. They hugged us and we kissed their cheeks and everyone smiled and all of our hearts warmed and every scrap of this was excellent fun. But like chess, the night provided some challenges.

The girls had grown accustomed to my doting parents. Our return meant stricter discipline and far fewer sweets and chips, among many other things. So after my dad and mom returned to their hotel, Annie and I engaged in a few hours of pawn-nabbing and check-mating with the kids. There were tears about teeth-brushing and hair-combing. More books to be read were demanded, and we caved (check!). Alarming noises were made about not having quite enough dessert, but then they drifted away, and the kids, thankfully, were in their beds with the lights out, and we nearly leapt into our own massive bed, traded quick pecks, and plunged into sleep.

SOME OF the porn-show swag was mildly amusing in a nonsexy way: Silly Putty in a red triple-X-rated egg, pens that lit up. Kid-friendly swag, we reasoned.

The girls played with the Silly Putty and the pens in the morning. Then Ginger slipped on her backpack, and we headed to her preschool in my beat-up Subaru. I kissed her on the cheek and dropped her in the breakfast room, a humid little space in the old church that held the preschool. Kids sat around big tables drinking milk and eating whatever was on the menu for the day (often things that we never would have fed Ginger at home, such as corn dogs for breakfast or deep-fried French toast from a box). Ginger never looked back to say good-bye, and I always suspected that that omission had something to do with the corn dogs.

And then I was at work. Annie had posted the photos we'd taken from the show on a website, and they were popular with my colleagues and among our FFF, or "triple F" (our far-flung friends). I was especially fond of the shot of me with the porn star.

"See!" we were suggesting to our FFF. "You think we're all cardigan sweaters and microbrews, sensible vehicles and potlucks, and just plain doing good. Wrong!"

In the middle of the afternoon, after several hours of tapping away on my computer, surrounded by my earnest and accomplished coworkers, I realized I was suffering from porn-show withdrawal. Everything seemed dull, tarnished, less than what it had been before the show. As I watched people shuffle around with their mugs of coffee, I realized that I did not want to be in this environment, that the newsroom had grown stale. I e-mailed Annie. She was experiencing the same thing. We wanted back! We craved people smoking in casinos and shiny porn stars and stark, beautiful, desert desolation and a fake Eiffel Tower down the street from a fake Egyptian pyramid and across from a fake medieval castle and a fake New York City skyline.

Since the girls were born, and certainly in Colorado, most of our time alone together had been spent outdoors and involved cabins, hiking, cooking over open fires, and so on. This time, we had played in what is arguably the least natural place in America—even the "culture" that tourists engage with in Vegas is artificial—and it had fueled us. We weren't ready to set aside the weekend's bright fevered dream for the Siberian reality of Denver in January.

By the time I got home from work, exhaustion had attached itself like an anchor. I wanted to plop onto the couch, close my eyes, and fall asleep. But we were treating my parents to dinner at a clubby restaurant in a highly yuppified area of Denver called Cherry Creek, a wealthy-casual hangout for divorced businessmen wearing khakis, dress shirts, and expensive watches, drinking scotch, and chatting with thin, Appletini-sipping blonde women who work in real estate.

I watched what I ate because I had to perform that evening. A gigantic meal, I knew (based on years of experience), might steal what was left of my energy and my libido. Annie, on the other hand, inhaled a grilled artichoke, an immense salad, a pile of handmade potato chips swimming in Maytag blue cheese, and a fat slice of cornbread shot through with Cheddar.

"Are you going to make it for tonight?" I asked, considering her feast with sharp envy.

"Of course!" she whispered. "I don't have to, you know, get it up."

I tried one of her cheese-saturated chips. "Mmm," I said,

reaching for another. Annie kicked my foot. I looked at her and shrugged. "What?" I said.

"Be careful," she warned. "You've got work to do." She then tossed a wink my way, an entirely inadequate peacekeeping gesture. I grabbed a chip, swabbed it in cheese, and inhaled it. Then another. And another. "I just might eat the whole thing," I whispered. "Be a good test. Can a man do it after filling his gut with fried things and cheese, not to mention beer, chicken, bread and butter, and maybe some chocolate brownie dessert kind of thing?"

Annie eyes veered from mischievous to concerned. "You're playing with fire, DJ," she warned.

"Right back at you," I murmured.

My parents had been chatting with each other about an upcoming weekend while Annie and I playfully sparred, but as I reached for my fourth chip, my mom swiveled her attention to our side of the table.

"So, you guys have to 'do it' tonight, don't you," she whispered, smiling.

Annie reddened. I squirmed. Mom and Dad watched us like an audience studying a magician. Would a rabbit pop out of a hat?

"Uh, yeah," I answered.

"Better watch what you eat, honey," said Mom. "Don't want to load up too much!"

"Uh, yeah."

WE DROPPED off my parents and said good-bye. They were taking a shuttle to the airport in the morning. I missed them intensely before we even finished dinner, knowing I would not see them again until sometime in the spring or summer. This parting added a veneer of wistfulness to the end of the evening, particularly during the drive home, that was not welcome in light of the upcoming scheduled activities. Had the marathon not been under way, the combination of exhaustion, a full (though not bursting) belly, and my parents' return to their Pennsylvania small town would have made a late-night erotic romp unlikely.

When we arrived home, the girls were asleep. While Annie drove the babysitter home, I quickly showered and readied the room. And then Annie and I were naked, struggling to get in the mood.

"I'd rather hit the sack tonight, to be honest," said Annie in the darkness.

"You got that straight," I said, yawning and eyeing the top drawer of my bureau, where I'd stashed my pile of Viagra. "If I put my head down and shut my eyes, I'll be asleep in no more than two minutes."

"I'm thinking one minute for me."

"You played with fire, and you got burned," I said. "All of that food. You thought you were immune."

"I think you're right," she said. "Although your abstinence doesn't seem to have helped you much, either."

"True."

"Let's do this," said Annie, sounding a bit like a football coach.

"Enough nonsense," I said, dismissing thoughts of a little blue pill. "Time for sex."

I began with an oral proposal and then floated inside, at which point we fulfilled our carnal obligations for the day. We wrapped our arms around each other and squeezed. With my limbs and torso and head, my heart, my spirit, and probably even my damn shadow feeling exalted and potent, teeming with tingles—a feeling far removed from the postdinner lethargy that had settled over me—I savored the ascension of the orgasm and then its completion.

We lay facing each other, between the sheets. Annie stroked my arm.

"We nailed it," she said.

I yawned again. "It ended up being good, too," I said. "Surprising."

We listened to the wind rattle the windows for a few moments before rolling over on our sides for sleep.

"Oh, I forgot to tell you—maybe letting the kids play with that 'kid-friendly' swag from the show wasn't our best collaborative effort," said Annie. "I found the Silly Putty egg in Ginger's backpack. The one she takes to school."

"Good God," I said, feeling as if I'd just been roused into wakefulness by a scorpion sting. "That thing had three X's on it, right?"

"Correct."

Ginger was 3! She believed in faeries! She drank juice and milk from little waxy cups at school. She slept with a stuffed penguin. She was scared of owls! And she places a pornographic egg—something I actually gave to her—into a little purple backpack with flowers and "Ginger" inscribed on it. This did not lighten my heart. This did not compel even a wan smile. I found nothing subversively ironic about the whole thing. I felt like a dad who had really screwed up.

"You don't think she passed that around, do you?"

"Doubt it," said Annie. "I'd have heard about it."

"Yeah, from the police."

"Note to self," said Annie. "Anything even remotely connected to the sex industry shall remain far from our kids from now on."

OUR PROGRESS at this point was merely fractional, but people at my office already were voicing amazement about the feat.

"How the hell are you keeping it interesting?" asked one colleague.

"Aren't you exhausted?"

"Have you ever thought about, you know, bringing other people into the relationship to mix things up?"

I definitely was feeling a bit lethargic, but group sex? That would wake me up, sure, but then I'd be freaked out for the rest of my life. So no.

"Never," I answered. "That's not part of the adventure."

Like most humans, Annie and I are jealous people. I'd written stories about people involved in "polyamory," a practice where couples let their partners have romantic relationships with other people. Not just swingers-style sex, but love-letter-writing, bouquet-of-roses presenting, whisper-on-the-phone-until-dawn romance.

"Why should that intoxicating feeling of new love, of fresh romance, never happen again after you've found a partner for life?" the "polys" asked when I interviewed them. The answer: because this would lead to a nation of people walking around weeping, consumed with violent fantasies, or both.

If Annie had a "relationship" with another man, I'd take the weeping route. We had discussed the whole "swinger" idea before, in the context of our relationship, and the conversation, sparked by my research into the "polys," didn't last long.

"I couldn't handle an 'open relationship,'" said Annie. "It would make me feel, I dunno, less than special."

"Believe me, there's no way I'd sign off on it," I said. "You having sex with another guy? Even if we, for some crazy reason, agreed to such a thing, I can't imagine it would sit well with me. Actually, I can't imagine I could stay married to you. It would fester. It would mess me up."

"Me too," said Annie.

So flesh-and-blood naked people would not be joining us. But people on video would, although Annie had begun to regret that decision as we walked around the porno convention and witnessed, over and over again, Pringles-can Neanderthals attacking a swollen-breasted woman.

"And this would appeal to women because . . ." she'd say, mantra-like, as she walked the aisles.

Nevertheless, we'd scooped up free DVDs at the Expo, mainly because we've cherished this motto, one we've protected and burnished since we met: "Free is best." Free cubes of cheese, free coffee, free key chains, T-shirts, Frisbees, Silly Putty eggs marked with three X's, lighters scrawled with "Pussy": If it's free, we're taking it.

That night as the girls slept, dreaming of talking lambs and top-hatted dolphins, we slipped a porno disc into the DVD player. Pringles-can halfwits rose like so many genies from a rubbed lamp. I'm not what you would call a Pringles-can man. I found the procession of proud baseball bats passing before Annie's eyes intimidating. I asked whether looking at them made her lust after one of those telephone poles.

"I'd hate something that big," she responded. "There really isn't anything pretty about genitals," she added. "They're all sort of ugly when you get right down to it. The most sensuous things on women are her boobs and brains, and on men, well, it's just their brains. In porn you get a lot of fake boobs, and next to no brain. How do women get all worked up watching it?"

I could have pressed Annie on this point, asking her to catalogue the widths and lengths of all of the penises she had . . . handled . . . prior to hooking up with me. I could have requested quality-in-bed summaries of all of her previous lovers, and cross-examined her answers: *So, you're saying that boyfriend in college had a sixteen-inch penis, but you're also alleging that he was lousy in bed. Please detail, precisely, how he failed.*

But that, I thought, was a category of chat not worth pursuing. What would be the point? Annie liked having sex with me enough to suggest we do it for one hundred days in a row. Our relationship, after fourteen years of making love, remained strong, and our sex now was improving rapidly. I did not need the introduction of nagging doubts, or the specter of an old boyfriend with a sixteen-inch schlong, to help me understand, or improve upon, our sex life. To put it directly, this sort of thing might fuck me up.

You may be thinking, *A wasted opportunity! You should push yourself during this marathon! Explore every aspect of your sexual relationship!* But sex, fourteen years into our relationship and only nine days into the marathon, had already soared from the sidelines into center field. And every experiment has its limits. Orgies? No. Leather masks? No. That style of sex so popular in porno, one we'll call "backdoor" sex? We had discussed that once during the training period. I was not especially drawn to it, but it didn't repel me, either.

"So waddya think, Annie," I said during one of many conversations about the upcoming marathon. "Shall we give it a shot?"

"No way," said Annie. "I don't find anything erotic about it. Grosses me out. Not other people doing it, just the idea of *me* doing it."

This brings us back to the porno on this tenth day of lovemaking—Team Pringles had taken turns with backdoor sex— and a conversation that was borne out of the cinematic sex.

"The thing is, none of this is real, I think," I said. "It's all role playing. The women could be lesbians, and the men could be bored to tears with the violence. It's make-believe."

"True, but that doesn't make it less lame," said Annie.

"There's all kinds of role playing in porno, though, not just this sort of thing," I said.

"The violent, demeaning stuff is the absolute worst," said Annie. "I don't find anything sexy about women being belittled and humiliated. I'm sure I'm capable of liking some porno. I just haven't seen anything that really gets me going."

"The violent stuff isn't high on my list either," I said. "But what about role playing in general? Anything ever grab you?"

"You mean like having you dress up like Goldilocks or something?"

"That's the general idea, although I've never considered donning a blonde-pigtail wig and a checked dress for the sake of sex," I said.

Annie winked. "You'd make a great Goldilocks. But I've never really thought about role playing. You the cop and me the woman who has been pulled over for speeding? You the pizza-delivery guy and me the frustrated homemaker? You the doctor and me the patient?"

"You sound like a porn aficionado," I said. "Does any of that appeal?"

"It's more like being a cliché aficionado, or a very occasional dabbler in erotica, but no, none of that does anything for me," said Annie. "I don't find it disgusting, though. Just silly. I'm not sure I could keep a straight face if you had a mustache, leather boots, and a blue uniform and then started making 'moves' on me."

"What about bondage?" I asked. "Light bondage. The sort of stuff that receives *Cosmopolitan* and *Vogue* approval?"

"Is that something you want?" asked Annie.

"If you desired it, I'd do it. I've got nothing against it. It might even be thrilling. But just thinking about it doesn't excite me all that much."

"It's not my thing," said Annie. "I don't want to be tied up."

"Again, I think I might just laugh," I said. "Like, I'd rather tickle you while you're strapped to the bed than have my way with you."

We gave the porno a few more minutes and then bailed. Annie yawned dramatically as we moved closer, as we began skipping—although it felt more like shuffling—toward the sex zone.

"Wow," she said. "Not. In. The. Mood."

I had met her yawn with one of my own and had to agree.

I stroked her arm lightly. Yawned again. My yawn inspired another one from Annie. It was like trench warfare, only instead of grenades, we tossed yawns at each other, pushing ourselves not closer to stretchers or victory marches but to an unheard-of mutual surrender. I grabbed Annie by the arms, clumsily, and we sort of teetered onto our sides on the bed. We stared at each other. I brought my lips to hers. But sparks did not fly. At first. In time, though, things between us heated up: The low-spark kissing turned passionate, our limbs entwined, and we bounced around on the bed with a moderate measure of liveliness, eventually trading orgasms.

"Still dizzy with sleepiness," said Annie, on her back and staring at the ceiling when we had finished. "But I've got to say: The more I'm getting sex, the more I'm loving it. I think daily orgasms should be mandatory."

And then we pulled the covers over our shoulders and rocketed into sleep.

SUPERB MEMORIES of Annie captured my imagination at work. A few weeks earlier I had interviewed a woman for a story about moms who love to smoke pot. The woman—a ganja-gaga momma—called to say I'd left a hat at her house.

"I'll bring it to the restaurant where I work," she said. "You can pick it up anytime."

On this frigid day I went to retrieve the hat, the first thing Annie had ever knit for me, a stout green cap with white and black designs ringing the crown. During the walk, memories of an early encounter with Annie drifted into my brain.

As already established, the first time I saw her, in the break room of the publishing company where we both worked in the heart of Philadelphia, I gasped. She radiated. She cast an aura. I stayed with the miserable job for only four months or so and didn't see Annie much. But one afternoon toward the end of my tenure

I was out killing time on a cold day, taking a stroll. And suddenly, there was Annie, walking in the same direction. She was headed to a yarn store in the city.

"Wanna come along?"

"Sure," I said. I was in the middle of a particularly unhappy relationship at the time. We sauntered and chatted, and I remember understanding during that walk that my relationship was a disaster. Here was the kind of woman I needed to be with, walking beside me, with her purple woolen mittens and her little black wingtips and her black jeans. I left the company, and the troubled relationship crashed shortly thereafter. I called a mutual friend of Annie's and mine at the publishing house to snoop around for me. I wanted to know if Annie was dating.

"Sorry," the friend said. "She's with some guy from England who is a music 'roadie' or something."

Great, I thought. *He's rock-and-roll. He's exotic. He has that accent. I'm twenty-four, living at home, and working as a temp.* I didn't forget about Annie, but I muddled forward, going on a bunch of exceedingly unsuccessful dates, drinking too much, watching a lot of *Twin Peaks* and my favorite television show of all time, *Get a Life,* starring Chris Elliott as a 30-year-old paperboy living above his parents' garage. It spoke to me.

It still does.

During this confusing few years in the early 1990s I answered an advertisement in my hometown newspaper, the *Daily Local News,* for a freelance feature writer. I sent the editor some ridiculous short stories I'd written, but she called anyway.

"I'll give you a shot," she said. "Why don't you come to the newspaper and we can chat about an assignment."

The moment I stepped into the newsroom I understood I belonged there. I liked the sound of people clacking on their computers, the sight of books and papers piled high on reporters' desks, the smell of ink, the witty snippets of conversation carried out between and over desks. I kept working part-time at a theater company while I wrote freelance features for the newspaper. Then I got a "beat," a few rural communities to write about. I applied to graduate school in journalism at the University of Minnesota, received a teaching stipend, and began fantasizing about moose and hockey and snow. And then my friend called.

"I ran into Annie at 2 a.m. in a diner in the city a few days ago," she said. "I told her you rang, asking if she was seeing anybody. She said she wasn't dating the English guy anymore. She'd love to go out with you."

"Awesome," I said, my heart pounding. "I'll call her right away."

"Don't bother," said my friend Sue. "She just quit her job and left for West Africa."

"West Africa?" I said.

"Yeah. Senegal, Sierra Leone. Some other places. She and some friends are just hanging out for a month."

As I said—she likes her adventures.

A few weeks later she returned from Africa, and we went on our first date. A few months later, we were living in separate apartments in Minneapolis—Annie was ready to move with me to the Land of 10,000 Lakes, but not yet ready to share an apartment with me. Among other things, her grandmother would be crushed if her only granddaughter was living in sin with some boy. We ended up getting an apartment together the following year, but we had two phone lines—one for Granny to call, the other for everybody else. It was during our two-year entombment in Minnesota ice that Annie had knit the cap. And now, nearly fifteen years later, I had it again, after a short spell in the house of a pot-smoking mother.

It was a pleasant walking reverie, and I'm not sure if all of the sex helped coax it from my memory archives. Either way, I hailed the images and sensations of those early years together in Philadelphia and Minneapolis, dawdling over them as though for warmth as I cut through the frozen January afternoon.

That night, Annie could have used some heart warming.

She had capped her day with Girl Scouts.

Surreal, alarming clown smiles never left the faces of the strange troop leaders, who led a gymnasium full of confused girls and parents in rousing games of bingo involving different Girl Scout cookies, Annie said later. Annie had been a Girl Scout as a kid, but it never took, and she lasted for only a short while, until she was kicked out of Girl Scouts. She envied the Boy Scouts of her brothers. For them, "Scouts" meant sleeping in tents, making fires out of sticks and dead grass, learning how to properly launch arrows using bows, and spending entire weekends canoeing down rivers. For Annie, "Scouts" meant making cupcakes, selling cookies, sewing pillows, and learning how to cobble together a variety of "crafts." If you ask her about Scouts, she'll say she was "gypped," but she will add that if Girl Scouts could become more like Boy Scouts, she'd turn into an enthusiastic advocate. Now, as an adult, Girl Scouts had rushed back into Annie's life. Many of Joni's friends in elementary school were in Girl Scouts, Joni wanted to join, and Annie saw an opportunity, which can be summed up as: *I will change it from the inside!*

When she first laid out her proposal to me, I felt a combination of affection and fear: I found her zeal for reformation exceedingly cute, but I also suspected she was setting herself up for failure. Girl Scouts, after all, is a large organization. Sure enough, despite Annie's best efforts, her troop remained mostly fixed on crafts and, of course, Thin Mints and Samoas. Her stabs at transformation were met with uncomprehending shrugs. *Camping?* The experience exhumed bad memories for Annie, and it frustrated her, a combination that did not lead inexorably to unbridled carnal appetite. So when she arrived home from the cookie bingo extravaganza, she reported the whole thing was "the oppo-site of arousing."

"Might be a tough one, tonight," she said, sighing, as we shepherded the girls up the steps for the nightly routine: the sto-ries, the repeated commandments ("brush your teeth," "brush your teeth," "brush your teeth," "comb your hair," "comb your hair," "put on your sleeper," "put on your sleeper," "put on your sleeper"), the spats between sisters over, for example, who has a cooler toothbrush, and so on. With that many-act play finally dispatched, we climbed into bed and for a while ignored the sex dangling over our heads. We turned on our laptops and poked around on the Internet looking at news, weather, answering e-mails, whatever. We read magazines. We batted small talk back and forth. We looked at the clock. In about an hour, the day would pass.

Annie put down her yoga magazine. "I'm sleepy. I feel lazy. It would be so easy to turn out the lights and roll over. Again. Just like the other night."

"The night you said daily orgasms should be mandatory?"

"That's the one," she said. "That was the post-sex high talking. I was sex-stoned. Now I'm just beat."

Twenty minutes later, we lay side by side, staring at the can-dlelit ceiling. We had started with mild petting and gentle kissing, a basic erotic arithmetic that usually led rather quickly to racing libidos and consummation. This night, though, our libidos stalled. We broke off the standard sex prelude and talked about this and that for a spell, neither of us verbally acknowledging the disrup-tion of the normal chain of events. After five or six minutes I again brought my lips to Annie's. We petted. After what felt like far too much time but was probably four minutes, those elements finally reacted together in the desired fashion: glints appeared, then smoke. Soon my robe was open, and our hands were groping each other, Annie's lingerie was discarded on the carpet, and we were, as they say, "preoccupied." A few minutes and two orgasms later, we were asleep.

"GOOD LUCK tonight," said the food editor as I left the office at the end of the following day. She's a classy wit, that one, with a sly smile and devious laugh. Many of my colleagues were interested in Annie's and my project; the food editor was one of the more zestful parties. Another coworker, whom I had told about the project the previous week, reported that she and her husband were so inspired by our venture that they had upped their sex regularity. She also asked me for "pointers."

"How," she e-mailed, "are you doing it every single night? What have you learned?"

We'd been at it for nearly two weeks straight. What *had* I learned?

Before I answered, it registered that somebody was tapping *me* for sex advice. This, without question, was a first. Before responding, I dawdled over the thrill.

"Don't wait for 'chemistry' to lead you to sex," I eventually wrote. "It's great when all of the elements combine and suddenly you're having a romp. But if you rely on chemistry, you'll have sex only once in a while, if you're lucky. Plan on sex. Understand in the morning that in the evening you won't spend the night watching TV or surfing on the Internet or talking on the phone. You'll have sex." (A side note: During this phase of sex escalation between the colleague and her husband, she got pregnant with her fourth child.)

One point I'd failed to divulge: If you're at the tail end of two weeks of daily sex, as I was, you might need an evening espresso. When I poured myself a hot little cup of caffeine at home that night, something I'd never done before, Annie lifted her eyebrows. She alternated her gaze between the espresso cup and my groin.

"Oh, don't worry," I said, fixing my gaze on her breasts.

After giving the girls long baths and interring them in their bedrooms, Annie and I were starting to get ready when we heard the fateful "click" and Joni walked into our room, asking if she could sleep with Ginger. In theory, there is something magical and sweet about sisters flopping together in the same bed at night. In practice, however, at least in our household, it rarely worked. They would whisper and giggle and play, but this never led to sleep. The Dance of the Happy Sisters inevitably led to the Clash of the Shrieking Siblings.

But Joni's request was so steeped in sugar, so very Shirley Temple Meets Cindy Brady, that we relented. Yes, we were a couple intent on a mission entirely removed from the doll-and-dress-up world of our children. Yes, we had serious adult matters to attend to. But we remained parents too, of course, the caretakers of our own little elves, and these elves possessed enormous powers of persuasion. We both understood that by allowing them to hang out together this late into the evening, we were break-dancing on a tightrope. We realized this decision had the potential to complicate our drive toward the fulfillment of certain fleshly pleasures. It did not matter. The elves had their arsenal of spells, and we succumbed. And minutes later we could hear them laughing in Ginger's bedroom.

Then we heard another "click," and Ginger stepped into our room—we had not yet locked our door for the presumed and pending festivities—asking for "faerie dust," talcum powder in a decorative purple canister that we sometimes sprinkled on them. I escorted Ginger back to her room, and there was Joni, pretending to be asleep on Ginger's bed.

"OK, this isn't going to cut it," I said to Joni. "You need to get back to your own bedroom."

She freaked out. She stiffened her back, making it difficult for me to carry her. She kicked, punched, growled, shrieked. I deposited the wolverine—like most magical elves, she was capable of "shape shifting"—in her own bed and returned to our room, but I could hear her sobbing in her bedroom. Annie and I shook our heads and traded worried glances. Annie began rising to deal with them, but I urged her to remain in bed.

"You've handled them all day," I said. "I've got it."

I went to Joni's room, sat on the edge of her bed, and tried to comfort her. Nothing in particular, of course, was upsetting her. We chatted about a variety of things having nothing to do with the spark that set fire to the bedtime routine, which was my signature strategy—*Just change the subject*—for dealing with foundering young girls, a category of humanity with which I'd had no experience before becoming a father. I grew up without sisters and, like most boys, didn't fully appreciate girls until they no longer were especially little. Eventually Joni calmed down, and I returned to our sanctuary, with its lit candles and incense.

"I don't know how parents have sex on a regular basis," I said. "So much work, so much time spent on being in charge. It's exhausting."

Annie held up a sex instructional video I'd received as swag at work, the sort of thing publicity types had been sending me with greater frequency since I'd started writing about sex. "Tonight?" she said.

Annie had hated the hard-core pornography, but she loved this: silicone-free women and men who were *not* Pringles-can excons. Some of the guys were total geeks. One of them must have been the inspiration for Will Ferrell's *Saturday Night Live* "lover" character. This bushy-bearded guy actually squealed in the video when he orgasmed. We sat on the bed and watched, exercising our funny bones. By the time the credits began rolling, though, we were ready to get naked. But if you are linking the porno with our mutual desire for sex, I implore you to stop. The squealing man made us laugh but failed to leaven our carnal drives. We managed to do that on our own.

THE NEXT morning we headed to theater camp in downtown Denver, another species within the genus "child activity" that blossomed in the family ecosystem we'd hatched. This tiny world contained things like work and adult pleasures, of course, but increasingly, like alien and invasive plants, things hinging on the edification or development of children muscled into the family environment, crowding out most adult species of distraction, such as simply walking around and checking things out. Even birthday parties, at least some of them, suggested in their invitations that the presence of parents would be most nifty.

We could have bailed on all of it, of course, as many of our moms and dads had. But in the context of child rearing, an air of guilt seemed to pervade not only our little family ecosystem but many of the other family ecosystems we encountered. Currents of competition, too, swirled around everything. Here's what I mean: *Look at her clap her hands to "Shoo, Fly, Don't Bother Me!" I believe she is a musical prodigy! I can see her performing a violin solo with the New York Philharmonic! Time for music lessons! If we don't start now, the children of more attentive parents will fill those Philharmonic slots, and our child will lead an unsatisfying life, and we will be to blame!*

Sound ridiculous? It is ridiculous, but there's nothing fanciful about it. Let's say there are 80 million families with young children in the United States. If even a quarter of these families formed guilt-and-competition-fueled family ecosystems, then there are 20 million families having discussions similar to the one offered above, and they are holding forth in this manner at least, let's say, four times a week. Which means conversations like this happen about 4 billion times a year in the United States, although I'm guessing the number is much higher. Either way, you get the point. The family unit has become, for many, the achievement hive.

To be fair, we do love our children quite a lot, and this love, too, contributes to the evolution of the achievement hive. We want the best for them, period. So, like many of the parents around us, we vined our little family ecosystem with activities, we flowered it with lessons, and we creatured it with camps and athletic competitions— anything connected, in theory, with building self-esteem, confidence, brain power, artistic prowess, or expertise in a sport.

Theater camp brought together small packs of children running circles around their free-spirit teachers. Ginger was studying beginning theater—at age 3! Yale Drama School, here she comes! Joni, who had been through many theater camps, was into "circus acrobatics." Parents weren't invited to Joni's class, so we stayed with Ginger and about a dozen other parents and their kids in a little room with an almost audaciously wholesome female teacher. We sat down "criss-cross-applesauce" style, in a circle, and introduced ourselves to the other moms and dads, something I don't recall my parents ever doing. While I sat, not to brag, in a paragon of criss-cross-applesauce, my eyes immediately were drawn to one of the moms: makeup, long hair sculpted into place, blue jeans tight, breasts pneumatic. Her lips? Shiny. *Is she in porn?*

As the preschoolers toddled, the apple-pie teacher tried coaxing them to use their imaginations to become different things— kings, elephants, whatever. In a later class, the *parents were encouraged to take part in the activity,* and I played a witch. (In a parenthetical whisper, I feel it's only right to disclose that *I actually enjoyed cackling, riding a broom, and stirring a cauldron before the preschool audience.*) Regardless, in this class, as the kids crawled and meowed and flapped their arms like wings, I snuck glances at the taut pillows pressing against the porn star's silk blouse, catching the occasional sway, finally discerning the outline of a nipple.

When the woman stood up, I of course carefully studied her back-side (remember my fondness for pretending to scrutinize the bark on a tree while in fact marveling over a cleavage spectacle). I re-spected the tightness of the blue jeans, which were more like a sheath than a loose cotton covering.

Probably not porn, I thought. *Not much porn production going on in Denver. But an escort. A professional escort. No way she doesn't have a beeper.* This question persisted for the rest of the class: *What part of the sex industry is she employed in?*

Later, Annie admitted her thoughts had drifted to similar ter-ritory. Although in Annie's case, it wasn't the sex industry so much as everyone's genitals. As we all sat in a circle playing pat-a-cake, she said she couldn't stop thinking about what the adults were packing beneath their jeans and sweaters. Two weeks of sex, and I was seeing porn stars. For Annie, strangers were canvases for geni-tal art. If we somehow pushed our way to week 14, would we be sexualizing clouds and refrigerators?

WE WENT straight from the child-activity genus to another famil-iar one, errands. Costco. A liquor barn. A grocery store. Before yielding to the gauntlet of errands, we'd imagined a day filled not with trudging down windowless aisles but with hiking along mountain paths, a species that was squarely within the genus "adult pursuit" but usually involved the kids, to their great dis-pleasure. Still, the edification-of-the-kids angle did not escape our trekking endeavors; we thought of weekend hikes as "our reli-gion," as our family's version of attending a spiritual service, com-plete with the grousing kids and the earnest parents who not only enjoy sitting in pews and listening to someone talk about a book, but also believe it will benefit the children in years to come.

But something inexplicable yanked us off the highway en route to the mountains, when we passed the peninsula of big-box stores. Some disturbing force, a black art, persuaded us to trade wilderness astonishments for shopping deplorables, a decision the kids cheered wildly.

During the drive home, after a few hours of navigating immense carts down sterile aisles, devouring samples of whatever they'd heave our way—fulfilling our "Free is best" motto—grabbing boxes and bags, jars and bottles, waiting in endless lines with antsy kids, I began fantasizing about the simple pleasures of our cozy sex den.

The home high jinks unfolded in a predictable manner—some sweetness involving book reading, movie watching, playing games, and being silly, some sourness involving teeth brushing and going to bed. As soon as the kid stuff ended, I cranked up the space heater in the bedroom, put on shorts and a T-shirt, and commenced lifting weights, doing crunches, and performing push-ups while Annie puttered around downstairs.

"Looking good," she said when she entered the den.

"That's the idea," I grunted as I curled a dumbbell. I flopped onto my back and did seventy-five crunches broken up into sets of fifteen. By the end, my abdomen felt as though it had been injected with sulfuric acid: I was covered in sweat, gasping, my veins popping out of my biceps, forearms, and neck. I stood up and Annie examined me.

"I like the hard body," she said.

"I don't think I yet have attained 'hard-body' status, but I'm trying," I said. I popped into the shower for a minute to shed the sweat, and then we ran an extremely hot bath, dropped into the water a "sparkle" bath bomb, and slipped into the tub. We had bottles of India Pale Ale; we had candles; we had patchouli and lavender and ylang-ylang oils in the water. We just about melted.

"Another week down," said Annie. She gently stroked my hips with her feet. "I'm beginning to think the only thing stopping couples from doing it every night—or at least us—is sheer exhaustion."

"You ever worry the desire wouldn't be there?" I asked.

"Not worried, although I am curious about it. There have been nights already where I didn't have any desire for sex; all I wanted was sleep. But once we started getting into it, the desire showed up."

"If you stand up to the fatigue, it falls to pieces," I said. "It's a cheap bully."

"Exhaustion is a cheap bully. That's *awesome*," Annie said. "That knowledge alone is worth this experiment."

Before sinking into the bath, I had retrieved a box of massage products I'd purchased a year ago for Annie's birthday, promising her I'd "get into" massaging her. The box had remained unopened. The reason? Yet again, the bully fatigue. I'd plan to massage Annie, but my bones and then my head would plead exhaustion, and instead of kneading her sore body I'd read and sleep. It bugged me now that my combination of forgetfulness and apathy and lethargy had denied Annie so many well-deserved back rubs. I wondered: If I had massaged her more routinely, would that have led both of us to more frequent sex? Annie positively adored massages; most times I had given them to her, just being so hands-on with her nakedness had aroused me; a few times, at least, this had led to sex.

This night after the bath, she lay on her stomach on the bed. I played a CD she had bought during the week called *Tantric Lounge,* which sounded sort of like East Indian music, only with synthesizers and Western beats. I poured some of the massage kit's cinnamon oil into my palm and began caressing. The heels of my hands searched for taut muscles in her back and pressed. I used my hands to squeeze her calves and thighs, her biceps and shoulders and derriere, the soles of her feet.

"Massaging you turns me on," I told Annie after we had floated from massage to sex to just hanging out. "I became very horny the minute I started rubbing your back. What about you?"

"Hate to break it to you, DJ, but when I'm getting a massage, I'm not thinking about sex. I'm thinking about how much I love massage," she said. "I think it's a guy thing."

"What?"

"Guys are much quicker to associate touch with sex. Like, you're massaging me, you're touching my skin, and therefore you are thinking about turning the massage into a 'move,'" she said.

I shrugged. "All true," I said. "You got me. Does that bug you?"

"Not at all," said Annie. "And you know, every once in a while, massage will turn into sex. Just don't count on it."

"Unless the massage happens in the evening during the marathon."

"Correct."

4

Screwing Ourselves Together

Outside of the big bang that is responsible for their creation, kids have nothing to do with sex, but raising them does contribute to declining sex lives. We'd wound our lives tightly around them for the previous seven years, slowly building around us that ecosystem teeming with juvenile-happy species in the genus "child activity," in addition to the vibrant world of species in the genus "child responsibility," such as bedtime sagas, doctors' appointments, and the containment and manipulation of volatile moods.

All of this family management, combined with work and middle age, crammed our lives as never before with responsibilities and appointments. When we were younger, time stretched before us, blank, every morning. *How shall we fill this day, dear?* I might ask. *I know, let's play backgammon for a spell, then just walk around and check things out,* Annie could reply. Time was a vacant vessel, awaiting our infusion of merriments. But now, how we would spend most of the hours in our days was preordained when we opened our eyes in the morning, and the majority of those hours were dedicated not to our own whimsy, but to work and child rearing. We loved our children, and would not have traded our grommet-thick world for life without them. But there's no denying we sacrificed the pursuit of a lot of adult pleasures on the altar of child rearing.

When you're left with a pittance of time every week in which you are free to be selfish, you must be choosy. It's 9 p.m. on a Tuesday, and now is your time. You have maybe ninety minutes before you will be asleep. You could play backgammon; you could watch TV; you could read; you could talk; you could have sex. Not all of them, of course. Maybe two. Probably just one. And within the realm of reasonable activities, only one of them, for most of us, requires physical effort as well as a certain, sometimes tricky, emotional intimacy: sex.

Annie and I had largely jettisoned that adult pleasure on weekdays after we started having children. In fact, weekday sex was in decline even before then, once we both had careers and were tired after work. But now we'd had sex on fourteen consecutive days, many of them grueling weekdays. How had we managed?

So far, we hadn't traded much kid time for our sessions between the sheets. Instead, we dedicated most of our "free time"—the minutes bridging the kids' bedtimes and our drift into dreamland—to pursuits of the flesh. What we sacrificed for the sake of sex was evening aimlessness: sitting in bed and leafing through magazines, reading books, turning on the TV and clicking around the stations, watching videos, surfing the Internet. Before the marathon, these activities often marked the extent of our nighttime pursuits, and, frankly, this suited me swell. Exhaustion kicked our asses every day; every night we desired a gentle waltz into sleep.

The switcheroo required by the sexathon was not effortless. After the daily workday march, it sometimes was a stretch to continue forging ahead instead of happily fading. But the bright pleasures of the marathon far surpassed those of the quick spiral into twilight. Sex really can vanquish weariness if given a chance. The question I toyed with as we started week 3 was, What about boredom? Given the volume of sex we'd accomplished already, as we thrust further into the adventure, I imagined Annie thinking: *Great. There's that penis again. *Yawn*.* I'd not tired of her bouncy breasts or her honeyed dominion, but I wondered: *Would I?* I never before found anything dull in these elements of her anatomy, but I'd never explored them with such regularity.

We were reengaging with ourselves, introducing something novel into our midlife. Gratification, we decided, was something to manage, not to eliminate. By coddling ourselves, we were buttressing our bonds, and if the pursuit of daily sex eventually led to the thinning of some of the species within the "child activity" genus, so be it. There's nothing worse for kids than parents with threadbare and steadily unraveling unions.

"You know what we're doing?" said Annie. "We are screwing ourselves together."

That day, we hired a babysitter, a yoga instructor named Vicki, to watch the kids while we planned to sit in a coffee shop to talk about our progress with the marathon. We wandered outside Stapleton, which was so thick with parents and children that the only "fancy" restaurant had an entire corner dedicated to kids, complete with toys, cushions, and picture books. Have fun trying to enjoy that $24 piece of salmon lacquered in a lemongrass-coconut glaze while little Jimmy and his brother Caleb push trucks around the floor until they decide to play Spider-Man. Families tended to pepper the only coffee shop in the 'hood—a Starbucks, of course—and we wanted something removed from this world, someplace that wasn't a variation of our own household. Like explorers in distant lands, Annie and I drove around the more bohemian-looking neighborhoods in Denver until we spotted what looked like the right place. From the street St. Mark's Coffeehouse looked warm and bustling. As soon as we opened the front door, we knew we'd found our hangout. The coffee was rich and distinct, the music, highly eclectic—most certainly not the result of any corporate mandate—and the crowd couldn't have been more interesting: an old man playing chess with young hipsters; a pair of guys in mohawks speaking a language that I could not decipher, although I suspected it was Hebrew; women in pigtails and army boots.

Armed with laptops, Annie and I decided to sit apart for a bit and do some reading about sex for the project. I'd look over at her all by herself, reading, and get aroused. She looked so sexy. And cute. That's her style, to me, sexycute. I e-mailed her my observation, sitting twenty feet away, and I saw her eyes brighten when she read the message.

"I'm melting," she wrote back.

"Me too," I responded. "I can't wait for tonight."

"Right back at you."

Annie and I discovered coffee shops before Starbucks conquered America, in the early 1990s when we lived in Minneapolis. Now *there* was a city that understood lounging. The city's espresso emporiums seemed to have been around forever and were packed with dreadlocked people decorated in tattoos and piercings—a personal style taken for granted today but charged with insurrection fifteen years ago. Neither of us had experienced such an accomplished café culture before, and we took to it immediately, spending hours sitting across from each other in Muddy Waters, the coffee shop across the street from our house, where we played backgammon and drank coffee. When it's minus-twenty degrees outside and the five-day forecast predicts high temperatures never rising above zero, what else are you going to do? We flirted with cafés in Albuquerque, but we befriended a bunch of high-spirited, hard-partying oddballs. Nightlife and desert hikes occupied our time there, not hanging out in cafés.

After five years in Albuquerque we moved to South Florida, where it was hard to find espresso, let alone a café devoted to it. By then our lives were spinning around young Joni. In Washington,

D.C., house hunting consumed most of our weekends. In Baltimore, we sank into our house, rarely feeling the need to trade its charms for those of the neighborhood cafés.

"Why didn't we think of this before?" asked Annie that Sunday as we sat among the Denver bohemians. "We spent seven dollars on coffees and a big cookie, we paid for the babysitter, and we have three hours alone, just hanging out. Together. Had we gone out for dinner, we'd have spent more than this entire excursion on the drinks alone."

Here's why it hadn't occurred to us before, something I didn't understand at the time but now do: It had been a long since we had devoted so much effort to each other, and this embrace of *us* was advancing to other corners of our life together. Every night we were consummating our couplehood. This had consequences, and so far they were most welcome.

We went experimental that night after the girls were in bed. Satin sheets?

No. Salad.

"I need to stay nimble," I said to Annie as we drove home from the coffee shop. "I wonder if eating very lightly, for dinner, will make the sex that much easier?"

"Worth a shot," said Annie. "Big meals, I think, do slow down the machinery, for both of us. Makes us sleepier. You want to have salad tonight?"

So we prepared food that I've never been able to treat as a meal. A plate of greens with feta cheese and toasted walnuts. A loaf of bread with some good olive oil for dipping. I eyed the girls' bowls of macaroni and cheese as I chewed my greens. I envied them, but I walked away feeling sated, and surprised.

"I feel like a friggin' leprechaun," I said. "Light as a feather. I've got, like, zest."

"Of course," said Annie. "You're not using energy to digest a porterhouse, a baked potato, and three beers. Your body is happy. I'll bet it will thank you later, too."

When we started dating, my culinary expertise, not to mention my culinary ambition, did not stray far from macaroni and cheese from a box. I did not hesitate to eat fast food of any sort. I drank Coke like water. I grazed on sweets like a Guernsey cow wandering through a Vermont meadow in July. Annie, on the other hand, made bread from scratch. She dreamed up complicated menus, which she then prepared. She knew how to properly cut a mango (something I'd never tasted until Annie introduced me to one). Cobbling together a pile of scones came as second nature to her. And when it came to soup, she was like Cézanne at work on a canvas. She had been a vegetarian since ninth grade, and she believed food and health (and now, apparently, sex too) were linked intimately. Being around Annie, I quickly became interested in learning how to dice an onion and knead dough, and I gleefully yielded to the pleasures of the kitchen. Cooking became one of my principal hobbies; it was something Annie and I cherished doing together.

Annie wore a slip that evening. The *New York Times* that week had proclaimed slips as the new sexy thing. Prior to our experiment, she likely never would have noticed the *Times* article, much less squeezed into a slip based on the article's breathless enthusiasms. "The *Times* is right," I said. "The slip is very sexy. Who knew?"

After another twenty-minute round of weight lifting and a shower, I put on my silk robe and began pawing through the bag full of sex-show swag, which we kept hidden on a high shelf in our closet.

"Porno?" Annie said, sounding less than bubbly.

"One of those moist towelettes," I said. "Supposed to enhance erections. I want to experiment. Keep things interesting."

"Interesting?" said Annie, her voice tinged with concern and worry. "You bored?"

"Nope," I said. "Just interested in trying some of this stuff we got at the show. For the sake of the marathon, at least. See if it does anything."

Buried beneath DVDs, magazines, vials of lube, condoms, and much more, I finally found the foil packet containing a product called Keep Dick Hard. I read the list of ingredients.

"Caffeine," I said. "And pepper!" I paused, rereading.

"I don't know about this," I said. "*Pepper?*"

"Will it move from your penis to my vagina?" said Annie, sounding appalled.

We both stared at the packet.

"What the hell," said Annie. "What's the worst that could happen?"

"Besides otherworldly pain?" I said, ripping open the packet, withdrawing the white, wet towelette, and, with no ceremony, swabbing. We sat cross-legged on the bed, both of us admiring my penis. I don't believe we ever had gathered around my penis before, in the manner of mycologists on a field trip discovering a rare and prized variety of chanterelle.

"It tingles," I said. Then my slightly tumescent penis began to swell and then to harden.

"It's like watching Sea Monkeys grow," said Annie. "Just add water."

She lay back. "Here goes," she said. "I'm either about to have fun or get my reproductive organs lathered in pepper."

I entered the castle tentatively, cautiously, like a lost knight uncertain about the political affiliations of the royalty enthroned within.

"How's that," I asked as my . . . sword . . . reached the end of the . . . scabbard (sorry).

"So far, so good," reported Annie. "No evidence of pepper. Yet."

We went at it gingerly and steady for a good ten minutes, with no sign of discomfort.

"I think we're good to go," said Annie. "Hold on." She turned perpendicular to the bed, hanging her head over the side of the mattress. I kissed her highly exposed neck. Eventually we flopped onto our backs and panted.

"*Loved* the position," said Annie.

"I got good leverage," I said. "And I loved nibbling your neck."

Something poked my spine. I reached behind and retrieved a Polly Pockets doll, one of the little dolls that our daughters spend hours dressing up in tiny outfits.

"She looks like a porn star," said Annie. "Almost no clothes, tiny feet, big boobs, and even bigger hair."

"Speaking of porn stars," I said, flinging the plastic doll from the bed and gazing at my still-raging erection, "I wonder if they use these towelettes?"

"It seems to still be working," said Annie, pointing, then climbing between the sheets and pulling the comforter to her chin.

"It's tingly but also numb," I said. "It seems somewhat beyond my control."

I followed Annie between the sheets, reaching down every minute to inspect the erection's ferocity. After about ten minutes, it started to flag. In another minute, it was gone.

"Whew," I said, looking over at Annie, who I assumed was at least half awake. But she was out cold.

Keep Dick Hard, I considered just before drifting off, was interesting. Was the sex any better than with an unpeppered, decaffeinated penis? I'm not sure the intercourse itself felt any better, although the introduction of the head-off-the-bed position was a pleasant surprise. In short, the sex was somewhat "jazzier," but I wasn't sure Keep Dick Hard had anything to do with it.

THE NEXT morning I plodded back to the office, coughing and blowing my nose.

The food editor asked me: "What happens if you're sick?"

I shrugged and said: "That's the way it goes. We have sex, sick or not."

She said, "You can't go over it, you can't go under it, you've got to go through it," a line from a kid's song.

Her summation was apt. There were no detours around sex. We had to go through it. This could have saddened me, but instead I felt puffed up. *Not even illness can stop me,* I thought. Which is not to say that I had become cocky. By this point in the marathon, as we approached day 20, I believed the goal of one hundred days was achievable. I was fully invested, but with big investments comes worry.

Take the hug. There was nothing encumbered, at first, about the tight embrace Annie delivered to me when I walked in the door after work that evening. The clutch, however, deepened without any sign of dwindling, and I began to think something bad might have happened. Selfishly, I thought: *I hope this doesn't mess with the sex.*

"Everything OK?" I whispered.

Annie answered, "This sex therapist recommends hugging your mate with love and real sincerity three times a day. He says this alone can enhance a sex life and, ultimately, a marriage. Welcome to day one of routine hugging."

"Hugging is good," I said, relieved. "I'm all for hugging."

HUGGING WARMED our union, but it was helpful in a practical way, too, for it was wintertime in Colorado, so it was frozen.

If you visit Denver in the winter, *shhh, don't mention the cold.* People up and down the Front Range (the eastern flank of the Rocky Mountains) champion the weather. Advertisers routinely exploit it to drum up business: "You deserve to enjoy our great

Colorado weather in style! Come to the patio furniture sale!" Coloradans never hesitate to go on and on about how it's much warmer in Denver than most people think, about how it can be seventy degrees in January, and yada yada yada. If you listen to them long enough, you think Colorado is really Santa Monica. "It's our little secret" is a favored phrase. What it means is "The rest of the country associates Colorado with snow and skiing, but in Denver the weather is actually balmy and clement. We don't need floods of people moving here. The sublime weather is our little secret."

No, the sublime weather is their little hallucination.

Even Annie sometimes lionized the weather. Occasionally, our divergent reckonings provoked arguments. But we both understood that our ongoing debate was really not about temperatures and sunlight. It was about place. I hunted for reasons to move the family back to the East's clannishness and happy claustrophobia. Annie dreaded yet another move, especially to a region where home prices were so high and congestion was so great (you say "congestion," and I say "happy claustrophobia"). She pinned the West's freedoms close to her heart.

Either way, performing for one hundred days during Denver's Greenlandesque winter did offer some advantages. Dusk's early arrival made it easier to put the girls to bed. The deep freeze nudged us into our own bed and begged us to warm each other.

Which we'd been doing for nearly three weeks.

That night, after a hot yoga session transformed me from exhausted and irritable to enlivened and blissed out, I showered, lit candles and incense, and moved straight into foreplay. Had this not been day 17, I doubt we'd ever have had the bright idea to have sex on an exercise ball. But we knew we had more than eighty sessions to go, and we were feeling more adventurous, sexually, than ever before.

"How about here?" I said, pushing the ball to the center of the floor.

"I'm game," said Annie, sitting on the ball and spreading her legs.

With my angled erection leading the way, I came to her, working to fit myself inside.

"Hold on!" said Annie as I pressed into her. "Whoa!"

The ball rolled to the side. We both listed, our hands first waving around for balance, then reaching down to soften the blow we both were sure was coming. We hung there for a few moments without falling to the floor before managing to right the exercise ball.

"That was exciting," I said.

"Maybe there's a better way?" said Annie.

"We could try pushing it against the side of the bed," I offered.

Voilà. The ball bounced her hips up and down, sliding me in and out of her warm utopia with great force and rhythm. It was wild. We pushed the ball back to its resting place, a corner in the bedroom, and flopped on the comforter, still panting from the intense burst of exertion.

"We'll have to do *that* again," said Annie.

We lay together silently for a while.

"What do you think of cock rings?" said Annie.

"Actually, I don't think of them," I said, startled. "In addition, I don't like thinking about or, God forbid, actually pronouncing those two words together like that."

"The marathon led me to the Internet this afternoon, where I spent thirty minutes looking for cock rings for you," she said. "I almost bought one, but I didn't know if you'd really like it."

"You know the swag bag has one, right?"

"Oh, that's right!" she said. "Glad I didn't get you a new one. Are you going to try it?"

I shrugged. I did not like talking about this device. I did not

like thinking about this device. And when Annie said the words—
cock ring—they appeared in my mind's eye as if scrawled in fire.

"I'M WATCHING some chick give some guy a blow job right now."

That's what the guy on the other end of the phone said, the
porn-industry entrepreneur I was interviewing for a story about
mobile pornography. Sometimes I really liked my job. I encountered characters.

"Who wants to watch pornography on a little screen?" I asked.

"Men who like pornography. It's porno in your pocket." He
(and other industry guys) argued that you don't need a TV, you
don't need to be sitting in front of a computer. You can have
porno with you wherever you go. It will revolutionize the industry.

"Think about stalls in men's rooms," the blow job–watching
fellow said. "Guys can look at porno in the middle of the afternoon, at work, in the bathroom, and do their thing."

The more he talked, the more I believed him. I relayed this
conversation to Annie that night, including the bit about the
bathroom, and Annie recoiled.

"So this dude thinks men will get into sitting on toilets in
stinky public restrooms, watching porn on cell-phone screens,
and whacking off?" Annie said. "Unbelievable. I cannot imagine
any woman doing that. It's stuff like this that really shows how
different men and women are."

"For the record, not only am I never going to watch porno in a
bathroom stall, I'm never going to watch porno on a cell phone.
Just FYI," I said.

"Duly noted," said Annie. "And assumed, of course."

"Of course. But I do think we should check out some allegedly
'couples-friendly' porno on the laptop tonight. We don't like the
violent porno, but we should give softer stuff a shot."

"Sounds OK, I guess," said Annie. "I'm not hopeful, but you never know."

We clicked into a website for which we'd been given a free "day pass" during the Adult Entertainment Expo, a site that championed its couples-friendly porno. Within minutes, however, it was clear that "jazzing it up" wasn't in the cards for us, because the staged sex was dull, an interminable spectacle of gentle foreplay moving toward gentle sex and gentle moans that sounded like bad actors following stage directions for sounds meant to convey the sense of swooning. It amounted to something like the opposite of hard-core porn, with its extravaganza of violence. For Annie and me, at least, neither worked; it was like having to choose between a glass of grain alcohol and a shot of water.

That night, I showered and lathered my body in a moisturizer that smelled "musky," an undertaking that had become routine since the beginning of the marathon. I assumed Annie would prefer smooth to rough skin, and I believed she would appreciate an aroma described as "musky," because marketers often associated muskiness with manliness. (I'm still not sure what "musk" smells like, exactly, but Annie said she did indeed appreciate the musk.) We ended up having the sort of sex you rarely encounter on video. We took it slow and deliberate but shot through with sparkle and lust (instead of torpor mixed with overdramatic demonstrations of "swooning"). The sex was a fitting complement to the day. It had started snowing in the morning, and the snow continued falling as we climbed into bed. The snowfall hushed and cloaked. It said, "Go inside and have warm sex."

After the hearthlike sex, Annie regaled me with the results of a study she had conducted during the afternoon. Annie wanted to know how many times a year the average American couple made love. After much noodling around on the Internet, she determined that the answer was probably 36.

"Most women don't like to have sex during their periods, so that eliminates one week out of the month," she said. "And even if they do like to have sex during their periods, it seems that most people have one weekend a month where it just doesn't happen, for whatever reasons: exhaustion, sickness, too busy, not in the mood. That leaves three weekends a month. Most couples, I think, have sex on the weekends. And it's usually just a Friday or a Saturday."

"Three times a month," she said. "Thirty-six times a year. By the time we're done, we'll have three years' worth of sex under our belts!"

"How scientific of you," I said. I fooled around on the Internet myself, looking for answers. "OK, you might be on to something," I said. "The studies don't agree, surprise, surprise. One says the average couple in their forties has sex one and a half times a week. That's way over your number. But in another study," I looked at my computer to get the number, "forty-five percent of couples report they have sex just a few times a month, which fits into your scheme. Either way, couples aren't having much sex."

"I'm sticking with the thirty-six number," said Annie. "People lie in studies. I know there are couples who have been together for a long time who still have sex constantly."

"Like us," I retorted. "But really? You know couples like this? Who?"

Annie hesitated. "Well, I've read about couples like that," she said. "I guess the only times, in recent years, that girlfriends have talked about their sex lives with me, they're responding to our sex marathon. And the ones who talk say they have sex like us. Used to be more. Wish they did it more. Wonder if they're doing it enough."

"So it's possible we're the only couple, among our friends, that is having a lot of sex?"

"Yes!" said Annie, her voice lit with enthusiasm and relish.

Annie's competitiveness was something I loved about her, although loving this "about" her isn't the same thing as loving being competitive "with" her. I don't like running with Annie, for example, because inevitably she turns my precious constitutional into a race. I like losing myself in my head during runs; Annie wears a watch and tries to beat her best times. When we ran together—difficult with kids, but we always managed it during beach vacations with our extended families—we'd tread side by side for a while. I'd admire the cresting and crashing waves, the petulant terns and skittish ghost crabs, and the tangles of green seaweed. Annie, too, probably did all of that. But at some point she'd begin inching ahead of me. Then the competitor took over. As she moved farther away, she'd toss quick glances over her shoulder to see how far behind I was. Sometimes she grinned.

We woke up to another milestone: twenty straight days of sex. The afternoon was cold, but it was Friday, so it had that going for it, too. The newsroom, as on most Fridays, maintained a lighter air than the rest of the week, which led my colleagues to launch into much ribbing about the sex marathon. I received a few arch e-mails from my FFF, too—for example: "Is your weekend screwed?"

These jokers, I thought, are headed home to their spouses, and at some point many of them will do the deed, the anticipation of which may explain, in part, the explosion of levity that happens on Fridays. Yes, not reporting to work for two days is huge, and so are the ski trips, the dinner parties, the sleeping in. But there's the sex, too.

I arrived home to a happy house: Everyone, even the 3-year-old, understands the advantages of a Friday, the start of more than fifty hours of family time and no work. For the kids, it means a much larger share of Daddy's and Mommy's attention. For Annie and me, it meant solid family time, a full sinking into the genus "child activity," which, despite my earlier (accurate) description as something occasionally harrowing and taxing, is also enormously rewarding and often, simply, fun (consider, for example, my role as the witch).

When I got home, we made pizzas. Then we read to the kids and played a game of Uno with Joni once Ginger was in bed. Finally, Annie and I were alone in our bedroom, and I lifted weights and tortured my abdomen for a spell. We cranked up the space heater and showered, then pawed through our sex-show swag and came up with a virility thing that you place on your tongue and let dissolve. It tasted like cinnamon. We also retrieved a sample of lube and two porn videos.

"Aphrodisiacs, lube, and porn," I said. "All at the same time."

The porno failed miserably, which was not remotely surprising given Annie's antipathy toward that form of entertainment and my growing boredom with it. In the first video, guys on a bus entice allegedly anonymous women to come on board for money, and things quickly turn hard core. If you have daughters, you watch this sort of thing and think: *Oh my God, keep sociopathic men like that away from my precious angels*. The second video featured lots of bondage and leather and whips. It didn't do anything for either of us. After a few minutes, we switched it off.

"I'm totally turned off and tuned out with porno," said Annie.

I agreed with her. For most of my life I'd paid little attention to porn, in part because the very idea of buying the stuff in a triple-X store was embarrassing enough—and forget about ducking into the "adult" section of the local video store, where the neighborhood moms (*Hi, Sheila!*) and their kids were carting around *Finding Nemo* and *A Bug's Life* videos. Only when porno began populating the Internet did I really check it out. The daily sex with Annie hadn't turned me against porno, but it had made porno seem rather redundant and awfully excessive. Not only was I already doing it every day with a real person, but I very much *wanted* to do it every day with this real person—this Annie. Adding porno to our blaze was like tossing a Kleenex on a bonfire: It accomplished nothing.

It didn't take long on this happy Friday, after bailing on the pornography, for Annie and me to throw a few logs of our own on the coals. Did the cinnamon aphrodisiac thing I had dissolved on my tongue work? I wasn't sure. The ramrod erection did not flag, the libido felt carbonated, the sex splendid. But I could not determine if the aphrodisiac had anything to do with it.

THE WHOLE Girl Scout cookie thing was like a casino for Joni. Like her mother, Joni is extremely—almost pathologically—competitive. She blossomed into a card shark at age 6; by 7, she was begging us to play for money, which in her case meant allowance savings. She encountered the game Risk and took to it immediately, driving herself ruthlessly toward world dominion and brutal dictatorship. Joni's compulsion to win extended far beyond Uno and Sorry. Wherever we drove, she played the "slug-a-bug" game, which involves counting Volkswagen Bugs and adding up the points to determine a winner. If we were anywhere rural, the wildlife game got added to the mix: one point for squirrels and farm animals, more points, on a rising scale, for foxes, coyotes, moose, elk, and so on. When the minivan was parked in the garage after returning from anywhere, she sped out of her seat, ran to the back door, and announced: "I'm the first person into the house!" After dinner, she often raced to her bedroom and flung herself into pajamas. "I'm the first person in a sleeper," she'd shout as she ran back down the steps, an announcement that often caused her younger sister to burst into tears.

"That's not fair!" Ginger would cry. "Joni gets a point!"

Selling Girl Scout cookies works like this: The more you sell, the bigger are the rewards, and the greater are the bragging rights among your fellow Scouts. Joni desired total victory—purse and power both. The Arctic cold sent some of her competitive drive into hibernation as we drove around our neighborhood, looking for a good place to park the car and start knocking on doors. But as soon as we began the sugar-hawking sojourn, the competitor reappeared like an Amazon princess. The Amazon's killer instinct amplified when I introduced a new game: We would "call" whether someone would answer the door after we rang the doorbell, and get points for each correct guess. Joni became hyper for points and increasingly desperate for home owners to order many, many boxes of cookies.

One woman opened her door, and a snarling gray standard poodle appeared at her side. "Now, now," she said, patting the dog's head. It leapt beyond the threshold and ran at me.

"Now, now," I said, holding out my hand for the dog to sniff. Chomp. Poodle fangs pierced my flesh.

"Holy shit!" I yelled.

The woman freaked and coaxed the barking dog, which would not remove its satanic gaze from me, back into the house. She bought a big load of cookies because she felt bad. My hand ached, but I could tell that Joni was thinking: *Score!*

We knocked on a lot of doors, we sold a bunch of cookies, and then we headed home. Soon Vicki the babysitter arrived with Romeo, her gigantic, muscular dog, whom I'd never seen before. I flinched. It hadn't been a good dog day for me.

Later in the day, I called my mom, wondering about her weekend.

"I'm so proud of you, honey," she said at one point. "That you can do this day after day after day."

"Thanks, Mom," I said, uncomfortable as usual with this subject, which never went unmentioned in any conversation I had with anybody in my family.

That night, after Annie and I spent a few hours hanging out at the coffee shop together (followed by a pizza dinner with the kids, a video, some book reading, and then bedtimes), the sex, again, took some work. Annie said she wanted to "veg" in front of a video, "any video.

"Something two hours long. Something I can zone out to, fall asleep to. And then wake up tomorrow. Sorry."

This time, I was more geared up for a romp, and the critique stung.

"C'mon," I said. "It's fun!"

"Not always."

Ouch.

"Well damn," I said. "Then why are we doing this?"

"Because our sex life is already improving. And I'm feeling closer to you. And this whole thing, I think, is going to work."

"But you seem to be getting bored," I said.

"I never thought it would be freewheeling every night of the week," said Annie. "I figured some nights would be great and others wouldn't. But pushing ourselves through all of it would teach us things. And it is."

"So you want to do it tonight," I said.

She paused, then smiled. "Yes. I want to. Soon. Not now."

I returned to my book, a guide to Kama Sutra sex positions. After about an hour of reading, peppered with the occasional chat, I reached over and stroked Annie's thigh. The half erection I had been carrying around for about an hour prior to Annie's "veg" announcement, in anticipation of the evening's festivities—and which had retreated after the "veg" thing—swiftly returned. We kissed sitting up, and I directed Annie to her back, where we kept pressing our lips together until Annie said, "Hey! I'm getting into this!"

I said "Yay," and soon we both were done with that chapter of the evening, lying in bed together and talking.

"We've done so much this week," I said. "Porno. Lube. Aphrodisiacs. Exercise ball. It's been a blast, don't you think?"

Annie revealed that she had been tense all day, worried that we'd grow bored with our evening escapades. "It's been awesome," she said. "But we aren't even a quarter of the way there, and I don't think we can keep pushing it further every night, as far as toys and stuff. I know we've talked about this already, but now it's really bugging me. Will I bore you?"

"Funny, I've had the same worry," I said. "It was one thing when we had a couple of quickies during the first week, when we did it while exhausted, while lacking all desire. But what happens when these sorts of episodes start stacking up? Once, three times, whatever. But if three morphs into a baker's dozen, and then from there it just mushrooms, do we lose all enthusiasm for sex?"

"I'm thinking long-term, too," said Annie. "I mean, what if we force ourselves to go through with this, but by the end we are so sick of each other that our relationship is actually in worse shape than it was one hundred days earlier?"

"That would be a disaster," I said.

"Well, DJ, I don't think that will happen. I can tell you that right now, at least, I'm not bored with you, or our sex life. In fact, I'm jazzed about it."

Long pause. Annie cleared her throat. She gently struck my arm, then shrugged her shoulders and lightly raised her hands, palms up, a gesture simultaneously conveying "I'm waiting" and "What the fuck?"

"What?" I said, clueless.

Annie rolled her eyes. "You're now supposed to tell me that, you know, just as you don't bore me, I don't bore you."

"Of course!" I nearly shouted. "No boredom! No! For example, my penis vibrates when I merely catch a glimpse of your cleavage."

"Good job," Annie said, smiling.

"Anyway," I said after a few minutes, "all of this stuff, this lube and porno and all, it really doesn't matter. We obviously don't need it to keep everything going. In fact, we haven't needed much. All we need is each other, it turns out." I turned to her. "Pretty cool, huh?"

Silence.

She was sitting straight up, but she was sound asleep. Despite the fact Annie had been talking just moments earlier, this did not stun me. Annie could fall asleep while riding a bike. I turned off the light.

5

Nasal Shrapnel

Where was home? We'd been struggling with this question since our first date. Having sex for twenty-one straight days didn't answer it, but it had compelled us to pay more attention to at least one room in the dwelling where we ate dinner and stored our stuff and slept. Three weeks into the marathon, the fussed-over bedroom had emerged as a star. We had transformed the room shortly before the kickoff and maintained the look and feel of the room ever since. Sitting on the bed and observing the landscape of cleanliness, order, and warmth, Annie asked: "Why didn't we do this earlier?"

"We've been in such limbo here," I said. "It's OK."

"No, not just here in Denver. I mean in general," she said. "How many bedrooms do you think we've had over the years?"

Good question. Annie started counting.

"OK, we had separate bedrooms in our first apartments in Minneapolis. Then we shared a bedroom in Minneapolis. So we're on three for Minnesota," she said. "Then we had that dumpy little apartment in New Mexico that we got kicked out of for having Eggplant [a cat]. Then there was the apartment at that complex 'The Lakes,' behind Hooters, Long John Silver, Pizza Hut, and Jiffy Lube. There was the townhouse we bought, then the house we lost our life savings on." She paused. "So now we're at seven. There was the Florida townhouse we rented, with its lizards and tick infestations, the D.C. apartment, and Baltimore. That's ten. And then there was the apartment in Denver. And now, this place. That's twelve bedrooms, and we've *never* showed any of them the care we're showering upon this one."

"I've gotta admit, it's really shaping up," I said. "I'm surprised we've managed to keep it so . . . orderly. But then, it's another by-product of the marathon. It's a sex den, and we're gonna make it stay that way."

When the kids went to bed and we finished with dinner and the dishes and the rest of our responsibilities, den shui invited us to luxuriate, to sprawl, to touch. We blasted the radiator-style space heater every night, making the normally cool room warm enough for nudity without needing to slip under the covers. I might shiver my way through another Denver winter, but my teeth wouldn't chatter in the sex den. Like the coffeehouse, the sex den had become a sanctuary. We weren't sure about Denver. We knew we'd leave the rental house. But the bedroom? That was different. It was our rock. And it was one lesson the marathon already had taught us, one we vowed to maintain long after we had ceased having daily sex.

The den's natural environment, though, was evening. In the morning, once awake, we were up and out, downstairs, immersed in child rearing, and then off to work, off to a child activity, or off to something else entirely. On this cold Sunday, we found a new species within the genus "child activity" and headed to the National Western Stock Show, an annual event in Denver that brings livestock-types from around the country to the city for a few weeks near the end of January. It reminded me of just how far I'd come from my boyhood home. We sat in bleachers in an arena and watched enormous horses pull sleds piled with sandbags across the dirt floor. We walked up and down aisles past booths selling western stuff—

cowboy hats, leather belts, fringed vests, toy horses, state-sponsored displays touting Colorado beans, dairy, cattle, and so on. Men tucked chewing tobacco behind their lips. Manure spiced the air.

"This event is the opposite of the Vegas show," said Annie as we passed women wearing American-flag-embroidered vests and guys with cowboy hats and trucker ball caps and beach-ball bellies. "Nobody appears to be pursuing this western lifestyle thing for a spell before moving on to something else."

"That's for sure," I said, as a guy in worn cowboy boots, a denim jacket lined with sheep's wool, and a gray cowboy hat ambled past, chewing on a long piece of hay. "I'll bet most of these people don't move to different regions of the country every few years, just for kicks."

"That would be like us," said Annie.

"Precisely."

"No, I think these people are themselves all the way to the stitching of their Wranglers," said Annie.

Although many of them clearly were not home in a geographic sense, most of the people filling the hall blended in with the ropes and spurs, the draft horses and monstrous American pickup trucks and sheep-shearing tools. Sex intruded on our stroll through Ranchworld—"I wonder if these folks have as much sex as the porn crowd?" whispered Annie—but we managed to dispel most of it, walking hand in hand while the girls played in a giant bin of dried pinto beans and climbed on a jungle gym and pleaded with us for French fries, which we bought and scattered on a newspaper, swabbing them in puddles of ketchup and mustard we had created on the paper while we watched the cowpokes.

Annie rested her hand on my thigh as we ate. The girls scooted a couple dozen yards away to inspect a big display of plastic horses and cowgirls for sale, and Annie squeezed my thigh. Then she winked. She's a big winker. I loved it when she winked. I put my arm around her waist and pulled her close.

"Giddy up, Winky," I said.

That night, for the first time since moving to Colorado, we showered together, which stands as a truly pathetic admission. Here we had a gleaming bathroom described enthusiastically by the real-estate folks all around us in the sprouting subdivision as a "five-piece," meaning a toilet, two sinks, a separate bathtub, and a shower. The shower stall occupied as much space as a decent walk-in closet. It even had a bench—we'd never had a shower seat before—which of course could aid any stab at shower sex. Nevertheless, I had showered alone, and Annie had showered alone. Until tonight. We lathered, we slid our hands across our slick bodies, and we tiptoed toward the sex zone.

"Mmmm," said Annie, kissing me lightly. "This is nice. We haven't had shower sex for a long time."

"And this is a good shower," I answered. "The best out of twelve. It's even got the bench." I ran my hands across her back. I reached down and cupped her cheeks, lightly squeezing fistfuls of flesh as she kissed my neck and fondled my quickening stiffness. She stood in the stream of hot water and smiled as she crooked her neck and invited the water to massage her face, to stream down her long hair cascading toward the ground. And then I abruptly untangled myself and stood washboard straight, startling Annie. She nearly slipped.

"What the hell?" she said. "What are you doing?"

"I'm sorry, honey, but it's, you know, it's my nose thing."

"Oh my God, you're going to do that thing you do in the shower? *Now?*"

"Yeah," I said. "Suddenly, I really have to."

The shower door opened. She was gone.

Colorado's exceedingly arid climate had transformed the inside of my nose from a happy terrarium into Death Valley. Rattlesnakes and scorpions would kill to nest in my nostrils. Every morning I spent about ten minutes standing in steam, inhaling moisture into my desiccated, brittle nasal passages, and then exhaling the desert life that had accumulated during the previous day and evening. Sometimes the cache of crust grew suddenly painful, and excavating it became urgent.

"Sexy," said Annie when I stepped out of the shower. "No wonder we haven't showered together."

"Sorry," I murmured, scurrying to the bed and slipping under the covers, the room dancing with candlelight and incense smoke. This unfortunate episode points toward a possible problem in our relationship, a complication centered squarely on my wee head. Had the shower encounter happened early in our relationship, it never would have occurred to me—it would have been beyond the realm of possibility—to purge my nose with Annie so naked and so hot beside me. You must be thinking, *You idiot! What were you thinking?* I had grown too comfortable with our relationship; I took Annie's love and adoration for granted; I did not stop to consider the ramifications of my broadcasting of nasal shrapnel.

Were the tables turned—had Annie pulled such nonsense—I would have reacted with disgust. Which is how Annie responded. How she managed to actually sleep with me after that, I do not know. I did, at least, note her reaction, her panicked retreat from the shower stall, and this stuck with me. *Don't do that again,* I said to myself. *Jackass.*

After both of us warmed up in our cocoons, I emerged and turned on, via a laptop, WFMU, our favorite radio station, an almost fetishized spot on the dial for many music fans, a station based in New York with a highly eclectic range of DJs and programs. And then we sat across from each other, kissing and hugging and petting, both of us nude.

"Why don't you get on your stomach?" I said, by way of peace offering.

Annie looked at me warily.

"That's a good start," she said.

I poured grapeseed oil into my hand and commenced massaging. I explored her back with my palms, pressing with more weight than seemed wise, but she responded with enthusiasm so I continued. She eventually sat up, poured a dollop of lube into her palm, and gestured me onto my back.

"Nice," I said, smiling widely. "Despite the whole shower thing."

"Very despite," she said.

She kept going, and going, and going, and I lay back and lost myself in pure pleasure, despite the music, which had changed from something . . . musical . . . to the sound of a stick striking the side of a table.

Bang!

Click!

Thwack!

Notwithstanding the racket, I could have orgasmed, but decided that might not count as sex. So far, we'd had intercourse every night. I wasn't about to change the rules unilaterally at the start of week 4.

"Great ride," said Annie. "Surprising, too, after the shower disaster."

"I think the massage helped, despite your claim that massages and sex are, in general, not intimately linked."

"In tonight's case, it's possible," said Annie.

We stayed up for a bit, reading. As usual, Annie fell asleep with a book in her lap. I placed the book on the floor, and Annie woke up.

"Unh, did I fall asleep?" she asked, rubbing her eyes.

"Of course, honey," I said.

I turned out the light.

THE FOLLOWING day, Monday, day 22, I couldn't even listen to the radio on my way back from work. The noise interfered with my meditation upon my failure to identify Denver with home. Where were we headed? My best answer was "Beats me." Such an approach to life can be liberating and romantic, especially when you're 25. At 40 with two kids, it was disorienting and not welcome.

Earlier in the day, from the office, I wrote Annie: "It's like having smog in my brain." I dragged my ass home through Denver's winter desolation and immediately popped ginseng and maca root, hoping that together the alleged aphrodisiacs would awaken and brighten my curdled spirit.

I was unaccustomed to depression. Like my father, one of the sunniest people I ever encountered, I tend to shrink from upsetting things and grasp at nearly anything that pleases. But our time in Denver had come with clouds. The sex was improving things, but it did not erect (heh) an impregnable wall. Sometimes it was difficult to emote bright enthusiasm for Annie and the kids. I didn't shroud their world in fog, but they all sensed the occasional shift in mood. On this Monday night, the kids seemed a bit off-kilter. Joni and Ginger were arguing with unusual ferocity about the rules of a game of their own invention. Their sourness, combined with my own, brought Annie down a few notches, too, as she stood before the stove, making spaghetti and homemade sauce for the family.

During dinner, the kids stepped into new arguments about absurdly trivial things (e.g., who had the more colorful napkin), I barely talked, and Annie toiled to coax the meal into something placid and pleasant. I recognized the effort Annie had put into the evening, so at its conclusion I did not hesitate to tackle the dishes. I did this anyway whenever Annie cooked (which was every weeknight and many weekends, too), but sometimes it took me a while to grab the sponge and start wiping.

"Relax," I said to her. She plopped onto the couch and read to the girls while I scrubbed. Then I read Joni some *Harry Potter,* and Annie regaled Ginger with some Dr. Seuss. We trudged into the bedroom, feeling wiped out.

"So tired," I said as I climbed into bed, again ogling the bureau drawer holding the Viagra hoard. "God. I could just collapse."

Which is precisely what I did the instant I slipped between the sheets. I dropped my head on the pillow and stared at the ceiling. It was the best sensation I'd experienced all day. Annie quickly followed my lead, lying beside me on her back and gazing up. We lost ourselves to small talk and gossip about our FFF for a good half hour. And then Annie said, "I know you're down, honey. I can lift your spirits. I think."

She kissed me on the lips, then traveled down my bare chest, kissing me all the way. Fireworks did not explode the instant she began kissing, but novel tingles—unique for this lame Monday—began buzzing different parts of my body. She moved back up, and we kissed on the lips again, holding it for longer.

"Thanks," I whispered. "It's been a crummy day. Climbing into bed was the highlight, and now it's getting better."

We kissed and petted some more, and eventually the inflation began in earnest, becoming somewhat of a pressing matter. And then we were joined and having a happy frolic. At some point, Annie rolled onto her side while I remained above, sort of straddling her top thigh.

"Sideways sex," I said. "A brand-new position."

"Yeah," said Annie. "It's cool. You feel . . . stubbier."

"Stubbier?" I said. Given the context, this was not a winning adjective.

"In a good way," she said, sensing my alarm. "A good way, honey. Keep doing what you're doing."

THE SEX drug lasted through the night and across the next day, dispatching every wisp of ennui that had haunted the previous afternoon. With my mood bubbly, I took a shower after the kids were asleep and rubbed myself with a moisturizing bath bar bought by

Annie that would more aptly be called a "sparkle bar." By the time I finished, I glinted like an alien, shimmered like some forest sprite flitting through a stand of enchanted apple trees. I entered the bedroom and shook my body in front of Annie.

"I'm all sparkly."

"What a turn-on," said Annie, grinning. "Sparkleman."

While we talked, we lay on our backs at opposite ends of the bed. We pressed our feet together sole to sole, swinging our legs back and forth in unison.

"Foot massage?" I asked.

As I kneaded and she groaned, it occurred to me: Billy rubs her feet, too.

"So," I asked her, "are foot massages akin to sex with you?"

"Oh, most definitely," she purred, her eyes closed, her mouth curved into a smile.

"Interesting," I said, alarmed. "You know, Billy massages your feet all the time. And I'm going to have to just blurt this out: He's one of the best-looking men I've ever encountered, although don't take this the wrong way."

"Don't worry."

"So, do you get off on Billy massaging your feet?"

"You mean, beyond the massage itself? Because I love the massage."

"The fact that it's Billy doing the massage. How does that influence things?"

"Well, as we discussed earlier, massages do not lead to sex fantasies. Massages lead to nonsexual happiness. But I'm not blind. Billy's not exactly Ernest Borgnine. And if Ernest Borgnine were massaging my feet, it might bum me out a bit."

"So you like that it's Billy?"

"Yes, but like I said, I'm not lying there thinking about having sex with him while he's massaging my feet."

"But other times . . ."

"No," said Annie. "No other times. I don't dream about having sex with the guy when he's rubbing my feet, and I don't think about having sex with him when he's teaching, and I don't fantasize about doing him while I'm doing the dishes."

"Cool."

"But I definitely notice that he's hot."

This conversation would not have happened weeks earlier. And if it had, I think my jealousy might have gotten the better of me. But this night, at least, the ripples of anxiety turned glassy, and I dropped the whole subject.

ON THIS sex anniversary day—number 25—I went to work and Annie lined up playdates for the kids: She planned to take back-to-back yoga classes to mark the milestone. While she stretched, I returned from work, picked up the girls from their playdates, and brought them home, where things moved along at a somewhat swift, unruffled clip. Dinner, no problemo. Stories, they liked them. Joni found it amusing that her mom was doing a whole three hours of yoga. Three hours, I'll venture, seems like at least an adult week to most young children.

I tucked the girls into bed, turned off their lights, and migrated to the bedroom, where I began dwelling on a dilemma that had confronted me just as I left the newsroom: My boss sent around an e-mail saying we would have our first staff meeting of the year the following day. I had planned to stay home, not only to celebrate the one-quarter mark but to get some rest. The night-after-night sex did rejuvenate and energize me, but it also stole sleep, because Annie and I ended up staying awake later than normal. Contemplation of the suddenly fraught situation—to bail either on the staff meeting or on the day set aside for celebration and recuperation—dragged me down, delivering me to a familiar place: bummed-out about "home."

Annie returned from her back-to-back nearly glowing, but soon after her arrival in the bedroom, hope for intimacy withered.

"Glad you had a great yoga session," I said. "I may have to go to work tomorrow. There's some meeting I should go to. But I feel rotten, I'm exhausted, and I'm just down."

"Down again, huh?" she said, as she stripped off her yoga clothes. "You just can't shake this, can you? It's not you. I'm not used to it. Are you down because of the meeting, or something else?"

"The usual," I said. "I wish I could move back to Baltimore today."

Annie sat on the edge of the bed while I talked. Her eyes told me this worried her.

"It's so odd to me," she said. "Granted, I'm not nuts for the neighborhood, but to me, at least, it feels so good to be here in the West."

I nodded, barely acknowledging her comment. She tiptoed to the shower. I roasted in self-pity. *I give up,* I thought. *She wins. She can have her precious West. Guess I'll just have to live my one life way out in the middle of nowhere.* This marination in ego persisted after she returned to the bedroom, where I first ignored her and then reported with great sarcasm that I'd be "delighted" to "spend the rest of my life" in "a place sharing many attributes with Upper Mongolia, including a lack of trees and an unforgiving, parched climate."

"This is nuts," said Annie, "I've done enough child rearing today. Whenever you return to the land of adults, let me know."

I will spare you the rest of my embarrassing tantrum, the tick-tock of the half hour I spent on the bed wallowing in woe, the dejected musings that captured my head as I showered. Let us just say that this lasted for some time, until Annie entered the room again, got into bed, and started talking to me, which is what competent adults do with each other. In addition, Fair Annie said "I'm sorry" to me, which not only was unnecessary but was in fact improper. Apologies are things that are "owed." An apology that does not serve to satisfy some sort of debt is not an apology at all but a misguided verbal signal. If somebody were to ask you for the time and you responded, "Penguins live in the Southern Hemisphere," this remark, for example, would be another misguided verbal signal.

So she said she was sorry, and I came to my senses and told her that was not necessary, that I owed her an apology, which I then delivered.

"I wish America weren't so big," said Annie, a phrase she'd copped a decade earlier and used every few months. "Why can't the West be only an hour from the East?"

"I would enjoy that," I responded. "Then the West would be, like, Lancaster County, Pennsylvania, which would put me closer to my family, and I would have no reservations whatsoever about living in the West."

This conversation spread out for some time—until 11:30, to be precise, which gave us only thirty minutes to have sex before the next day officially arrived. With the argument behind us and the time before us diminishing rapidly, we finally lurched forward.

IN THE morning, after I decided to skip the staff meeting, Annie and I took the girls to their different schools. Then I visited the yoga studio with Annie, who had the idea that on this day we should, for the first time, practice yoga together, at the same time. Had the decision been entirely mine, I most likely would have selected to do something other than yoga. For example, go find some good fish and chips somewhere, wash down the fried things with a Guinness or three, and then come home and have sloppy-tipsy sex.

However, I felt that the previous night's apology did not sufficiently pay the debt I owed Annie. In fact, her unnecessary and preemptive apology made me feel as if I owed even more—maybe not double but clearly much more than the simple "I'm sorry" that I'd tossed into the ring. This could have been genius on the part of Annie. Regardless, I agreed to the yoga without even offering alternatives. I acquiesced immediately, so there we were, sweating in the room with a bunch of people from the 'hood. Ninety minutes later, I understood the wisdom of Annie's choice: I felt vigorous. I felt limber. I felt very horny.

Fortunately, the yoga had excited Annie, too. Upon entering the empty house, we nearly raced up the stairs. We each showered (taking a shower together would have made great sense, but I had tainted that erotic experience), and then we embraced between the sheets, in the sex den bright with sunlight. Soon, we lay side by side, panting.

"Great way to start the day," I said. "Yoga and sex."

"It feels like I've spent the day at a spa," said Annie.

We had planned to do something like take a walk. Instead, we curled up in bed and awoke a few hours later. We hadn't napped together in a long time, possibly since leaving Baltimore two years before. We relished it—a Thursday afternoon, alone in the house, sex and a nap, and then a bunch of hanging out doing nothing, a variation on a theme of "walking around and checking things out."

COULD WE have largely remained in our house for the duration of the marathon, never having sex anywhere other than in our bedroom and the Vegas hotel? Could be. But thanks to Annie's shrewd "brainstorm" before the marathon kickoff, we planned occasional weekend getaways to, as Annie put it, "keep everything interesting." New places, even mere motel rooms, always seemed to improve our sex life.

In fact, the course of our lives had been shaped, in part, by sex we'd had on a vacation. We'd been grinding through a Minneapolis winter in the early 1990s while I was in graduate school and Annie was working for the University of Minnesota. In the Land of 10,000 Lakes, winter encompasses April and can even threaten May. We needed sun and warmth, so Annie planned an April trip to New Mexico, which sounded reasonably warm as well as, by American standards, exotic. The plane landed late at night, and we woke up to brilliant desert sun and snow-blanketed mountains.

We spent the next few days skiing, drinking margaritas, and soaking in the sun. In every atmospheric faux-adobe motel room, we had excellent sex, sessions between the sheets that were energetic and spirited and long. Sex like this was not unknown to us in Minnesota, but it didn't happen day after day as it did in New Mexico. What had sparked five days of especially effervescent sex, of memorable lovemaking? The high elevation? The sun? The skiing and tequila? We didn't know. But months later when we decided to flee Minnesota, Annie said: "We could just point our car south, depress the gas pedal, and not stop until we reach New Mexico, you know."

"Deal."

It is not an exaggeration to say sex drove us to New Mexico, where we launched careers, made great friends, embraced nature as never before, and conceived a child.

Sex had precisely nothing to do with our moving to Denver. But the upcoming weekend retreat was linked directly to our carnal pursuits. Shortly after yoga had enchanted Annie (*enchanted* would be too strong a word to describe yoga's effect on me, but I would not quibble with "pleasantly surprised"), she'd found the ashram, with the swamis and the meditation and, most important, the mountain cabin. We both thrilled to small spaces with rough-hewn walls, scant insulation, and cold floors. We like feeling as though we are "roughing it" when in fact we are living the way most people in America lived just one hundred years ago. Like our trumpeting of a "free is best" motto, we championed cabins and, in fact, rarely met a "room for rent" that we didn't like. Mere contemplation of a mountain room for rent, not to mention the sex we'd have in a presumably cozy room (and, yes, the yoga), tickled my brain.

Ginger didn't attend preschool on Fridays, so while I worked on stories from the office, Annie spent the day with the elf, playing games, running errands, preparing meals and snacks, and so on. She also hatched a plan related to our room-for-rent-in-the-mountains weekend, a sly and simple strategy. She took Ginger to the grocery store and bought Eggo waffles. I admit this sounds inconsequential. But you must understand that junk food, like Eggo waffles, does not dwell in our house. Waffles? Of course. We make them from scratch, with whole grains, ground flaxseed, organic, hormone-free milk and butter, and free-range eggs, and we douse them with real maple syrup from New England or Canada. But to our children these discs of labor and love do not compare to Eggo waffles, which are mass-produced by what I imagine are gleaming machines in Battle Creek, Michigan, and have been a presence in my mother's freezer in West Chester, Pennsylvania, since 1971.

Joni, in particular, adored Eggo waffles, although Ginger was no slouch in her demonstrations of Eggo devotion. The salient point here is that Eggo waffles had never dwelled in any freezer of Annie and Doug Brown. Now, suddenly, they did. Their presence, Annie hoped, would please the girls so much that they would forget about our absence during the upcoming weekend. We were leaving the house Saturday morning and returning Sunday afternoon, and the girls were staying home with the nanny we'd scored thanks to one of Annie's friends. We were worried, not because of doubts about the nanny's competence but because of the girls' possibly negative reaction to being alone for twenty-four hours not with a grandparent or an aunt but with a stranger.

Shortly after prospecting for Eggo gold, Annie hunkered down with Ginger at the library while I worked at the office. Few things gladdened young Ginger like a couple of hours at the library, sitting on a parent's lap and listening to stories. Sometimes, too, she'd find a shelf full of children's books and shoo us—actually, shout us—away: "Go! I want to read!" Of course, Ginger had no idea how to read. She could look at pictures, though. Annie took advantage of a Ginger excommunication by browsing, whereupon she found a book of quotations. Shortly after, as I walked toward a Vietnamese restaurant for lunch in downtown Denver, my phone beeped.

> *Graze on my lips; and if those hills be dry,*
> *Stray lower, where the pleasant fountains lie.*

The text message, lines from a Shakespeare poem, was my first ever. It charged the lunch hour.

"I feel so techno-savvy," said Annie that night in bed after tucking the kids in (and alerting them to a morning surprise to coincide with their introduction to the weekend nanny). "And literary. You know what I was thinking? It's possible that was the first time that quote was ever used in a text message. And I'm certain it marked the first time that someone used it in an inaugural text message."

"You're feeling competitive again, aren't you," I said, grunting through another round of squats and push-ups at the end of the bed.

"That's me." She smiled and blushed.

"I love it," I said. "I mean, my God, you're getting excited about text messages!"

"It's true," she said. "I do get these little thrills. I can't help it."

"I know," I said. "You can't help it. Which explains why it's so you."

"WHAT'S THE big surprise?" asked both Joni and Ginger soon after they woke up. Annie opened the freezer, whipped out the yellow box, and both girls gasped.

"Oh my God, WE HAVE EGGOS!" shouted Joni.

"Mama, can I have an Eggo . . . no two Eggos . . . right now?" squealed Ginger.

We did not buy the "syrup" that contains high-fructose corn syrup, maple flavoring, and other stuff—this potion is the girls' preference—because like most parents, we do have our limits. But it didn't matter. The girls lost themselves in their Eggo waffles, oblivious, it seemed, to the pending departure of Mommy and Daddy. Their remove from this event, which we had assumed would at least disorient their little world, seemed even more pronounced several seconds after the nanny arrived. The smiling woman immediately plopped to the ground—to girl level—and began engaging our children with games and stories. We handed the girls presents that Annie had picked up earlier in the week—a few Polly Pocket dolls, some books—rained kisses upon them and shrouded them with hugs, and waved frantically as we worked our way to the door.

"So long, girls!"

"We love you!"

"We'll be back in a flash!"

"You're going to have so much fun!"

They pulled themselves away from the nanny briefly to acknowledge our exit—some weak waves, a few distant "bye-byes"—and then we were in the minivan, gunning the thing west and north into the Rocky Mountains.

"Eggos were brilliant," I said to Annie.

"They seemed to work, that's for sure," said Annie. "Something worked. They weren't even ruffled by our leaving for the weekend."

I nodded solemnly. "This has the potential to be a touch upsetting," I offered. "But the alternative—our exit spiraling the girls into paroxysms of grief—is clearly worse. I think, given the circumstances, we came out ahead."

Within moments the whole episode—a paroxysm of indifference—became eclipsed by the blur of talking that persisted until we reached Boulder, where we stopped at a supermarket to buy seltzer water for the ashram cabin. Except for those parents who have full-time nannies, or those who live within a broad family network, time for daylight adult talk between spouses is exceedingly limited. Considering that Annie and I actually liked each other quite a lot, we did not dither when these opportunities sprang up. So I drove and Annie knitted a gray scarf and we talked about FFF gossip, summer vacation plans, the skiing we had yet to do in Colorado, and so on.

Soon, ALPINE nature enveloped us—pine boughs bending with snow, massive boulders, views of the Continental Divide. And then we pulled into the entrance to the yoga ashram, a compound of sorts, rustic buildings scattered throughout the woods with people who clearly were part of the permanent ashram community—men with long hair piled atop their heads in makeshift buns—smashing ice on the trails between cabins with long metal rods. We stopped at the office, and a blissful young hippie lass listening to sitar music handed us our keys, told us how to find our cabin, and urged us to come to the temple that evening, adding that blue jeans and yoga clothes were not permitted. On a wall behind her, a sign warned "No smoking or alcohol is allowed at Shoshoni."

"Uh-oh," said Annie as we walked to our cabin. "All I brought are jeans and yoga clothes. And I want to go to the temple tonight."

We unpacked our bottle of California Shiraz-Cabernet shortly after stepping into our frigid, bantam cabin. On the walls were posters of Hindu gods, including one of the elephant-god Ganesh behind the bed. A big evergreen log extended across the length of the ceiling. I cranked up the heat immediately, and then we walked back to the office to ask the hippie about the no-jeans policy.

"We want to go to the temple tonight, but I don't have the right clothes," said Annie. "Does this mean we can't go?"

"Happens all the time," said the woman behind the desk. She pointed to a box full of gauzy, patterned skirts, the kind women wear to Grateful Dead concerts. "You can wear one of those."

Annie grabbed a blue skirt that looked like a tapestry, and we headed back to the balmier but still chilly cabin. We stripped and crawled between the sheets while the guys outside chipped away at ice. Grinning, we pulled the covers to our necks and braided our warm limbs.

"I love that we're at an ashram." I said.

"You just like saying 'ashram.'"

"True," I said. "What do you want to do?"

"The same thing as you," she said, reaching down and giving me a squeeze.

She brought her lips to mine, and everything started to warm.

LESS THAN an hour later we bundled up and walked through snow and ice to an industrial outbuilding for the yoga class. About twenty people filled the plain room, including a white guy with enormous brown dreadlocks like stuffed pythons dangling down his back, and a colossal man with a shaved head and skinny mustache who looked like a comic-book villain. Annie told me he leered at her the whole time she was doing her yoga practice.

Typical villain.

It felt good to stretch, but by now we both were used to our own yoga studio's pronounced swelter. The sauna heat there rid our bones of winter cold and loosened our muscles and ligaments. The ashram studio was cold, but I had brought along my ancient blue sweatpants with five pockets, in case the yoga room was too frigid for shorts. (*Hey, pal! Nice to see you again!*) The yoga session was more a lengthy meditation on a few poses than a procession of bends, folds, and twists. In short, it did not compare to the stuff we were doing in Stapleton, although I suspect yoga aficionados, real sticklers for yogic authenticity, would argue that the ashram yoga was far superior.

After the session, we rushed back to the cabin in the darkness, changed into non-yoga, non-blue-jeans clothing, and walked through howling wind and single-digit temperatures to the temple. The schedule said simply "Meditation." We expected a spare room with people sitting silently on cushions.

We opened the door. Candles flickered everywhere, and smoke from incense wafted across the big space framed with huge logs. Gigantic statues wreathed in garlands and surrounded with busy shrines holding Polaroid photographs, conch shells, and, oddly, Butterfinger candy bars (among other things) dominated the front of the room. Massive photographs of Indian yogis loomed. People indeed perched on cushions, but instead of silence, a band of chanting ashramites wearing white and orange robes played unusual instruments like the harmonium and the ukelele. It was loud.

Annie and I found cushions and marveled at the scene until a tall, skinny, bearded fellow in a white robe stepped to the front of the room, knelt, bowed, and then sat cross-legged and closed his eyes. The music stopped. He opened his eyes and smiled, then talked for a while about "ego." He said we all would have to put aside our egos for the night and dance. *Dance?* I like to dance, but only somewhere dark, and in complete anonymity. For Annie, it's even worse: She doesn't know how to dance—that is to say, her mind and body do not merge with music for the purpose of collaboration (i.e., "You, music, provide the beats and I—Annie—will command my limbs to follow your path, and we will have fun together. Capiche?"). We danced once at our wedding, and only because everybody squawked us to the middle of the courtyard. We held each other and moved—calling it "dancing" would be a stretch—to a song arranged by Tommy Dorsey and sung by Frank Sinatra in 1940, "The Sky Fell Down." It was our one concession to familial pressure but, despite our misgivings, one of the highlights of the wedding. However, I'd steeled myself for that. Dancing never flitted across my mind for the night of meditation. I began jonesing for a little silence.

Then a lass with a nest of curly locks, a flushed face, and a blissed-out smile appeared, holding in her left hand a tray with candles and in her right hand a little bell. She approached the frieze of statues and altars and began swaying, holding out the tray for the gods and ringing the bell. She put aside the tray, grabbed a horsetail brush, and danced while waving it before the gods. She did the same thing with a red umbrella, a peacock fan, and a scarf. Then she handed the tray to somebody in the audience and distributed the rest of the props to other people, all of whom moved to the music and waved their items in front of the gods as they shuffled from one end of the room to the other. *Oh my God*, I thought. *One of these hippies will hand me one of those things. And people will expect me to dance for a bunch of statues.*

Unbidden, an image of Andy Kaufman gamboled into my

brain. I saw him grabbing the red umbrella and capering to the front and dancing around like a lunatic, losing himself to the wild environment, the cold wind shaking the temple, and the weirdness. A woman handed me the horsetail brush as the people in robes belted out a thundering chant to Lord Shiva. And I became one with Andy Kaufman. I pranced to the front, stood before a statue of Ganesh, the elephant-god, and shook my hips. I raised both hands and waved them back and forth slightly. I closed my eyes and saw Andy Kaufman with his startled-doe eyes and unruly hair. I envisioned him holding my horsetail brush and not waving it limply, cowardly, but sweeping the air with it, flapping his arms and rolling his eyes back in his head with devotional delirium.

With the image running cinematically through my brain, I felt my arms above my head wave wider and with greater force. I felt my hips draw broader and faster circles, my head pivot metronomically on my neck and then loll back and forth in arcs. I lifted my face to the rustic ceiling and opened my eyes. I twirled. I faced Ganesh and waved the brush before his visage, now moving in step with the Lord Shiva chanting. I slowly bounced across the front of the room, visiting with gods and brandishing the brush like a painter gone mad, decorating the air with angled plumes and deep waves, zigzags, and quick curlicues and slaps.

All of these theatrics may have been inspired by Andy Kaufman, but I must add that I was not engaging in mockery. I found the whole Hindu ceremony to be, and I hope this does not offend any Hindus, quite a gas. I felt happily liberated up there before the row of gods, waving the brush and moving my hips. In many other contexts (in fact, in any that involve me dancing in neither darkness nor complete anonymity), I think a sour self-consciousness would have flooded my being, But here among the earnest and kind Hindus I felt nothing but, to put it dramatically but truthfully, joy.

When I reached the end of the line, for the first time in ten minutes I took note of the rest of the room. I was alone in the front. A shudder traveled up my spine, but then I looked into the audience and saw Annie, laughing silently on her meditation cushion. Dancing, I moved toward her, and the chortling ceased. Fear rooted in her eyes; her face went slack. I could almost hear her pleading in her head: *Please, DJ! Don't give me the brush! For God's sake, no! I cannot dance!*

I am not a cruel man, and I love my wife with great passion. Nevertheless, as I moved toward Annie Who Fears Dancing Above All Else, I understood what I had to do, which of course was to give Annie the brush, which would compel her to rise and "dance" before the gods. My determination did not arise from any innate brutishness. In truth, I imagined that she, in the end, would appreciate participating in this unusual ceremony, although I also understood that her appreciation might come only after the passing of time, which could mean the next day or the next year. Regardless, Annie was the yoga disciple, she was the principal engine behind the evening's temple event, and she simply could not escape this kaleidoscopic marvel without taking part in its centerpiece.

So, with the ends of my mouth rising almost to my ears, I handed her the brush.

"Enjoy thyself!" I whispered.

Bless her little nondancing soul, she floated up to the front in her gypsy skirt, and I felt a certain warmth that comes only from love as I watched her trying to fit in with the rest of the enthusiasts, several of whom had followed me to the front as I concluded my mad romp. The devotees kept chanting, and it was rhythmic. And Annie moved at the same time. But was there a harmonious melding of mantra and motion? Nope. Annie jerked her body around independent of the music. She gently flapped the brush toward the gods. She bobbed her head. She shifted her weight from leg to leg. She neither smiled nor frowned but maintained a pure blankness: a

Mona Lisa flat-line mouth; expressionless marble eyes; a furrowed brow betraying the great effort she was investing in projecting nonchalance. The music ended while Annie "danced." All the participants returned to their cushions, and the skinny guy appeared again.

"Good job!" I whispered and squeezed her thigh.

"Thanks a lot!" she whispered back, grinning wildly.

Fortunately, as I had hoped, the delivery of the brush had not angered Annie, but instead had given her a little thrill. The bearded, robed man urged us all to repeat to ourselves a certain Hindu chant, and then he stopped talking. We all sat quietly for a long time, listening to the whistling wind tremble the trees and shudder the walls of the temple. Then the guy in charge stood up, and it was over. Somebody opened the heavy door to the outside, Arctic air whipped into the temple, and we filed out into the darkness into a night that somehow had grown even colder, and ate dinner in the communal dining area. Some of the people who lived at Shoshoni served veggie lasagna, garden salad, barley salad, garlic bread, and key lime pie, all of which was excellent. People squeezed into the dining room, an odd, ragtag assembly. Hippies, the bald villain, retirees. A woman who sat across from me revealed she was from Siberia.

"*The* Siberia. The real Siberia."

She must have felt at home.

We rushed through the brittle cold to our warm cabin, where we immediately unscrewed the wine bottle, filled the cups to their rims, leafed through magazines, and cuddled. We did not have sex because we'd already done that in the cabin, while the guys outside chipped away at ice.

"So you were OK with the dancing?" I asked.

"It had its moments," said Annie. "I mean, I'm pretty certain I didn't actually dance, but I'm glad you made me go up there, even though at the time . . . Let's just say it wasn't a high priority."

"I knew you'd never do that on your own," I said. "But I thought you'd appreciate it, once you were up there. In addition, I wasn't sure how the Hindu gods would react, not to mention the ashramites, to a guest who failed to participate properly."

"Good point," added Annie. "Maybe one of the gods would curse the marathon." She took a sip of wine and said, "That was amazing. That whole thing. So colorful. And loud. Definitely not the sort of service I grew up with."

Annie was raised extremely Episcopalian. As a child I visited a rural Presbyterian church only occasionally—probably, on average, six or seven times a year. The biggest religious influence on me was the two years I spent at Westtown School, a private Quaker school near my home. I had basically flunked out of fourth grade, my parents were worried about me, so they tapped their savings—I did not grow up wealthy—and sent me for two years to an elite prep school, where we sat in "meeting" every Tuesday afternoon. The Quaker meetinghouse I attended had pews that were arranged in a circle and rose like stadium seating. There was no priest or preacher, no patriarch or matriarch, to lead the "flock." Instead, people stood and spoke whenever the spirit moved them. The service, for the most part, was silent, not a state familiar to many 10-year-old boys, and I don't think many of us while sitting in peace contemplated Ecclesiastes or even, say, much of anything outside of, in my case, girls, motorcycles, television, and rock stars. But even dwelling on those things became dull quickly, and at first I dreaded this weekly descent into quiet. But by the end of my time at Westtown, I'd grown to appreciate the solitude.

And now, I respected at least one Hindu ceremony.

"Without question, it wasn't boring," I said to Annie.

"Nope," she said. "I mean, c'mon, a six-foot statue of an elephant wearing a necklace of flowers? A laughing Buddha? Peace and love and selflessness? What's not to like? I do have to admit, however, that I was suspicious at first."

Organized anything tended to irritate Annie. In third grade she stopped singing "Jingle Bells" because she found it too "rote." She ceased repeating the Pledge of Allegiance in fifth grade because she had learned that people in Nazi Germany had been forced to recite patriotic pledges.

"I was totally into the Hindu ceremony, though," she said. "In fact, I'm totally into this: the yoga, the food, the community, the temple."

"I know what you mean," I said. "I was all Mr. Las Vegas after that trip, but now I'm Mr. Ashram. I like this better than Vegas, which definitely surprises me. I definitely want to come back here."

"Me too," she said. "And I'm with you on the Vegas thing. One thing I've got to say, though: I still have my problems with meditating."

"So I'm guessing you didn't, you know, actually meditate?" I asked.

"If that means sitting there thinking about absolutely nothing, the answer would be no."

"Have you ever really meditated?"

"I've tried, but I always fail at it," said Annie. "I can't think of nothing."

We huddled in our warm room, drinking wine from plastic cups and listening to the cold world outside whistle and groan and rattle. We talked of our girls, wondered how they were handling the nanny, and admitted that we missed them despite being gone for only ten hours or so. This "missing," however, should not be confused with feeling a great need to have them with us at that instant. We were content, for now, to be adults in a place revolving around grown-up pursuits, as opposed to those that involve zoos, birthday parties, or crayons.

"I'm so happy right now," whispered Annie.

"Me too," I said. I could hear Annie's breath thicken as she plummeted into slumber. I sat on the bed in the dark and tried to meditate—to not think—but the thoughts won. They refused to leave. *You're already home!* they insisted. *This is home. Annie is home. Joni and Ginger are home. What's home? Love.*

6

Catcalls of the Past

We woke up in a cabin in the cold mountains, with no kids in sight, and, I hesitate to report, it would not be out of line to describe the feeling as "euphoric." This may have had less to do with the absence of kids than with the presence of additional sleep and a wake-up that did not involve the preparation of several breakfasts followed by a rush out the door to soccer practice. We were not prepared to spend these valuable hours filing from one activity to another.

Great gusts of wind drove snow from the roof, and it spiraled and spun like the ghosts of dervishes. We watched the dark evergreens bend on the sides of the surrounding mountains. It was all rugged and stirring, and we could have gone straight to breakfast, then to a swami lecture, and then to a round of breathing exercises, among other things. But we did none of it. Instead, we stayed in our warm cabin and had sex.

"Let's try that interesting lube I picked up at the show," said Annie, rising from bed to scamper across the cold floor to the toiletries bag, from which she withdrew a packet of lube that allegedly exhibited "clitoral stimulating" properties. Shortly after applying it, as we began kissing, Annie reported that the lube manufacturers may have confused "stimulating" with "inflaming."

I considered offering that to inflame is probably to stimulate, that the terms are not mutually exclusive, but quickly concluded such an observation had the strong potential to stimulate severe annoyance in Annie.

"Hold on for a minute, honey," she said. She closed her eyes. "I think it's getting better. Hold on." Another thirty seconds. "Aaah, there," she said. "The pain is gone. I'm not sure if it's stimulating, but at least it's not hurting."

"Inferior lube," I muttered as I fit my body into hers comfortably, my kneecaps pressing into the warm backs of her knees, my hand on her hip, my waist cupping her derriere. I ran my hand along her hip, then down to her thigh and up to her ribcage. I pressed myself into Annie, and she pressed back, a sign, I felt, that I was welcome to, you know, toss the spoon. I hesitated for a moment, because spooning, like cuddling, appears to be championed with particular fervor by women, although I am not suggesting here that most or even many men are opposed to spooning. But spooning seemed like the sort of thing women, and from experience I knew this included Annie, enjoyed for its own sake with more brio than men: a long cuddle, an epic spooning.

From time to time, Annie and I had discussed this over the years, this dislocation between men and women when it comes to spooning, cuddling, or any variation thereof. I never ridiculed these forms of touch, but they didn't come naturally to me. Annie, on the other hand, cherished anything that involved our bodies being pressed together for extended periods of time without even a hint of sex. Among many guys, especially when they are in groups and without women, the very word "cuddling" is used like a judo throw. I don't think there's any mystery here: Guys like to verbally spar when they're hanging out. Instead of saying, "Hey, I love your outfit," a guy might instead shout to his buddy when they meet in a bar: "Hey, asshole. What's up with the pink shirt? Trying to look like a ballerina or something?" A healthy portion of the brawling often revolves around feminizing one another, and it's in this context that "cuddling" is wielded like a surprise move, one meant to toss the other guy onto his back.

So I think it's fair to ascribe a predisposition against cuddling and spooning to guy culture at large, although I suspect things change when guys are alone with their wives or girlfriends. I'd never been much of a cuddling-spooning basher in general, so the transformation was not dramatic when I left Guyworld for Annie. But still. I can't imagine defending cuddling-spooning while snug in Guyworld, but I was prepared to trumpet its benefits while with Annie.

On this night in the ashram cabin, I did not want to be accused of rushing from what Annie might be savoring as an emotional massage to what she might see as "just" sex. We had tossed the spoon before, and Annie never had cautioned me ("Hey! What are you doing? I thought we were spooning?"), but then again, I always had given the spoon its due before making the move. So despite what I believed to be an invitation to dispatch the spoon, I persisted with the arrangement for a few more minutes before ditching the activity, and then, suddenly, we were having sex.

It was an excellent romp, the two of us nearly covered entirely by the sheets and blankets as we went at it, playful and smiling and clearly feeling a touch giddy with our solitude and our atmospheric ashram cabin. Eventually, we grew warm enough to continue the session above the bedding, never mind the chilly room. At some point I asked Annie if she would be interested in getting on top but facing away from me, a position I herald because of the view but one Annie never suggested and never seemed especially enthusiastic about. Although during our years together we had launched into a lot of sex, probably upwards of a thousand sessions, give or take, that healthy volume of sex had not led to much discussion about each other's sexual preferences. We did it, we liked it, but we failed to spend much time talking about it. A month into daily sex, however, the deed had become such a routine part of our lives that the hesitation that had stopped me from verbally exploring sex fell away. I had a feeling the position wasn't top shelf for Annie, but I wasn't sure. So I asked.

"It's not my favorite," she said. "It makes me feel too exposed. Maybe it's all of that ass on display."

"But I love your ass!" I said.

"I don't."

It was a constant with Annie. "I'm chunky," I'd heard her say repeatedly over the years. She wasn't. Annie wasn't plump, pudgy, or Rubenesque. She wasn't skeletonic, either. She was perfect. But in her mind . . . chunky.

"Do you want to look like one of those model wraiths?" I'd ask her. "Bones and flesh? Definitely not my favorite look."

"No, I don't want to look like them, exactly," she'd say. "But maybe something between my current state and theirs. Why is that so hard?"

"So that's the problem with that position," I said. "Why didn't you say anything before?"

"It's not a big deal," said Annie. We were sitting cross-legged across from each other. "I don't hate it, and we don't do it that often. It's just that in our list of positions, it does not rise to the top."

"In fact, it's your least favorite," I said.

She nodded. "Anything that makes me think about weight makes me insecure," she said. "And insecurity and making love don't get along so well."

I thought about what she said for a few moments.

"You know what gets me?" I asked. "Performance. If I think I'm not performing well in bed, it makes me insecure. Which messes with my performance, which makes me worry about it even more, which messes even more with performance. Vicious cycle."

"I've never noticed your performance varying all that much, to be honest," reported Annie. "I don't see ups and downs . . . so to speak."

"Well, that's good to hear," I said. "Frankly, I think it all goes on in my head. Lots of insecurities up here." I rapped on my forehead with my knuckles.

Annie scooted herself closer to me. We leaned in for a lingering kiss.

"You have nothing to worry about," she whispered.

"Neither do you."

We climbed under the sheets again for warmth and to grab onto a little more alone time before hurtling back down the mountain to our house.

"I liked that talk," said Annie. "It's good to be open about this sort of thing."

"Maybe it was the whole spiritual thing. Or something," I said. "Of course, it's possible the round of openness has nothing to do with the ashram, but instead has a lot to do with having sex every day for a month."

"Either way, let's keep being honest with each other about everything. Not just sex," said Annie. "Maybe we don't reveal the whole truth as much as we should, you know? Maybe we keep too quiet about stuff."

We eventually packed up our stuff, washed away the wine-residue evidence, bought a CD of the Shoshoni ashramites playing the kind of music they performed at the temple, and drove off, back through a hyper-January landscape, along a road layered with fresh snow and ice, down steep mountain slopes.

SHORTLY AFTER lunchtime we opened the door to our house, and there they were, the girls and the nanny, sitting on the floor playing Candyland. "Hi girls!" we nearly shrieked.

The nanny stood up immediately, greeting us with a smile, and clearly prepared to detail for us the highlights (and lows) of the overnight. But the girls? They glanced up for a moment, offering little more than a collective "hey" before returning to the game.

Annie and I traded looks that could be interpreted as bemused, although a discerning critic might argue that a more insightful evaluation would stress a mixture of relief, chagrin, and discomfiture. We had imagined something more frenzied: a homecoming charged with juvenile gaiety; at the very least, a return marked by what is widely known as a sigh of relief.

"Guess the Eggos worked," I said.

"They do love those Eggos," said the nanny. When she left, we cuddled up with the girls on a couch and reviewed the hours they had spent with the nanny. This exercise could be confused with a hunt for independent corroboration of the nanny's account, but in truth it was just an excuse to hear the girls' voices.

That night, after a day spent sitting around the house with the girls and doing little more, we agreed that the girls' successful overnight engagement with the nanny opened, as a relationship counselor might put it, "new windows of opportunity" into our marriage. The chagrin and discomfiture that colored our initial reaction to the kids' response to our return had leaked away, leaving relief, yes, but also adding something you could call ambition.

"This means we can go away for weekends without depending on visiting family to watch the kids," said Annie. "This is huge."

We had removed ourselves from anything resembling a rut during the ashram weekend; we'd engaged with our suddenly weird world like stoners let loose in a penny-candy store. This sort of thing, we knew, was relationship balm. But when you are depending on family to watch the kids for a night, and the nearest family is a two-day drive away, it limits the field of possibilities. This had been our life in Colorado. But no more. And if not for the marathon, we never would have sprung for a nanny.

"Let's go away again soon," said Annie right after we turned out the lights and rolled onto our sides.

"We've got that hotel trip coming up," I said in the darkness.

"Perfect," said Annie.

HOURS LATER, while I was sitting at my desk in downtown Denver, my mind kept drifting back to the weekend in the cabin, to the wild Hindu temple with its brilliant colors, to the dancing, the music. To several friends who asked about the ashram, I responded, archly: "I think I'm Hindu."

"With a particular fondness for the Tantric teachings," quipped one FFF in an e-mail.

My "I think I'm Hindu" line was delivered as a joke but not with sarcasm. It would be a tad much to claim the two days had changed my life, but it also would be perfectly reasonable to say the time there had influenced me. The people who lived in the ashram, the folks who regularly visited for inspiration and peace, received something valuable and important, something powerful, from their connection to the temple. Annie and I touched this electricity for less than twenty-four hours, and now we wanted more.

"Are you thinking about the weekend?" e-mailed Annie in the middle of the day.

"I am. I think I'm Hindu," I wrote back.

SOON I was grabbing my coat and keys, and offering the litany of good-byes and waves that I offered every day as I left the office, the maze of desks and hierarchies where I dwelled somewhere on the periphery. And then—snap—I sat at the center of an entirely different world, one of magic elves and a captivating enchantress. This was a much more tactile place—a hot stove, books read aloud, hands soapy from dish washing, children kissed on foreheads—than the comparatively antiseptic environment to which I had just bid adieu. I found the land of faeries much more satisfying than its standard alternative—the office—but this does not bespeak a dislike of work; I just preferred family life to the office. In addition, the preference is not influenced by the idea that faerie life is easy and office work is difficult—that work is work and everything else is . . . not.

The patches of life squeezed in before and after the workday were rigged with exhausting demands, with toil, and this first workday evening after the glide through so much ashram exotica was no different. Dinner. Dishes. Bedtimes. And so on. And then, showers: Annie first. By the time I finished with my quick shower and slathered dollops of musk lotion over my body, a cold India Pale Ale sat sweating on my bedside table, and Annie, wearing a beguiling black slip and holding a beer in her hand, sat crosslegged on top of the bedspread, waiting. We kissed and within moments stepped into that other, most excellent, world: a carnival Tunnel of Love, a roller-coaster ride on rose petals. Here, again, we lost ourselves for a spell.

"Damn," Annie said moments after we had returned to earth. "Hot. Great."

"Just straightforward good sex, no?"

"*Yes.*"

Could Annie observe the workings of my brain, she'd see something like a bodybuilder after a good round of iron pumping: squeezing his fists and flexing his biceps; gazing into a mirror at the mounds topping his shoulders, his muffin-tin abdomen, his pomegranate calves. I asked Annie if she felt pride after a good session.

"I don't know . . . It's more complicated with women," she

said. "It's a good question. I want to give it some thought. I'll e-mail you something."

Happy and proud, with the lights turned off, I rolled to my side and pulled Annie close to me, spooning her from behind.

I RECEIVED the e-mail in the middle of the next afternoon.

"I never thought much about pride, and how it relates to good sex," it began. "A memory. I was in Philadelphia, probably 22 years old, I had just walked out of a deli and was thinking of something that made me smile when a young man caught my eye. I blushed and he looked at me and sang, 'I can see clearly now the rain is gone.' And then he walked away. It was one of those moments when a stranger touches your life forever. I went from feeling anonymous to feeling sexy in a matter of seconds. And another time was in Minneapolis and a man on the street catcalled to me, 'Shoooooorrrrrtttt and petite! Yeah! Just the way I like 'em!'

"I was at once embarrassed and secretly thrilled. I never think I'm being noticed in a sexual way, and it was clear that's exactly how this guy was seeing me. I have clung to these two anonymous comments for decades, calling them up when I needed a little self-esteem boost, those bad-body days during your period when you feel bloaty and poofy, or those early days of pregnancy when no one knows you're pregnant but everyone thinks you're a little chubby. Those are the days I call on the catcalls of the past to buck me up."

It went on.

"Pride during sex. It's kind of like doing a job well. When I see the satisfied look on your face post-orgasm, I sometimes think, 'Damn, I'm good.' Or, 'Who knew it was that easy?' But pride is different for women because I think the mechanics of the male are so much easier. It's like addition versus calculus. A biscuit you pop out of a vacuum-sealed can versus one you delicately mix from scratch. It's been said before, many times, and it's true—men are easier to get off than women. We're complicated down there.

"But it's also when you notice me or tell me I'm beautiful or say, 'That thing you did with your fingernails sent me into a different space.' Now that's when I feel pride. Like, wow, I can still turn on my husband merely by my looks, or just doing something simple with my fingernails. But the actual orgasm? Nah, that's too easy for pride to fill me up.

"And then there was the time I was practicing setting up my big farmers' market tent in the garage to get myself ready for my first day selling pasta up in Boulder. I was struggling to erect the tent and didn't want any help from anyone—not that I was being pissy or anything, but because I knew I wouldn't have any help at 6:30 a.m. the next day. Later, you told me you were getting turned on watching me set up the tent. Now that's pride. I was in an old T-shirt and an ill-fitting pair of jeans and hadn't done anything with my appearance, and you're turned on? My thought at the time: Score!"

I wrote back, thinking to myself as I tapped on the keyboard: *This e-mail exchange never would have happened before the marathon.* "You're so right about the biscuit thing. There is no doubt the mechanics of the female orgasm are much more complicated than that of the male. And I *did* find you so sexy getting that tent off the ground!"

FEBRUARY BEGAN with the word "pee pee" bouncing around in my slumbering brain.

I woke up.

Pee pee?

I noticed Ginger beside us in the bed; she had crawled in during the night. We locked the door during the deed but always unlocked it afterward, largely because of Ginger's nighttime peregrinations. We welcomed them because we understood that someday she would cease her midnight travels, just as Joni had done, and then, unless we had another child, we would not again hear a young person sleep-breathing beside us in bed until, if we were lucky, we were grandparents. Of course, we'd also have to wait until our dotage to lie in bed looking at a 3-year-old, watching her say "pee pee," and then coming to a certain realization.

I looked down on a puddle of warm toddler pee metastasizing across the sheets.

I shot out of bed and grabbed Ginger, who was sopping wet. She started crying, waking Annie, who rose and stripped the bed. I peeled Ginger's sleeper from her shaking little body, dropped her in a warm bath, and cleaned her up, all of which might sound uncomplicated, but then, you know, you just had to be there. Screams, flailing limbs, splashing water: This was not a proper way to begin a day. Then Annie trekked downstairs and had her own "uh oh" moment. Joni was downstairs arranging muffin liners on a cookie sheet.

"Oh my God," Annie whispered to me when I came down the steps just a few moments behind her. "The muffins! I *completely* forgot. It will break her heart if I don't make them. But we don't have much time!"

Annie routinely baked homemade muffins for Joni's class. She wasn't fond of the processed snacks the school served the kids, so at least once a week, she reasoned, they'd get something wholesome, albeit sweet. It clearly registered as an exercise in pride for Annie. She had half an hour to mix and bake twenty-five muffins and then have them cool enough to squeeze into a container. Amazingly, she pulled it off, as well as making Joni's lunch, writing a little "I love you" note for her lunchbox, getting dressed, picking out clothes for the girls, and gathering notes for an early-morning meeting with her boss, whom she was seeing in the office this morning.

"Damn," I said as she got into the minivan with Joni. "What you just did is unbelievable."

"I know!" she said, and she winked at me.

My FFF started contacting me now more consistently, curious about my progress. One week? No biggie. Three weeks? Not such a huge deal. But a month? One guy, a hilarious Chicago journalist who had written for a bunch of publications in New Mexico over the years, called and asked, "Are you sore yet? Burning?"

Another friend e-mailed me, "You deserve an award for January alone."

This response did wonders for my ego. Behind my wild opinion of myself, though, was a more grounded understanding of the previous month of sex. An achievement, of course. And, like most achievements, difficult. Trying to squeeze it in between work and child rearing was growing tiresome. Take the evening that followed the pee-pee morning.

I made the girls dinner while Annie did the yoga thing, her second session of the week (she usually managed three sessions a week, including Saturdays and Sundays, and I probably averaged two). Ginger wanted a smoothie for dessert with "a lot" of berries, so we pulled a sack of berries out of the freezer, put "a lot" of berries and yogurt and orange juice into the blender, and whirred away. I poured Ginger her glass of smoothie, turned my back, and within seconds she started to shriek. I whipped around and saw the second growing field of liquid of the day, only this time it was bright purple and spreading across the beige carpet. The voice in my head yelled "Goddammit!" but I kept my cool with Ginger, although now my blood was racing, my pulse was thumping, and I was pissed that Annie wasn't home to help me cope. Joni deployed, grabbing dish towels and mopping up the mess. I consoled Ginger. She was hysterical about the spill, completely out of her wits.

After much playing with Ginger's stuffed animals—a nighttime game affiliated with Ginger Whispering wherein I animate

her pillowy penguin and furry fox with voices and movement—
and three or four storybooks, I turned off Ginger's light and then
traveled to Joni's room, where I read twenty minutes of *Harry Potter* before turning off her light, too. By the time Annie returned, I'd
been child rearing nonstop for more than two hours—not a remarkable stretch of time but certainly not a relaxing way to cap a
long and taxing day at work. It was about 8:30, and nothing would
have soothed me like sleep. Not sex and then sleep, but just sliding
into bed, turning out the lights, and closing my eyes. The sack of
Viagra? It loomed. If I had opened the drawer and a dazzling gold
light had shot out of the bag, filling the room with a blinding and
stupefying shimmer, I would not have been surprised.

"We had quite the night," I said and filled Annie in on the spill
and the tears. I no longer felt anger toward Annie—that spasm of
jealousy arrived and passed all within a few minutes of the smoothie
disaster—but I didn't exactly feel roaring with libido, either. I
wore the "sexy" pajamas and the Thurston Howell III robe that
Annie liked on me. Annie slipped on some new lingerie she had
bought on clearance at Target for $3.98, and she climbed up beside me on the bed.

"I've got a question for you," she said.

"Shoot," I responded, preparing myself for a query about, say,
weekend plans or a potential change in coffee brands.

"Do you want a blow job?"

"I like this whole pushing ourselves thing," I said.

The pre-orgasm tingling began almost immediately. I stuck
with it—in other words, I just sat there—for as long as I could,
and then I withdrew myself from the situation.

"It's your turn," I said.

I grabbed a bottle of foot-massage lotion from the bathroom
vanity, poured it into my hands, and began pulling her toes, grinding my knuckles into her soles, squeezing her heels.

"Yes," she said over and over again. "YES."

"Love ball?" I offered.

"Absolutely," said Annie, and she pushed the exercise ball against the bed and got on top. And so we bounced. At some point I scooted her off the ball and onto the extreme edge of the bed.

"This works," I said as we did the deed.

Later, we traded observations about the new position.

"It gave me great angles," I said. "Total access. It was like the VIP position."

"It took us fourteen years of sex to figure that out?" Annie said. "I can't believe we never had end-of-the-bed sex. Why not?"

"The marathon rocks," I said.

"WOMEN AREN'T going around looking at DICKS all day!"

The woman whose voice was shrieking on my voice mail absolutely hated my story about mobile pornography. She could not believe that such a thing existed. She could not accept that people would actually pay to get pornography on their cell phones. But during the extremely long, rambling message, she must have said the word "dick"—and thrown in a few "cocks"—twenty times. She lingered over the words; she articulated them with great relish. I lived for messages like that, and you get them from time to time when you're a reporter at a newspaper. You get calls saying you got something wrong (you hate those); you get calls from people who positively love every word in your morning story (you love those); and then you get the kooks. I savored the kooks. I always welcome jolts of weirdness.

Cheered by my morning waltz with a kook, I hopped into the car and drove north to Boulder to meet with a naturopath who, for a story I was working on, was going to tell me all about herbal libido enhancements. Boulder appeared almost cinematically atmospheric when I finally beheld the little flower of a town, shrouded in clouds and fog and pushed up against the towering Flatirons, a rock formation that looks like a row of old-fashioned laundry irons sitting upright, their points in the air. From afar, it looked like a Lord of the Rings vision, some shire of sorcerers and hobbits and thatched-roof houses. And then I entered the snowy village and drove straight to the office complex—needless to say, no dragons or bejeweled swords—where the naturopath had an office. The practitioner, who, given his line of work, could pass for, say, a druid, was a tall, middle-aged chap who prefaced our conversation by ripping into the American diet.

"It's the root of most of our health problems," he harrumphed.

I told him I got the idea for the herbal supplement story when I was in Vegas at the Adult Entertainment Expo and saw people hawking them all over the place. He shellacked pornography too, and then we started talking about sex and herbs and "erectile dysfunction." He told me that ejaculate is full of zinc and that if you plan to ejaculate a lot, you need to keep your zinc levels boosted.

This guy, I thought, might be helpful for my personal sex project. So I told him about it, and he became most excited.

"What an opportunity for researchers!" he said. "Is this by any chance part of a study?"

"Nope," I said. "No study. Just me and Annie."

"That's unfortunate," he said. "It's a good idea either way, however. I'd think it would be very educational."

"We hope so," I said.

He urged me to make an appointment with a specialist in Chinese medicine: "These guys know everything about herbs for male virility." He also advised me to set up an appointment for a "zinc level" test—one now and one for after we were done with the project. I told him I'd do both, but I didn't do either, because I didn't have the time or the cash for Chinese herbalists or zinc tests. The zinc issue, however, stuck with me. That night, additional and unusual effort on my part was needed to get the ol' machinery humming. Had I depleted my zinc? Had the naturopath's comments rearranged the furniture in my head, introducing a nagging worry about zinc levels, a concern silently and invisibly rocketing straight from my brain to my groin?

"Everything OK tonight, honey?" asked Annie as I struggled to raise enough desire to consummate the evening. My kissing was awkward, and my strokes were clumsy. The timing was off.

"Dunno," I said. "Everything feels out of step. I'm not feeling very horny."

"Interesting," said Annie. "Tonight, I'm the one more juiced for doing it."

"I'm glad for that," I said. "No boredom?"

"Not a bit. But you seem awfully bored. I need to work on that."

We returned to kissing, but Annie accompanied it with some most excellent rubbings and strokes, as well as an approach to kissing that you might say was informed with a bit more *conviction*. It took time, probably something approaching ten minutes, but she coaxed an appetite out of me, and we finally managed.

"Whew," said Annie. "Sometimes this takes a lot of work."

Just before plunging into slumber, I considered our latest happy milestone: We'd completed day 33, one-third of the way there!

The next day, I bought a bottle of zinc supplements.

FRIDAY BEGAN shortly after midnight, to screams. We rushed to Ginger's room. Her lights were on. Her pajama pants were off. She was shrieking, inconsolable, on her back, kicking, her face glazed with tears, her pillow wet with them. She'd had a nightmare—a rarity in Gingerworld. We sang and rocked her back to sleep, then returned to our own bed. We woke up in the morning exhausted. Predicting severe fatigue for evening sex, I sauntered over to TJ Maxx at lunchtime, a quick walk from my office. About a year earlier, Annie and I had discovered that a small square of chocolate was all we needed for dessert most nights, and during our first week of sex we noticed that little shots of chocolate provided the excellent fringe benefit of awakening our fizzling-by-the-minute nighttime brains. Shortly after first discovering the pleasures of evening chocolate, I'd also found that TJ Maxx carried an eclectic and sometimes fabulous array of sweets, including, occasionally, exquisite chocolate bars that sold for $5.99 at Whole Foods but $1.99 at TJ Maxx. While scrounging for chocolate, I found red boxer shorts emblazoned with Playboy bunnies. I bought them to wear on Valentine's Day. If not for the marathon, the mere thought of buying Playboy bunny boxers, not to mention the act of buying them, never would have crossed my mind. I also bought a box of old-fashioned penny candies for the girls' Valentine's Day presents.

All along—in the car, walking to TJ Maxx, later doing research in the public library for a project about pornography that I was just beginning for the *Post*—I'd been doing an exercise that I hesitate to disclose for fear of ridicule not only from male friends but also from the male community at large. Let me stipulate here that this exercise—like the weight lifting, the musk lotion, the pocketless pajamas, the occasional morning runs, the Thurston Howell III robe, the huge glasses of orange juice I drank every morning (the doc had said I needed citrus for the sake of Annie's "balance"), and my increased delivery of massages to Annie—was borne out of a desire to please my wife, this woman who *had the idea of having sex with me for one hundred consecutive days*. And so, for Annie, I had been doing Kegels, exercises that strengthen various muscles around the sexual organs.

Annie had been performing them for years. I'd never considered doing Kegels—they seemed like something for the "women's only" world, like tampons or eyeliner—until I read a few books that said men should do Kegels because they can increase erection strength and permit men to hold their ejaculations for longer and longer periods of time. The achievement of both of these, especially in light of the marathon, was something to seek out and celebrate. So I did Kegel exercises, and of course did not tell anybody but Annie, who responded: "I love Kegels! Good for you!" which, I hasten to add, was not a response that exactly buttressed my sense of manhood.

At some point during this afternoon of Kegels, I considered how central my penis had become to my life during the past thirty-three days. I found myself thinking about my penis all the time: *How are you right now, pal? You're the star, friend. Just stay positive. You can do it.* This night, I thought, should be a good test of the libido and its supporting cast of one—the penis. We were joining Tucker Shaw, the *Post*'s food critic, a guy who had spent an entire year photographing everything he ate and then publishing a book about it, for dinner at a nouveau Cuban restaurant. So tonight would be Annie's and my second "date" of the sexathon that demanded sex after dinner and drinks. If the hydraulics were beginning to gasp without booze or big meals and after sitting on the bed with Annie for long periods of time gearing up for an erotic interlude, how would they respond to a rushed, late-night commitment, challenged by cocktails and saddled with food?

Annie startled me when she appeared at the bottom of the steps in our house, sheathed in patterned stockings, a revealing black top accentuating her cleavage, her hair lavish, her lips succulent. The girls fluttered around their mother, telling her that she smelled nice, that she looked pretty, that they liked her hair, and so on. They bestowed praise, too, on my sport coat. Minutes later, the babysitter rang the doorbell and we were off, yakking while I drove, and then Annie ran her arm through mine as we raced along cold downtown sidewalks to the restaurant. Nothing could have made me prouder.

Hey, everyone! She's mine!

The food was wan, but the mojitos stunned. Annie was giggly and sly and devastatingly sexy, and she hatched an immediate friendship with Tucker, all of which drew me to her with even more urgency. I even found it cute when she spilled my mojito—Annie and I loved ordering cocktails at restaurants or bars but didn't make them much at home—across the table.

I failed to heed my inner counsel, who was wagging his finger and going on about how "substantial meals" are "not conducive" to "the consummation of a certain physical act." Blah blah blah. I ordered an appetizer. I ordered a big plate of protein—a piece of fish—nesting in a pile of carbohydrates. I consumed dessert. I probably would have ordered the same thing had Tucker not been with us—my hunger had hijacked my scruples—but the fact that we were with Tucker sealed the deal. Tucker, or I should say the *Denver Post,* had the meal covered. This was an opportunity to fully leverage the very essence of our "Free is best" motto. I was unwilling to pass up a single calorie.

The babysitter, one of our yoga instructors, drove herself home. Annie and I showered and slipped into bed about 11:30, about an hour after we normally fell asleep. Food weighed down my stomach; two mojitos dulled my libido. We moved straight to sex: nothing oral, no advanced petting or foreplay, just a swab of lube. Bada bing. Ten minutes later, bada boom.

"Marathon sex," said a groggy Annie just before falling into dreamland. "Sometimes you do it just to do it."

She had a point.

THE NEXT night, I responded favorably to the vision of Annie's hot lingerie, to her freshly pedicured red toenails, to her marble-smooth thighs. As the visual stimuli marched through my brain an audible one, too, arrived. I heard a slight buzzing sound, just as the show Annie and I were watching on DVD came to a close.

"What's that noise?" I asked.

Annie whipped out Two Fingers and a Thumb from beneath her robe and grinned: "I'm ready!"

With both of us fully stimulated, we conspired to consummate love session number 35.

This is becoming wild, I thought after we'd finished. I was planning to save the sack of Viagra my doctor tossed at me until I really needed it, but now I just wanted to up the ante.

7

Scat

"You're acting like a freak," reported Annie.

At exactly 7:11 p.m. the following night, I finally pressed a little blue pill from its cardboard container and swallowed it. By the time the girls were in bed, about an hour later, a parched, pinched sensation fluttered into my throat, and my eyes and attention darted like hummingbirds on a delphinium farm. It felt as if I'd just finished one too many espressos. In the shower His Lordship experienced volts of lightning-bolt energy and soon emerged as a mysterious new appendage that worked independently of my brain. When I reentered the bedroom, Annie was wearing sexy French lingerie, and when she bent over to get something, my new buddy Autonomous Appendage moved straight toward her. The amour commenced. I don't recall ever feeling so driven toward sex—it was a possession more than a desire. Twenty minutes of blur later, it was over and I collapsed: a spent internal combustion engine, a satisfied dog.

Annie pointed toward Autonomous. "What do you think? Is he gonna calm down?"

I looked down. "Awfully . . . taut, isn't it?" I said.

"Yeah, and it isn't even beginning to droop."

I propped myself up on my elbows and waited for one

minute. Three. Six. No change. Would Autonomous finally submit to my will and go to sleep? Would this *possession* require some sort of formal exorcism—chants, holy water, a shaman—before drifting away? After ten minutes, I began to worry: You will recall the emergency room, the kid with the busted arm, the man beside them who represents all that is curdled in America. At about the fifteen-minute mark, though, Autonomous tripped, then fell, then plummeted into sleep, and I followed him.

THE NEXT day at work I told one of my colleagues about my date with Viagra, and he asked, "Are you worried you're going to become addicted?"

I wasn't, but then I considered the notion. The pharmaceutical had tapped something primordial inside me. It channeled the caveman lost deep in the thickets of my 40-year-old brain. This club-wielding fellow remained as powerful as he had been in my youth, I think, but he didn't always arrive as pumped up, as it were, as he had been when I was, say, 16 or 20. I liked the grunting fool. I appreciated how he just showed up, grinning and ready to go, shortly after I popped the pill. I'm not sure about addiction, but I could grow accustomed to having him around, and the pill made that connection awfully easy.

Annie enjoyed the crackling-with-energy version of Caveman too, but there were limits. Two nights in a row, for example, would be one night too many. So after work, as the kids played with their Polly Pocket dolls and dress-up clothes in the basement, Annie said she was "glad" that the previous evening's incarnation of Caveman would not be making a reappearance.

"Right?" she said.

"No Viagra tonight," I answered. (Out of politeness I whispered to Caveman, *Sorry, buddy*.) "Why 'glad,' though?"

"It's just that I'm totally spent," she said. "Beat. I'm psyched for sex, but I'm not so sure I could take the, you know, pounding."

"So there was a noticeable difference?" I said.

"Yeah," she said solemnly. "You were especially energetic. It was fun, but not the kind of energy I want to experience every night. Sometimes, slow and easy is the best."

I welcomed this information. Had Annie said, "Gosh, I want you to use Viagra every night!" it would not take a psychiatrist or an English scholar to interpret the words to mean "Viagra is better than you."

"Hey, that's a new nugget," I said. "Slow and easy is best."

"We'd never talked about that before?" Annie asked.

"Not that I remember."

"Do you agree with me?" she asked.

"Nope."

A pause. A cocked head. "Really?"

"Don't get me wrong, I dig slow and easy, especially when I'm beat," I said. "But I like it best when we're really going at it. When we're having a workout."

"Interesting," said Annie. "Why?"

"It's like getting swept away," I answered. "I lose myself when we're having a wild romp. I like that."

"I know what you mean," offered Annie. "I get into that too. But I've got to come down on the side of slow and easy."

"Your turn," I said. "Why?"

Annie thought about it for a few moments.

"I feel closer to you when it's like that," she said. "I feel really connected. I like the super-lusty sessions, but I miss the connection. Sometimes it feels like we're sort of going our separate ways when it's wild. Like, we're lost to the excellent feelings, but we're not appreciating each other: our touching bodies, our breath, our eyes."

I instantly understood that Annie had a good point.

"That's true," I said. "I would miss the slow-and-easy nights if we stopped 'em."

"We both get off on the same things, I think, only overall we emphasize different approaches. I wouldn't want to lose the energetic sex, but, on balance, I want a little more of the slow and easy. With you, it's the reverse."

"Yep."

"And on that note, I'm off to another thing I love and I think you just like. Yoga."

"I'm in the 'pleasantly surprised' phase," I said.

Annie kissed the girls good night, and I then entertained them with a trusty old character, the evil witch (I'd been practicing), who sometimes stood in for my more standard character, the "troll." In the penultimate scene of each identical dramatic "short," the witch finally catches the poor, innocent children and places them in her big, ugly oven. Chuckles all around.

Eventually the kids were asleep, Annie was back, I had worked over my infinitesimally inflating muscles, and we hopped into a sultry bath swimming with loads of stuff, compliments of Annie—rose water, grapeseed oil, a sparkly bath bomb, patchouli, and ylang-ylang oils and Epsom salts. Candles flickered. Incense perfumed the room.

And then . . . Knock, knock.

"Who is it?"

"Ginger."

"Is this a knock-knock joke?" I said.

A pause. "What is a knock-knock joke?"

"Come in, Ginger," said Annie.

"Can I sleep in Joni's room?"

We said no, and she walked off, but then Joni appeared at the bathroom door, saying Ginger was acting "silly" and so she couldn't sleep. Obviously, Ginger had completely disregarded our "no." Sigh. We remained in the bath and by the time we emerged, both girls were sound asleep in Joni's room. That was good news, but bad news erupted shortly after we climbed onto the bed. I wasn't horny. Annie had on her fancy French lingerie. It didn't matter. I looked down. Nothing.

"Maybe I should have gone with the Viagra again?"

"You wouldn't want to become addicted to that stuff."

"Interesting," I said. "That topic, Viagra addiction, came up earlier today."

"You were talking about Viagra?" she asked.

"I told Frank I tried it, and he asked if it could be addictive," I said.

"What did you say?"

"I told him I could see someone getting addicted to the stuff."

"Like you?" Annie asked.

"Nah," I said. "I like it, but I don't want to depend on it, at least not for now. But if the equipment ever starts to flag—you know, someday, a long time from now—it's nice to know there is an alternative to not doing it. Just pop a pill."

Annie stroked the insides of my thighs as we sat cross-legged across from each other. And soon that familiar feeling of bubbling horniness—*I want to have sex*—emerged. She slid down to the end of the bed and massaged the soles of my feet for a while. Then she began kissing me, starting with my ankle and moving her way up to my calves, my knees . . .

THE NEXT day, a Tuesday, I wanted to investigate some of the local sex shops for the stories I was working on. I visited three of them, all near each other. My purpose was professional research, but the round of visits was not without personal interest. In Las Vegas, I had encountered an array of sex toys, and Annie had purchased one. I, too, came away from the convention with a sex toy, which I mentioned glancingly in an earlier chapter. I am going to blame my motto "Free is best." The toy was part of the hoard of swag we'd brought home. I'd snagged it, stuck it in a bag, and tried to forget about the thing, but whenever I'd dig through the sack-o'-sex goodies, it would taunt me: "Here I am! You've really *got* to see what I'm all about! Give me a whirl!" I resisted for a bit, but eventually shrugged my shoulders and submitted, fixing the device to my manhood one previous night during the marathon and having a romp with Annie. I am not describing the event in this account because, to put it directly, it's far too embarrassing— not the sexual act itself but the simple fact that I used this device during the sexual act. You are not crying out for details; I shrink from providing them—so let's leave it at that. I tried the thing once and liked it well enough to use it again, but I believed I had somehow lost it. So I visited the sex shops to conduct journalistic research, but in addition I wanted to replace the device that I thought was missing.

In the third sex shop, one catering to the local fetish community, with leather outfits crowding the showroom floor, I approached a tall, skinny, punk guy behind the counter and asked if they carried the toy I was seeking. He shrugged, then yelled across the room to another worker, a gaunt little lad with a mohawk and piercings all over his face: "Do we sell vibrating cock rings?"

"Vibrating cock rings?" shouted the other guy. "Hold on."

The words *in fire,* roared in my brain, flames licking my thoughts, charring forever the walls of different vaults and chambers, tunnels and anterooms. A horned, fork-tailed demon somewhere on a stone throne laughing.

"Sorry," the clerk screamed after scouring the shelves. "No vibrating cock rings."

The guy I'd first addressed shrugged again. "Too bad, man. I guess we're all out of vibrating cock rings."

"Got it," I whispered, barely able to lift my eyes from the floor. When I did, I surveyed the customers, hunting for disapproving looks, but none of them seemed fazed by Cock Ring Theater. In the end, I spoke *quietly* with one of the employees about the device. Because the shop didn't sell vibrating ones, he recommended a more traditional version of the device. I purchased it and used it several more times during Annie's and my adventure.

I also bought a pair of thigh-high white stockings emblazoned with hearts for Annie for Valentine's Day. I'd stipulated them during an early conversation about the marathon. Annie had signed off, but I hadn't yet seen Annie's legs sheathed in the hotness that is stockings stopping at the thigh. Why are thigh-high stockings so hot? I have no idea. Before the marathon, I had never surprised Annie with a pair out of fear that she would consider them the height of cheesiness, and we wouldn't have talked about them either, because back then we didn't really talk about sex. We just did it.

Armed with my new device and the stockings for Annie, I headed across the street to a pleasant coffee shop with an elaborate Italian espresso machine. I sat on a couch and sipped my excellent espresso with fresh energy and optimism. I rang my brother during the drive home, who detailed an achievement hive involving his family just as child-humid as our own—soccer, Scouts, school, karate, and so on—and, of course, asked about the marathon.

"You still 'up'?" he asked.

"Good one, bro," I said. "Yeah. Up. I've got no choice."

"You still liking it?"

"I am. I didn't know if I'd be sick of it by now, but I'm not."

"Good to know," he said. "I don't think I'd ever get sick of it."

"Think of it as 'news you can use.'"

"You're in that business," he said. "You should know."

That night, after the usual lineup of postwork responsibilities (a trajectory that comes to a significant point when the doors to both girls' rooms are shut), Annie held out her hand to pull me up from the couch.

"Follow me," she said.

We arrived in the bedroom. Annie closed and locked the door and told me to close my eyes. When I opened them again, she was nude. Her pubic hair, minus a thin strip, was gone. She had spent part of the day downtown, getting a Brazilian wax.

Oh. My. God. *Very* foxy.

"Today, I experienced great pain," she said. "And I do believe having another woman wearing latex gloves, holding my vulva, and pulling at my labia was the greatest humiliation I've ever experienced. And then I gave her a tip!"

"Damn, honey," I said. "Damn."

"It almost rivaled childbirth, although giving birth without drugs is empowering," she said. "This most definitely was not an uplifting experience."

"Wow," I said, observing her startling, almost ceramic, nakedness.

"I asked her if I'd get anything out of it. She said, 'You don't know about the benefits, honey?' She told me that sex will feel better with all of that hair gone."

"I can't wait to find out," I said. "I've got to say, I've been lifting weights, running, marinating in musk, and more, but none of that even comes close to having your pubic hair removed with hot wax. I'm in awe."

"Thank you, darling."

Then I regaled Annie with the story of my hunt for the device in the sex shop.

Annie laughed uproariously. "I wish I could have been there. And the kicker is, I know where your vibrating cock ring is. I put it somewhere safe, up in that hidden bag of sex-show swag, so the kids wouldn't find it."

"I could have been spared the announcements in the sex shop?"

She laughed. "Yes. From now on I'll be much more conscientious about keeping you apprised of your cock ring's comings and goings," she said. "Maybe your bout of cock-ring humiliation was the cosmos balancing my pain and humiliation with a burst of your own."

"Either way," I said, staring at her new nakedness, "I don't think pain and humiliation are on tap for this evening."

Annie wagged her eyebrows, and soon we both were naked and doing it.

"It's so much more sensitive," said Annie after the last ripple of orgasm passed. "It's amazing."

"It is," I said, and soon an orgasm crested over me, carrying me away.

"It's winter, it's cold, it's bleak," said Annie. "We need to keep laughing. Give us sex and give us funny. Before you know it, spring will be here."

It's funny about funny. It may be the least welcome intrusion into sex. Even anger, in some couples, apparently spawns hot bedroom romps (at least that's what seems to happen now and again in movies). But laughter? It sometimes spoils the spell. Yet humor is sexy. Take Hollywood. Annie finds Will Ferrell much hotter than Brad Pitt. It's not the beady eyes or thinning hair that excites her, but his sense of humor. I find Tina Fey incomparably sexy. She's a good-looking woman, but it's her razor wit (plus those mischievous eyes) that installs her in babeland, at least for me.

I have always made Annie laugh—I tell funny stories, she says—and that helps explain the intensity of her attraction to me: All I had to do was gin up some giggles, and she was mine. Who knew?

Annie isn't a life-of-the-party comic or a joke-spinning raconteur; she's more a wisecracking quipster, a sly wit. She's hot to begin with, but heat without fuel quickly turns cold, at least for me. She's got the juice, though—the humor, the liveliness, the merriment—to maintain her sexy smolder. Her overall cuteness, too, makes me laugh. Like the time my family first taught her our favorite card game, called Scat. I grew up playing the game, especially during beach vacations. Six or ten of us would sit around a table and play for hours and for money. The goal is to get "Scat," which involves having a series of cards in your hand. We explained the rules to Annie one night and started the game. About halfway through, she grinned, her eyes glinted—a familiar sparkle rooted in wild ideas about competitive triumph—and she laid her cards on the table, displaying them with a certain dramatic flair that said "Nyaa, Nyaa."

"Scat!" she purred, cocking her head and tossing her eyebrows nonchalantly, as if Scat were the most natural thing in the world. The problem, of course, was she by no means had Scat. Her hand, in fact, was poor. She sat there positively glowing, her competitive spirit crowned, throned, and sceptered. She glanced around the table, thrilled with herself, a queen lording over her court.

We all laughed.

"Sorry, honey," said my mom through a broad smile. "That's not Scat."

Annie's face crumbled. She panicked. "Yes it is," she said. "Look."

We looked. We shook our heads.

"I'm so sorry, honey," repeated my mom. "No Scat."

It happened early in our courtship and to this day, whenever we play Scat, somebody conjures Annie's mannerisms and voice and says "Scat!" And we all laugh.

Like Annie, I'm not immune to accidental-humor victimization. Annie is particularly fond of a story told to her by former colleagues at the *Albuquerque Tribune* (rest its glorious soul), my first full-time newspaper job. I received a 1099 form at work, and I announced:

"What the hell is this crap? Trash, trash, trash." And I heaved it into a trash can. Colleagues who witnessed the tossing urged me to retrieve the document. "You might want to deal with that," they said. "It's important. It has to do with your income taxes."

"Whatever," I retorted. I fished it out and brought it to Annie. My friends regaled her with the story a few nights later, and it caused her to laugh so hard she convulsed. This helps explain why Annie governs the family budget.

Another classic: We were living in our little townhouse in South Florida, and Annie was eight months pregnant. She'd gained about fifty pounds. She suffered through the astonishing South Florida heat, her steps plodding, her face typically flushed. She always seemed winded. And she had started to snore.

"You realize you're snoring, right?" I said one morning as we both lay in bed.

"Really?" said Annie. "How embarrassing. I hope I'm not keeping you up."

"Oh, don't worry about it," I responded. "It's not your fault. Heavy people snore."

A pause.

Heavy people snore. I'd just called my pregnant wife "heavy," she who'd left a place she loved and moved across the country with me while great with child, who lumbered through friendless days from one dispiriting strip mall to another, who spent weekend afternoons at my beloved beach even though she didn't much like sand, ocean, or sun. Fortunately for me, my comment quickly became just another in a long line of "harmless DJ malapropisms." Annie still invokes the line, probably every few months.

Heavy people snore.

I suspect that if not for this foundation of humor, the marathon never would have happened. We were having sex for one hundred straight days because we thought doing so would be a gas. Yes, we believed it might improve our love life. But in the end, if you were to conclude that "having a gas is the quintessence of this marathon," I would not argue with you. We were bored with Denver, alone, plodding along with our jobs, merging with middle age. We desired some laughs and thought a kooky adventure like this could add a bunch. Cock Ring Theater, no doubt, will remain part of our humor repertoire for a long time.

Like tonight, for example, this Wednesday after work: the kids in the basement playing with their dolls, Annie in the kitchen making a stir-fry, the house redolent of ginger and garlic. I was hanging up my coat on a hook in the small space between the kitchen and garage where we kept our jackets, boots, hats, and so on.

"Did you hang out with your buds at your new favorite store today?" asked Annie, who shot me a wink.

"Never again," I said, holding up my index finger dramatically, like a college professor making a point. "I'm not a sex-shop kind of guy, I'm sorry to report."

A few minutes later the girls came running up the stairs yelling "Daddy, Daddy," and then hugging me. As always, this was one of the highlights of my day.

"Hey, little people," I said, bending down to their level. "How's it going?"

They gave the same answer every day, "Great," which sometimes, of course, was not the case at all. Not until dinner would I have the chance to ask them more extensively about their days at school, an activity I anticipated with excitement every evening because of the nuggets of gossip about their friends that I would wrest out of them. This relishing of first-grade gossip may seem absurd, but if you have young children and never have received much gossip, try gathering some! It's fun!

It all started with Joni, when she first began attending preschool in Baltimore. At the time, I worked out of the house, and

Annie's job was taking care of Joni. We missed the office gossip to which we were accustomed, and a few months into Joni's first year at school we found ourselves grilling the little 'un about the passel of 3-year-olds in her class.

Sample conversation:

DAD: How was Nickie today?

JONI: Nickie? She brought a peanut butter sandwich today and she's not allowed because Madison is allergic so she had to throw away the sandwich and her mommy had to bring her something for lunch.

DAD: What? That's huge! OK, more details. First of all, set the scene. What was she wearing? Was the sandwich in a plastic bag? What—what *exactly*—did the teacher say when she saw the sandwich? And how—again, *exactly*— did Madison react?

Joni inevitably answered all of my questions. Three years later, I had office gossip and so did Annie, but we still positively thrilled to everything we could badger out of the kids, gossip-wise. And now that Ginger was in preschool, it was double the fun.

This evening, around the stir-fry, we learned the following from Joni: She'd had a falling-out with one of her best friends over something involving the friend's failure to participate in a game during recess (they "fell out" every other day). A "super annoying" boy tripped her on the playground, and a girl spent much of the afternoon pretending she was a dog. This is what we learned from Ginger: A close friend fell and cried. Another close friend did not know how to do ballet (Ginger demonstrated for us her friend's take on "ballet" and then offered her own, sensible version), and Ginger and the friend who fell and cried whispered to each other during nap time.

After dinner, I washed the dishes while Annie persuaded the

girls out of their clothes and into sleepers. Books were read. Sheets were tucked behind shoulders. Foreheads were kissed. And then Annie and I, at long last, were in our own bedroom. After showering, I donned the fancy-man robe and the pajamas, and Annie slipped into bed beside me in her Huit lingerie, a French bra-and-pantie set I had purchased at a fancy lingerie boutique in my Pennsylvania hometown just weeks before the marathon, when I was making a holiday visit. The set cost somewhere around $150. I'd never dropped that kind of dough on underwear, but I have to say that Annie did look especially smashing in the ensemble. But soon, of course, those pricey garments no longer hugged Annie's body. Instead, I did.

Later, as she slipped back into clothes—pajama bottoms and a muscle shirt—she first looked down at her Brazilian.

"I love it," she said, "but it has the potential for a preadolescent creepy thing going on."

"Before beholding your Brazilian, I did wonder about that. But now that my experience could be described as 'hands-on,' that worry is gone. It's not creepy. It's just one more thing that, for whatever reason, comes across as sexy. Like thigh-high stockings."

"Lipstick or earrings. Pumps," said Annie.

"Gym muscles," I said. "We could put together a huge list of things we do for the sake of attraction, none of which would be natural. So in *that* light, the Brazilian is a variation on a theme of eyeliner," I said.

She laughed. "Nice job," she said. "Brilliant justification for the Brazilian."

"I've got to admit, though—it's a lot cooler than eyeliner."

IT WAS also way cooler than the epiphany that struck me shortly after waking up the next morning. Today would be session number 40. I was 40 years old, so tonight's love dance would be my "birthday session," which would happen a good twelve hours later. But first I had a day at the office to put under my belt. When I returned home, I took a whirl with yoga. I was the only student to show up, so the female instructor suggested we do "partners" yoga. I had no idea what that meant but nodded in assent in the manner of a novice sailing student on deck with a salty captain who shouts, "Step athwartships while we reef, and mind the taffrail log."

Quickly, I learned that partners yoga meant we would massage each other's backs and then perform rather complicated handstands in which our bodies intertwined. I'd never intertwined with anybody during my brief yoga experience, not to mention lifting myself into a handstand, although don't get too impressed with this handstand business: The position involved the yoga instructor and I sort of leaning into each other; otherwise, I would have held the position for possibly two seconds before collapsing in a heap on the floor. As we essentially braided our sweat-glazed thighs, torsos, and arms, it did occur to me that something other than a good, healthy stretch charged this pursuit. Neither of us wore much in the way of clothing, candlelight colored the room, we touched for relatively long periods of time, and I wasn't accustomed to so explicitly touching women other than Annie.

I dutifully reported my yoga adventure to Annie. "Don't worry, I didn't, you know, 'get off' on it or anything."

"I never said you did," replied Annie. "It was just touching."

"Right. It was a lot more than just a slap on the back, but still, just touching."

"Did you feel anything?"

"Sexual? Nah. But I must say, I do feel very much in favor of sex right now. Maybe all of that touching reminded me of what's in store tonight."

Touching, the nonsexual kind, had emerged years ago in our

relationship as a rite, like reciting the Rosary, an activity we consciously pursued to remind us of our existence as a couple: not just two separate humans rocketing through life in different trajectories, but two parts of a whole. We often careered through days oblivious, in a way, to our couplehood, taking it for granted. Then one of us would approach the other for a hug, and we would welcome the fresh connection. This failure to touch properly had not been a problem for the past six weeks. Obviously, we pressed flesh every day in order to take another step on the marathon, but the hugging and hand-holding also happened more naturally. They didn't require proddings anymore; they just happened.

It was much easier to remember about touch with the kids. We'd compulsively pick them up and kiss their cheeks and hold their hands while we walked. They often climbed into our bed with us, not usually for protection from a nightmare but because we'd drape an arm over a back, or they'd rest their heads on a belly, or they just felt comforted by the sound of our breathing.

When I returned home to an extremely sick Joni—she had seemed fine when I left for yoga—nothing could stop my hands from clutching her little body and pulling her close. She had a high temperature and had been vomiting every twenty minutes. By about 11 p.m., she was vomiting yellow bile. She looked ghoulish. We gave her medicine, and she drifted off to sleep.

And then back to the den, now exhausted, to its restless candlelight and wafting aromas and luxurious warmth, where we tried to submit to complete dissolution, to fully relax despite Joni's feverish little body down the hallway. We sat silently beside each other, our feet touching, and read. No traded anecdotes about the day, no gossip, no wallows in politics. No television commercials. No music. Just the turning of pages. At one point I opened Joni's door to make sure she was OK, and I heard her deep sleep breathing.

We read for another fifteen minutes, but the clock told us we really had to get a move on if we were to consummate this day of sex.

"We probably should . . ." I said.

"Yeah, it's time."

We leaned into each other and kissed, long and passionately, and soon we were inhaling each other, somehow doing it close to midnight, on a weekday, after a long, taxing day and an evening complicated by a child's sickness. And by the time we were finished, we both experienced the familiar but odd sensation of being wide awake yet capable of plummeting into sleep in minutes.

"This truly is the best way to end a day," said Annie. "I sleep better."

"Me too," I said. "It's worth the effort for many reasons, sleep included."

"Check out this show about King Henry VIII," said Annie the following night as I slipped into my Thurston Howell III robe. I plopped onto the bed and became transfixed by royal imagery and the compelling story. Then I studied Annie as she watched the show. Her lips would part slightly and her eyes widen at the juicy tidbits—"And then they beheaded Queen Anne, Anne Boleyn"— and her attention never wavered from the screen. At some point a dramatic yawn captured me, one of those tripartite combinations of inhalations and gasps, and Annie's shoulders slumped. She pivoted her attention from Henry VIII to me.

"I guess I've got to get in the mood," she said, her whole body radiating dejection. "Let's put in that Tantric or whatever video."

I sighed, feeling the same. "Yeah. Let's try it."

Hard-core pornography championed men as ogres. The "sex-positive" tapes celebrated Muppet-men, and on this video we had a Muppet in a Hawaiian shirt, a Muppet with long hair in a silly-ass hat, a Muppet with a cheesy mustache and a horrifying haircut, and a fat Muppet with a good-looking blonde. At one point, the dude with the cheesy mustache and the horrifying haircut sat on a grassy hillock with a woman in a copper wig, and she started dancing around him. If Annie pranced around me like that, I'd laugh myself into the grave. There was absolutely nothing, not a scrap, not a smidgen, of sexiness in the dance routine. The other couples in the video become far too involved with feathers and gazing soulfully into one another's eyes. The video stirred not a thimble of carnality in Annie or me, but *damn* did we laugh. We became almost hysterical, our watery eyes leaking tears onto our cheeks, both of us bent over at the waist and slapping the bed.

"This is one of the funniest things I've ever watched," said Annie.

I wanted to shout at the screen: "People, people. There's something happy and dirty and healthy about embracing our inner animals during sex. I know you really want to make it all sacred—clean! spiritual! with purpose!—but I must tell you I think you're sorta' missing the point, or at least one of the points (and an important one)."

We turned off the video, I clicked on WFMU, and we curled into each other under the sheet and blankets, joking about the video. I stroked Annie's thigh and pulled her close, and within a few minutes we, as you might hear on cable television, were "kicking it up a notch."

THE DREAMY feeling that followed kicking it up a notch the evening before stayed with me the next morning, where at theater camp the teacher instructed the kids to paint their parents' faces. I jutted out my mug and said, "Ginger, go ahead," and she did, smearing yellow and blue and black and green all over my forehead, cheeks, chin, and nose. Even my hair.

Then on the way home, our minivan got a flat tire. I drove straight to the parking lot of a grocery store and called Annie, who alerted Triple A and then drove to meet us. Right before Annie arrived, a rough guy in a big truck arrived to jack up the van and put on the spare. I chatted with him for a bit, and he stared at me as if I was a strange bird, some sort of toucan fluttering around the prairie. At some point I remembered my painted face. *Ah ha!* I thought. *That's why this guy is treating me the way a vegetarian might confront a slab of ribs: with a mixture of revulsion and dread.*

Nevertheless, neither of us mentioned the paint. We just moved on. I placed the flat tire in the Subaru and drove with Joni to our neighborhood tire center while Annie waited with Ginger for the tow-truck guy to put the spare on the minivan. She would meet us at the tire place, where we'd have the tire repaired and bolted back onto the minivan. Then, if all went as planned, we'd continue with our Saturday, which involved a drive to Wyoming, one of Annie's treasured little trips. People in the shop gawked as Joni and I stood in line. I felt like a sandal-clad hippie freak gliding into a cowboy bar.

We got to the counter and the clerk cocked his head. A toucan?

I smiled. "My daughter this morning," I said. "She decided to paint me."

He laughed and dealt with our problem immediately, fixing the tire—a screw (hah!) had punctured it—and securing it back on the minivan. We stopped at the house briefly so I could wash my face, and then we all headed north into the heart of winter, to a Victorian bed-and-breakfast in Laramie, Wyoming, the home of the University of Wyoming.

For reasons I frankly do not understand, I'd long yearned to visit Wyoming, and we decided that poking into the state during its notorious winter would show us the real deal. Sprawl ended abruptly soon after we left Colorado. Civilization ceased. We turned west, and the tundra looked like a sea after a storm—not wind whipped and sharp but rolling, heaving, thrusting, and falling, and the color of iron. This was Western to its core: forbidding and desolate and beautiful.

WE PULLED into the bed-and-breakfast. The older couple who owned the place stood in the driveway, which wasn't something to celebrate because we had brought beer although we knew from their website they forbade alcohol in the rooms. I elected to not open the back of the minivan, and to not accept help from the man, until everything was stowed. They greeted us and then vanished inside the main house, and we scurried into the carriage house we had rented, a stand-alone building that looked like a garage. There was an upstairs and a downstairs, each containing only one room. The girls immediately migrated upstairs to the television. Our cable-free lives had turned hotels and Frontier Airline flights into kick-it-up-a-notch Shangri-las. Cable! Endless cartoons! The B&B's website had touted its game room, so Annie walked over to check it out and returned wide-eyed.

"You've got to see this."

She said it with such seriousness that the girls abandoned their beloved cable television and got in line behind us, their hand-holding parents, like ducklings. The ceilings soared. Everything was wood. The game room held a pool table, a Ping-Pong table, an air-hockey table, and a Foosball table. It had dart boards. It had stacks of board games, such as Life and Parcheesi. The room was a wonderland for the girls, who bounced from game to game. Joni became crazed, eager to learn every new game immediately and play her daddy and mommy.

The place played directly into a theory Annie had hatched years earlier, an idea I too had embraced. Entertaining oneself, so the theory goes, is preferable to being entertained. I grew up watching as much television as I wanted. The good news, I now think, is that in the 1970s there was less of it than there is today (although I do count my ability, today, to sing the theme songs of *Spider-Man, Hong Kong Phooey,* and *Kimba the White Lion* as "good news"). Consequently, I spent a lot more time playing and making up games than I did sitting in front of the box. Annie, on the other hand, was raised deep in the country. Her family, essentially, did not have television reception. During much of Annie's adolescence, she had to find ways to entertain herself. Not surprisingly, when we had kids, Annie's approach to fun centered on doing, rather than observing. I probably would have been more lax if the child rearing had been left entirely up to me. Good thing for the kids I'm not the only parent.

It didn't take long for us to figure out, when we asked our daughters about playdates at so-and-so's house and they would say, "We just watched TV," that kids who spent a lot of time at home sitting in front of the television were not good candidates for playdates. They would arrive at our house assuming that for the next few hours they'd be sitting in front of the TV, and they'd gulp when informed that watching television was not an option. Joni would lead them to the craft room, to the table loaded with paper and glue, scissors and yarn, and sparkles and markers, and start making stuff. Her playmates would sit and watch her, dumbstruck, unsure how to proceed. She'd try to rope them into staging little plays, or pretending they were Harry Potter characters, or building forts, but her efforts often flopped. The situation was reversed when Joni attended playdates at their houses—*Cinderella* again!—and these playdates depressed Annie and me, but we weren't playdate nazis. What went on, entertainment-wise, at the other kids' houses was largely beyond our control.

Things were different, usually, with kids who did not pickle themselves in television brine. Those were Joni's best friends because they could play. They were accustomed to hatching their own amusements; being entertained was a treat, a relished and appreciated one.

Loosing the kids upon the B&B's gigantic fun factory, this laboratory for kid-contrived diversions, warmed our crunchy-granola little hearts. The space itself spoke to this child-rearing foundation of ours: Everything was wood! The entire room was handmade! Ginger found the big piano. She sat on the bench, pounding keys and singing "I'm a princess" over and over.

We clapped.

"Yay, Ginger!" And she grinned and slammed the keys some more.

Back at the B&B, after inhaling burgers, pizza, and $2.85 microbrews in a restaurant in the miniature downtown, we sprawled across the big bed in the Heavily Victorian room and watched the Winter Olympics—skiing and speed skating. Joni fell asleep in front of the television, but not Ginger. We put *Alice in Wonderland* into the VCR—being entertained a *little* isn't so bad—and parked her in front of it while we showered downstairs, hoping to quickly and silently consummate number 42 in the loud shower stall.

You heard that properly. Not only did I say "shower," but I placed both myself *and Annie* within the stall. Ahh, *now* you're with me. Only a few weeks before, I had driven Annie from a shower stall by purging my nasal passages *while Annie stood hot and naked beside me.* Shortly after sizing up our sleeping quarters in the B&B—imagine a big shed stacked atop another big shed—we began to wonder about the evening's erotic festivities. The downstairs easy chair was a possibility, we thought, but the shower held great potential. If not for the echo of the nasal shrapnel, in fact, I think neither of us would have hesitated. But while the girls played in the game room and Annie sat on a bench watching them, I tiptoed toward a formal presentation, one that would resurrect the awkward golem known as Nasal Shrapnel.

"So in closing," I said to Annie, over the sound of a puck smacking the sides of an air-hockey table, "all things considered, the shower stall is the way to go. In my opinion, I hasten to add."

Annie studied me without grinning or betraying her reaction.

"You do make good points. I'm inclined to authorize this proposal. I think it goes without saying the whole nose thing won't happen."

"Of course it won't! In fact . . ."

"And if it does, not only will I never shower with you again, I will require paybacks. Let's say nightly massages, for at *least* one hundred days. Consecutive."

"Deal!" I said.

"That's just for starters."

I turned on the water while Ginger watched *Alice in Wonderland* in the upstairs big shed (and Joni slept). Steam quickly filled the stall, and we stripped and stepped inside. I instantly began soaping Annie's body in what I felt was a sexy manner. She released a few quiet "mmmms." But then, through the sound of the water, we heard Ginger coming down the ornate wooden steps. Annie stepped out of the stall, wrapped herself in a towel, met Ginger on the steps, and brought her back to the bed and the video. Meanwhile, I gave up on the shower, put on pajama bottoms and a T-shirt, and maneuvered under the sheets on the easy chair that was our destiny for the night. When we booked the place, we understood it had sleeping arrangements both upstairs and downstairs. When we arrived, we realized the downstairs arrangement was an easy chair.

Annie came downstairs and slipped under the blanket on the easy chair, hoping the video had finally engaged Ginger. But no.

Ginger crept back downstairs again. Annie, in pajamas, met her on the steps and brought her upstairs into the bed, where she lay with her and stroked her hair and willed her into slumber.

Meanwhile, downstairs, I didn't feel at all erotic.

At 11:20 Annie came back down the steps and crawled beneath the blanket.

"She's asleep," she said. "I think."

We started kissing and rubbing. I found it difficult to find a comfortable and practical position on the chair for sex—I needed good leverage—so I started twisting this way and that, nudging Annie a few inches to the side, sliding my knees to different areas of the chair. I grunted.

"How's this?" I whispered, with my right foot on the ground, my left knee on the seat cushion, my erection pointing into the air. Annie scooted closer.

"It's not gonna work," she whispered. "We need to get closer."

As desire, rather counterintuitively (consider the gyrations), percolated within my bones, I abandoned the foot-and-knee strategy for something a tad more daring: I climbed atop the chair, balancing myself on my knees and holding the back of the chair with my hands, with Annie beneath me. I inched myself awfully close to my goal—you go, yoga!—but then the chair bucked and actually threw me onto the cold floor, naked. I struck the side of a grandfather clock.

"That's actually pretty ironic," observed Annie after I gave a short, quiet laugh.

"Huh?" I whispered, on my back.

"The clock!" she said, pointing at the thing. "It's nearly *midnight*. Time is a-tickin'." She patted the seat cushion, inviting me back aboard.

This time, Annie sat on the very edge of the chair—another inch and she'd have been on the floor. Again leveraging my newfound yoga skills, I found a way to lean forward while holding the arms of the chair, with my feet on the ground and my knees bent, and, finally, enter Paradise. With minutes to spare, we fused. Annie looked at the clock and said, "Yay!"

Later, we cranked up the faux woodstove, piled into the high Victorian bed with the girls, and fell asleep in the cold, cold Wyoming winter.

8

The Power of Love

have a relationship with B&Bs that I like to think is akin to a coal lobbyist's association with the new Democratic chairman of the House Committee on Energy and Commerce: daydreaming of at least a few hard-fought victories, but wary. Very wary.

With B&Bs, I always imagine a room full of guffawing strangers sharing the arcs and textures of their lives with one another over jam-stuffed French toast, when all I desire is some whispering with the kids and Annie, some coffee and food, and maybe a few paragraphs of the newspaper. At the same time, however, I'm extremely fond of warm breakfasts. And the breakfast part of the B&B equation always seems free, even though the fee I paid for the room includes the extra cost for the breakfast. And to me, free—even when illusory—is best. So I woke up psyched about a "free" breakfast, but also wary, steeling myself for a room full of men and women ready to pounce on me with questions about my hometown, my career, my catalogue of likes and dislikes.

"I hope this isn't a chat fest," I said to Annie as we walked from our refinished-garage accommodations to the main dwelling and the dining room.

"I don't think you have anything to worry about," she said. "It didn't seem like this place was exactly packed last night."

We all arrived for breakfast in the ornate dining room. There was a counter groaning with warm oatmeal and cereals, coffee and fruit juices and bagels, and peach tarts were warming in the oven. We were the only guests. I did not escape arc-of-life banter, however, because the owners engaged us immediately with questions and conversation. But as usual, once I actually began speaking with strangers, I was happy about it (here is where my relationship with B&Bs differs, I'll wager, from that between the coal lobbyist and the new Democratic chairman of the House Committee on Energy and Commerce). The B&B owners were hosting a church group at the B&B shortly after breakfast, though, so we ate fast, loaded the car with the few bags we'd brought for the overnight visit, and split, gearing up for a two-hour drive back to Denver. I waved good-bye to the malevolent easy chair on the way out.

Once we got past the huge billboards on the industrial outskirts of Laramie warning people of the dangers of methamphetamine, the drive home—a different route from the one we took to the town—became wild, rolling grassy vistas punctuated with fields of gigantic and misshapen red boulders, buttes, and thickening stands of evergreens as we approached the Colorado border. Eventually, like all American landscapes, it skidded into strip malls, gas stations, and a cross-section of the nation's fast-food joints. There was an outlet mall. We stopped. At the J. Crew store I picked up several stupendously cheap items, including two bright orange things—a sweater and a shirt.

I held them up for Annie.

"Perfect," she said.

The checkout clerk, a stranger, praised my embrace of colors.

"Thanks," I said.

"Don't mention it," she responded. "You know, a guy came in here earlier, and he was actually angry about all of the colorful stuff for men. Do you know what he said to me? He said, 'No guy would buy these clothes but a homo.'"

She then handed over my sack of bright homo clothes.

"Talking with strangers can be dangerous," I said to Annie as we left the store.

Then back to the minivan for another hour of driving, this time along busy highways instead of winding mountain roads. Either way, we had the minivan, so driving with the whole family had the potential for pleasure, at least when compared to what driving with the whole family meant just a year earlier, when we carted around the kids in a white 1995 Subaru Outback.

In the Outback, the kids could touch each other. In the Outback, the distance between the kids' mouths and our ears could easily be measured in inches, requiring, maybe, a ruler and a half. Both of these things transformed what certainly had the potential for "placid rambles" into "arduous journeys" if not "descents into terror." There was the yelling, of course. But don't forget about punches, pinches, and kicks. And the throwing, obviously. The tears go without saying.

If not for a summer vacation to the Outer Banks, we still might have been shepherding the girls around in the Outback, or even—I clutch my chest just thinking about it—in a Volkswagen Bug. Before the vacation, we were looking to replace my tiny pickup truck with something more practical. Annie adored the VW Bug (the flower holder, I think, nearly sealed the deal). I experienced markedly less inner warmth at the prospect of a Bug—notwithstanding the flower holder—but this was to be Annie's car; I would get the Subaru she had been driving. Fortunately, when we arrived at the rental-car place in Raleigh, North Carolina, the guy working the counter said he could give us a minivan for the same price as the sedan we had requested. Annie and I traded shrugs and walked outside with the kids to our gleaming green machine. Before this inaugural drive, Annie and I both had scoffed at minivans.

"So suburban!" we'd sneered as we drove around our subdivision of plastic white-picket fences and shiny, five-piece bathrooms.

Somewhere around minute two of the drive out of the rental-car place, this haughtiness evaporated. The kids sat in separate, captain-style chairs, which were ingeniously placed far enough apart so that children sitting in them *could not touch* each other. When the kids talked, it would not have been out of line for Annie or me to cup an ear and say "Pardon?"

Very quickly, I turned to Annie and said: "I want a minivan."

"Turns out I love minivans," Annie replied, not missing a beat.

Weeks later, we were the proud owners of a new Honda Odyssey. And now, although the tense highway conditions kept the drive from becoming a "placid ramble," the trip was far from arduous. Annie and I agreed to play the kids' music—a combination of *The Lion King* and *The Wizard of Oz*—and they sat silently, looking out the window, as Annie knitted and we chatted.

"What do you think?" I asked Annie. "Was it worth it? One night in a B&B that was two hours away?"

"It was sort of rushed, but I'd do it again," said Annie. "If nothing else, it was cool to just be in Wyoming."

"That it was," I said.

We finally pushed the button that opened our garage door, filed into the house with our stuff, turned on the oven, and yanked a pizza out of the freezer. The girls marched upstairs to don their sleepers; then they played with some blocks. About the time the first argument between them broke out—about a certain purple block both of them wanted—the pizza was out of the oven and the fight fizzled. And then they were asleep in their rooms.

After showering, I poured cinnamon massage oil into my hand and massaged Annie for a long time, a good half hour.

"Your turn," she said later, fresh lube shellacking her hands. I lay back. The lube was not meant for aching muscles. Half an hour later, after graduating to lovemaking, we fluttered off to sleep almost effervescent with bliss, but it all leaked away from Annie during the night. She woke up sad and failed to shake her melancholy by the time I left for work.

"I'll be OK," she said. "Just dragging this morning. It will pass."

I drove Joni to school, but during the commute to work I couldn't stop thinking about Annie's heavyheartedness. So I made a detour; I swung by the house to deliver a hug.

"DJ," she said when I walked in the door. "What are you doing here?"

I walked toward her and put out my arms. "You need a hug."

She fell into me and clutched me close, and we held it for a solid minute.

"You don't know how much better that makes me feel," she said as we pulled away from each other. Her face had brightened; a smile filled her sweet face. "It's like you just warmed me up."

I'd never before actually made a detour to give Annie a hug. It's something I'd do again. It was Monday, day 44—a milestone for Annie, she said, because her birthday was April 4, or 4/4, and to Annie, her birthday is a High Holy Day. Every year, she starts talking about it weeks before the actual event.

An hour or two after the hug detour, I took a break from work and walked a few blocks from my office to The Brown Palace, a classic old establishment with superb service and a vanished-era, gilded sensibility about it. I booked us a room for the coming celebratory weekend—the halfway point—and instantly imagined myself, with great relish, propped up in one of those tall beds, a beer or a flute of champagne in my hand, and an exceedingly sexy Annie beside me. The very idea of "fancy sex"—sex in the classy room, in the hotel swarming with tuxedoed staff and monied guests—made me feel, as they say, "psyched." We'd do it twice, on Saturday night and Sunday morning, and joy cloaked my heart, I must admit, when I contemplated morning sex on Sunday followed by a precious night off. For now, though, it was finishing another day at work, child rearing, and then sex.

Back at home, the kids that night were happy, and then they were sad. Annie bought them a bunch of new clothes because they were swiftly outgrowing their wardrobes. This, naturally, pleased them quite a lot. Then, after dinner, they worked together building towers out of blocks, but Ginger kept knocking over the towers, which enraged Joni. I took Ginger upstairs for book reading and after a while Joni joined us.

"Joni, why are you making an angry face at me?" Ginger asked.

I looked. Sure enough, Joni was scowling at her sister.

Joni started reciting the litany of horrors that Ginger had visited upon her. "She kept knocking over my towers! On purpose! She doesn't pay any attention to what she's doing! She can't even build a tower!"

Then she got off the bed, stood in the doorway, and yelled: "I hate the world, I hate the world, I hate everything, I hate little sisters, I hate toddlers, I hate three-year-olds, I hate people who were born in September!"

I could have added, "Hey, honey, you forgot to mention people named Ginger." My standard strategy for dealing with young-girl emotional volatility—*Just change the subject*—wasn't especially appropriate here, given the dramatic explosion of anger and the tears gathering in Ginger's eyes. I scolded Joni for directing the inventory of hate toward her sister, and she stomped down the stairs. Ginger, now sobbing, required a dose of Ginger Whispering before I could kiss her good night and close the door.

By the time I arrived downstairs, Joni was crying on the couch. She had rebuilt her favorite tower, but it fell down just before I got there. I helped her rebuild it, I offered her some leftover apple crisp for dessert, and I let her watch the Olympics upstairs while I cleaned up.

We then watched the Olympics together on the bed. We took

turns predicting who would win each competition (and clocking points for who made the most right guesses), poked fun at a few of the costumes, talked about what it's like in the different countries, most of which involved me referencing the things I liked about their food ("Ah, Sweden. They love cardamom in Sweden, Joni. I love cardamom"). It was the kind of night I wished would happen more routinely. When I worked out of the house in Baltimore, I had much more time with her; bonding rituals occurred daily. In Colorado, I usually spent most of the day at the office and rarely arrived home before 5:30 p.m.

One of the greatest, though also most bittersweet, trips of my life took place in that old Subaru Outback, when Joni and I drove from Baltimore to Annie's parents' house in Missouri, on our way to a Denver apartment where we would live after four glorious years in Baltimore. I had been living alone in Denver, in a friend's house, for about three months (I drove out with my mom in my pickup truck, another trip that sits in the pantheon of "best trip ever"). One weekend in June, I flew back to Baltimore, packed up the house with Annie, and took off with Joni. Annie and Ginger would fly to Annie's parents' house in Missouri a few days later. Joni and I followed an old interstate, one that for much of the drive was a country road, a neglected highway that passed through maybe a hundred small towns, where Joni and I always ate in local diners and stayed in what Joni called "Sunny Days Inns" (Days Inns) because the logo looked like a sun. Joni, an unusually loyal little girl, picked the Sunny Days Inn for the first night and decided from that point forward that Sunny Days Inns were the only way to go. I have to hand it to her: We stayed in quite a nice string of Sunny Days Inns. The weather was June-perfect: flowers blooming everywhere, blue skies decorated with cottony clouds, the trees still displaying that light, young lime color instead of the dark-jungle evergreen of August. We listened to a tape of the play *The Frog Prince* probably 124 times, and we yakked and laughed and acted silly for days. I still have mementos from the trip: menus, brochures about things to do in, say, south-central Indiana, and chicken bones Joni saved after a fried-chicken meal at a country restaurant.

Now *that* was serious father-daughter bonding, a preface to a new life in Colorado, where I no longer worked out of the house, which is where Joni, at the time, assumed all daddies worked. By the time of the marathon, just eighteenth months after moving to Denver, I dreamed of repeating the trip one day with Joni, and of taking a similar long drive with Ginger. I also fantasized about spending more time with them at home.

"Good night, honey," I told her as she lay in bed. I pressed the top of the comforter to her neck, bent down, and kissed her on the forehead. "I love you."

"I love you too, Daddy."

An hour later, after washing dishes and straightening up the downstairs, Annie and I entered the bedroom and lavished each other with another round of lovemaking. On this night, possibly for the first time since we began the marathon, it seemed comfortingly routine, something like the DVD reward we used to embrace, effortlessly, after a long day thatched with the standard material: the work, the child rearing, the meal preparation, the cleaning up, the bedtimes . . . and then *The Sopranos*, courtesy of Netflix. Only now, the reward, which did verge on effortless, was sex.

"We're getting awfully good at this," said Annie. She gently stroked my arm with her fingernails.

It was an unusually meaningful Valentine's Day for us, given our project. Annie made me a cappuccino, and then we presented the girls with presents—Valentine's Day chocolates, heart-happy stickers and tattoos, books—before they went to school. They

grinned and hopped, so excited they could not contain themselves, a combo-platter of zeal involving the presents and the anticipation of a schoolday thick with candy hearts, Valentine's Day
cards (both girls had handmade cards for all of their classmates),
and cupcakes. I could have hopped myself. Ginger's preschool had
a wonderful deal: For $35 teachers at the school would watch
your kids for several hours on Valentine's Day night. We booked
the kids for the event.

Did we plan on going to dinner? Or to a movie? Hold on to
your seats. Lean close. I'm going to have to whisper this one.

Yoga.

You want to slap us. I understand. Here's my theory: We had
dedicated the previous forty-odd days to our bodies, fixating on
our physical selves as never before. It all began with the sex, and it
all revolved around the daily romps. The yoga, however, had in-
sinuated itself into the party; it had even persuaded us that it was
an accomplice to our daily exchanges of flesh. By this time in the
odyssey, our anatomies had rightfully gathered that they, suddenly, were in charge. They were like vice presidents after an assas-
sination: one minute attending state funerals and giving speeches
about business-friendly tax policy at chamber of commerce lun-
cheons, the next in command of the armed forces, having drinks
and dinners with foreign presidents, and thinking about writing
their memoirs. In other words, our bodies had taken over, and it
all was more a coup than a democratic election. They called the
shots, and for Valentine's Day they basically forced us to file into a
105-degree yoga studio and punish—I mean stretch—our bodies
for a spell.

Still, it *was* Valentine's Day. After work, I stopped off at the
local florist and waited in line as the crowd of fellows before me
dropped $100 each on elaborate bouquets for their wives. I bought
a single red rose. The woman who rang up my sale seemed appalled. Here was a room full of loving, attentive husbands doing

the right thing and plonking down big bucks on dramatic and aromatic explosions. And then there's this moron, with his single blossom. If she'd known about the yoga, I suspect she, like you, would have rolled her eyes. I wanted to tell her about the other gifts I had for Annie. And I wanted to inform her about all of the sex—today's session would make it forty-five straight days!—but I just bowed my head, paid, and got the hell out of there.

"Happy Valentine's Day, Mom," I said during the short drive from the store to the house.

"Must be a biggie for you," said Mom. "With the marathon and all."

Again with the sex reference.

"Uh, yeah, it's up there," I said. "What are you and Dad doing?"

"Your dad bought lobster tail and filet, and he's making dinner for me right now at home. He just opened a nice bottle of wine, too. So sweet."

"He's a keeper."

"I'll stick with him," said Mom, referring to this guy she'd met in ninth grade at West Chester High School. They both were the shortest 14-year-olds in their homeroom, my dad a farm kid, and Mom the daughter of a bartending father (the "Gramps" who later moved to Vegas) and social-worker mother. They began dating soon after they met, and except for a relatively brief "breakup" in eleventh grade, they've been together ever since.

"You guys know what you're doing, Mom," I said. "I miss you."

"Miss you too, honey," she said. "I love you."

"I love you, too."

THAT NIGHT Annie gave me a carving of Ganesh and a shaving balm that I liked. I presented to her the sexy thigh-high heart stockings I'd bought earlier (amid Cock Ring Theater), a face-cleansing product she loves made by a Colorado company, and the red rose. Then I revealed my Playboy bunny boxers, and she laughed. I'd worn them all day. At 6:36, we started. At 6:50 we had to be out the door to make the yoga class. Neither of us thought it was going to work, but Annie put this gauzy orange scarf over her face, making herself look vaguely Middle Eastern, and for some reason it powerfully aroused me. We went at it for a solid ten minutes. She did not orgasm; neither did I. We rushed downstairs, grabbed our yoga gear, and roared off to class in the minivan.

It turned out nobody else had the yoga-on-Valentine's-Day idea (surprise!). We were the only students, so we got a personal lesson from a fun-loving, middle-aged California hippie who had "spaced" that it was Valentine's Day.

As we walked back to the car, we agreed that this was the way to spend this holiday, not sitting in a crowded restaurant with an overpriced, "themed" meal, gorging on rich food and chocolate and cheap champagne, and waddling home, direct to the bed and sleep. Valentine's Day is a worthwhile holiday. But it's been cheapened, we thought, by extreme commercialization. It's love's only holiday. Love! Chocolate hearts, bouquets, Cupid-emblazoned cards, and toasts to "us" at restaurants are fine, but the spirit of the holiday seems to revolve around these icons, instead of its true heart—love.

"Let's do something like that next year," said Annie as we drove through the frozen night to the house, where I would drop her off before driving to the church where the girls were being watched. "I feel tingly and wonderful. Sex followed almost immediately with yoga."

"I've gotta say, it's a Valentine's Day I'll remember. In fact, I can't remember any other Valentine's Days. Can you?"

Annie brought her hand to her chin. After a few moments, she said she recalled that on several occasions we had prepared ambitious and romantic dinners for each other, complete with handmade and elaborate cards. This did ring a bell with me. But she could not remember the years, the meals, or the cards. Just that, at least a few times, we had tried hard to dignify the holiday.

"Not necessarily yoga every year," I added. "Although certainly something beyond my fallback position on so many things, which is fish and chips and Guinness."

"Needless to say," she said.

I arrived at the school about 9:15 to pick up the girls, which was fifteen minutes early. Every door was locked. It was dark inside. *Oh my God.* I ran around and around, knocking on doors, looking into windows. Nothing. I was about to call the police, but a custodial person opened a door I had been knocking.

"Yes?" she said.

Whew. "I'm here for my kids."

"There aren't any kids in here."

Heart-thumping terror.

"*What?*"

"Well, maybe in the back area. You can go check it out."

I rushed down dark hallways, opened a pair of double doors, and saw light coming from a room. I heard kids' voices. I don't recall the last time I was so taut with panic. Lots of things are important. For parents, nothing surpasses our children. They are raw love, innocent love, a love like the unknown energy that binds the universe: supremely powerful love, blinding love, love that cannot be understood or explained.

"Hi, girls," I gushed, love tumbling through my body and brain, spreading through my spirit like sweet breath, like a liquid warmth. They ran to me, surprised at my sudden appearance at the dark door.

"Daddy!"

I bent down and they flung themselves into my outspread arms, and I drew them close, kissing them on their little heads.

"Girls!" I whispered. "I love you so much."

I picked up Ginger and held Joni's hand, and we walked out into the frigid February night. But I felt nothing but heat, the cozy warmth of a mound of flaming oak in a fireplace, the steam incandescence of a coffee shop on a winter afternoon. No, that's wrong. It was a fire of a different order.

My heart owned this blaze.

THE HEART hearth smoldered well into the evening, coddling my sleep in ski-lodge snug. In the morning, though, I bundled up in several layers and steeled myself for Greenland on the tundra. It was frozen outside, and the forecast called for much more of the same. I spent the day at work dreaming of returning home and huddling beside Annie's hot body. I shivered on the long walk from the office to my car, my teeth chattered as the car warmed up, and I called Annie while I drove as soon as I felt some warmth.

"Hey!" I said.

"DJ!" she said. "You on your way home?"

"Yes indeedy," I said. "What's going on?"

"Cooking dinner. The girls are playing with blocks. We're just waiting for you."

"Any good gossip today?" I asked.

"Nada," she said. "Whole lot of nothing. Got lots of work done, though."

"Cool," I said. "Me too."

"Well, I'll see you in a few, right?" she asked.

"Absolutely, darling. See you in a few."

"Drive carefully. ILYSM."

"ILYSM."

I arrived home. Annie was busy in the kitchen, the kids were drawing on white paper with colored markers, and the house was roasting with stove and fireplace heat. Soon, Annie and I lay side by side, stroking and petting each other as we chatted nonchalantly about the day.

"I was thinking about Burlington today," I offered.

"Vermont?"

"I thought maybe it would be a good place to live. If we don't stick with Colorado, that is."

"Great food scene." said Annie.

"And cool to be so close to Montreal," I said, my fingers gliding across her thighs.

"But chilly!" said Annie, bringing her hands between my legs.

After a few more minutes of idle chatter—idle but extravagant with danger, given the topic ("Let's move!")—passion began elbowing away the everyday.

"Why don't you really—*really*—explore my Brazilian?" Annie asked, leaning back.

One glimpse of her on her back in those sexy thigh-high stockings I bought her, with that glorious Brazilian, and I felt something like ignition happening within my body. I gently stroked, and then committed to a thorough g-spot exploration. I'd read several books about women's sexuality, all of them with lengthy chapters about the g-spot, and they offered diagrams and complicated, step-by-step instructions. After a few minutes, Annie wriggled free.

"Sorry, honey," she said. "I know you're trying your hardest, and I know you've read all sorts of books, but the stuff with the fingers just doesn't work. Is that cool?"

I moved back up toward the top of the bed, dragging my fingertips across her body as I moved.

"Of course it's OK," I said. "The g-spot is complicated."

"It's best with sex," she said."

The vision of her in her thigh-highs was impossibly stimulating, and very porn—in a good way. I felt not a particle of disappointment about the failed g-spot expedition. I just wanted sex. Fortunately, so did Annie.

"I think I'm in love with it—my Brazilian," she said when we were done. "It's like I have a new vagina, a cool, hot, hip vagina. For once, me and my vagina are trendy."

"You know what?" I retorted. "I feel hip, too. I have a wife with a Brazilian. I'm getting some residual hipness from your very painful and humiliating process. So thanks."

"Don't mention it."

We sat on the bed and talked awhile.

"So, Burlington?" said Annie.

"Absolutely."

"Come close," she said, and I did. I pressed my kneecaps into the backs of her knees, my legs into hers, I spooned her derriere— unbidden, I must add—which I think of as marathon treasure, and wrapped an arm over her torso.

Do not fear. This is a story about one hundred days of sex, not one hundred days of homesickness. References to being "bummed out" about my dislocation from a previous, comfortable life have already threaded this tale plenty; I refuse to subject you to much more. Let me just say that the familiar and tiresome melancholy did infiltrate this week of sex, but certain insights also appeared. Here's the deal: I love my cousins unconditionally, and they love me back. I love my brother in an even stronger way, and his wife and kids and my parents. Walking into a room full of friends or colleagues pleases me, but it's altogether different from entering a competition-free cocoon of love, where we riff on shared memories of annual Jersey Shore vacations, and summers spent playing Dungeons and Dragons, and comic-book collecting, and inside jokes that nobody else would understand or appreciate. The cocoon is home. An energy, a force field, an environment charged with familial love, with memories and history and a comfort that can come, if you're lucky, with blood. Here, as they say, is the "takeaway" message: When we lived on the East Coast, I knew I always could drive to the cocoon and bathe in love. Now I couldn't, and this—much more than anything intrinsic to my life in beautiful Colorado—was corrupting my spirit.

I understood this after a brief e-mail back and forth with one of my cousins, nicknamed Bird, that reminded me of some especially good-old days. The exchange pushed a few tears down my cheeks, and once I had recovered I realized, finally, the true nature of the problem. Nothing was, in essence, about place. Everything was about people.

Without the sex, I think matters would have been much worse. It was like the pharmaceutical I could have taken, although it never really occurred to me that occasional bouts with the blues demanded clinical care. Regardless, this day verging on the halfway point left me awfully low. I didn't possess a shred of erotic energy when I got home. No desire for sex, no interest in sex, a complete void when it came to the topic. I wanted nothing to do with its gruntings and grindings, its pettings and posturings, its temperatures and textures. It was five degrees below zero outside. I wanted to fall asleep and then wake up on a tulip-thick spring day somewhere in the proximity of the Pennsylvania cocoon.

I didn't bother Annie with yet another report of wallowing in the blahs, but she figured it out anyway. It wouldn't rise. I gazed at the Viagra drawer.

"It will lift," announced Annie. "I can do it."

She nibbled my neck and blew into my ear. She performed magic with her lube-slippery hands, and ever so tentatively, like a buck venturing into a field during deer season, it rose. When it achieved a satisfactory measure of rigidity, Annie lay back, smiling triumphantly. It got hotter. I even hit the elusive g-spot a few times on this night that half an hour earlier I thought would, if we were lucky, amount to a few minutes of in-and-out followed immediately by sleep. After twenty-five minutes, with Annie on her back the whole time and lost in a fog of competitive exultation, we stopped. Sex, again, had wiped away the blues. It would not surprise me if I smiled while I slept.

THE LUNCH interview with the dominatrix the next afternoon didn't exactly lighten my psychological load, but I will say this: It helped me understand that, in the cosmic scheme of things, my complaints fell squarely into the "small potatoes" category. She appeared at the sushi restaurant wearing sensible shoes, a brown sweater, slacks. She looked like a middle school assistant principal. I asked her if she was in a relationship, and she answered, "Yes, I have my boy." I thought she was referring to a son, but she continued. "You know, my slave. I just call him boy. He lives in my house and does whatever I tell him to do. He cleans, cooks. Whatever."

The concept of "boy" dismayed me, and I hoped he wouldn't be at the house when we arrived, for we planned to cap the meal with a visit to her dungeon. What would I say: "Hi, boy"?

Boy held a full-time job, fortunately, so he wasn't there. I liked the dominatrix and had no problem with her line of work. But I could do without ever again visiting a dungeon. Among dungeon aficionados, the paddles, whips, hoods, prods, chains, gags, and the dark world of other stuff haunting every corner might have added up to an agreeable whole: *This is SO authentically and wonderfully 1980s Denver goth! Where did you ever find that perfect, leather medical examination table with steel stirrups?* But I'm more of a pub-aesthetic kind of guy, which, to be fair, can in fact share certain sensibilities with dungeons, albeit medieval ones (as opposed to those idealizing 1980s Denver goth): a hearth, lots of heavy wood, stone, maybe even a candelabra.

The dungeon jolt of weirdness was followed by an interview at a new "sex positive" sex boutique opened by a pair of local hipsters. Here, I found decor more to my liking. The wood floors in the turn-of-the-century house radiated warmth. A happy-hippie bell hanging from the doorknob tinkled when I entered. The wall colors whispered "apricot," "raspberry," and "moss." In addition, the sex toys sat in funky displays, and the employees grinned innocently and offered, in gentle, lilting voices, to help me navigate the store. After the interview, the woman owner showed me around, trying to find the right toy for g-spots. Obviously, my blossoming obsession with g-spot hunting hadn't waned. I decided to urge Annie to visit the store and bought her a pair of Hanky-Panky underwear instead of a g-spot tool. Meanwhile, the owner's husband encouraged me to try Cialis.

"But just take half," he said. "It's pretty strong."

So I went home, and, after playing a wide range of games with the kids—Candyland, troll, blocks, and so on—and after a taco dinner and dueling bedtimes, I slipped into our bathroom, popped a Cialis tab out of the metallic-backed sheet holding five of them, split it in half, and swallowed. I positioned the box containing the Hanky-Panky underwear in the center of the bed, and Annie noticed it immediately when she entered the room.

"For you," I said.

She grinned, opened the box, and oohed.

"It's supposed to be very 'in,'" I said. "Hanky-Panky underwear."

"I've heard of it and coveted it," said Annie. "This is fantastic! Thank you so much, DJ."

As she extended the thank-you into a kiss, I noted to myself the power of the gift.

Half an hour later, with the pharmaceutical racing through my bloodstream, Annie and I took a long and extremely hot bath with another sparkly bath bomb. I sprawled in the heat and steam, but at one point stood up abruptly and left. I thought I was going to faint. I sat in bed and hyperventilated. Annie emerged from the bath, confused.

"What happened?" she said.

"Dunno," I said. "Suddenly, I thought I'd pass out."

"Wow," said Annie. "The Cialis?"

"I think so," I said. "That and the hot water. It overwhelmed me. My heart raced."

"You OK now?" she asked.

"I'm fine. Perfect, in fact."

I shot my eyes down toward a blossoming erection.

"Passing out would have been a bummer," said Annie. "Imagine the effect it would have had on completing day 48."

The Cialis kicked in, but not with the same intensity as the Viagra. Good ol' Autonomous Appendage failed to make an appearance, instead sending his nephew, Excitable Accessory. We started kissing, we paced through a variety of positions. The Cialis was pumping now, the sex was hot and strong. Excitable Accessory did not taunt me in the manner of Autonomous Appendage—I did not fear a hospital visit for treatment of a defiant erection, for example. Instead, I descended immediately from post-sex beatitude to an understanding, just moments after opening my eyes in the morning, that I had suffered through a night of restless sleep.

As I labored to invoke vigor with espresso, Annie and the girls took off for theater camp and then Girl Scout cookie selling on this Alaskan Saturday. And I drove to a bagel place in a strip mall I'd read about. I'd not tasted a respectable bagel since leaving Baltimore, where if you go to the right delis you find chewy bagels with sharp crusts.

The Denver deli's ambience did not arrive, edict-like, from a corporate headquarters somewhere: "Make it look like an urban loft! Use lots of metal and wood!" Nor did the bagels come in fla-vors such as Georgia Peach Melba, Sonoran Frittata, or Gobble Gobble Cranberries and Stuffing. The lighting was fluorescent, the aesthetic Formica. And the point? The best bagels in town. They even had good salt bagels, my favorite. Here was something real. It was the bagel-deli equivalent of what I wanted for Valen-tine's Day—authenticity and heart. These people cared about bagels. They made them with love, like nobody else in the state.

The bagel mood-lifter was followed by a round of Saturday yoga that boosted me even more. And to top it off, Vicki, the in-structor, gave me a black stone called "jet" that she said was good for dealing with celibacy. But . . .

"It's also perfect for the opposite of celibacy," she said. "What-ever that would be called."

I dropped the little shark-tooth-shaped stone into my pocket and knew I would carry it around with me forever, or until I lost it. I'm superstitious. I latch on to objects for irrational reasons.

Annie went to a salon to color her hair. She hadn't done that in more than a decade, but recently her hair had been boring her, bothering her, making her feel unsexy. After hours of the Olympics and many rousing rounds of indoor troll with the girls (more ovens), Annie returned, the nanny arrived, and we were off to The Brown Palace for days 49 and 50. The outside temperature was four degrees. I dropped Annie at the front door, parked, and then walked across the icy sidewalks to the warm hotel.

We brought along cheese, bread and crackers, olives, and a French wine that we'd been sitting on since my thirty-fifth birth-day, when Annie presented me with thirty-five bottles of wine.

"Hey, 1994, that's the year we got married," she said, looking at the bottle.

I said, "Really?"

You never know how a slip like that will play out: anger, laugh-ter, maybe disgust. I waited, shrinking. I got a little of all three.

She laughed. It was sardonic and not entirely innocent. She also shook her head slowly, a gesture meaning "That's just so unbelievable that I'm at a loss for words."

"Remember how drunk you got?" I offered, spying an opening. "You know, speaking of wine."

"Where?"

"At our wedding."

"Yeah."

We'd traded the vows we wrote for each other on a stage in an old church that had been converted to an auditorium for a Santa Fe museum. For most of the guests, it was their first trip to exhilarating New Mexico, where the weather cooperated (the weather does that in New Mexico). My parents danced the jitterbug like it was nobody's business, guests ate dessert from a profiterole tower instead of a wedding cake, and my dad ruled like an emperor in his suite in the hacienda-style hotel, regaling my friends with drinks and cigars. Annie and I have made plenty of mistakes over the years (during the marathon alone, you will recall the triple-X Silly Putty episode), but our wedding wasn't one of them. Annie wore her mother's white dress, and red pumps, which matched her ruby lips. Just being in her presence made me drunk, but still we inhaled beers, cocktails, and many glasses of New Mexico's Gruet champagne. At some point, the clasps holding the back of Annie's dress vanished, and she stumbled around holding it together. During that magical weekend, the hotel was a mere technicality. It held our bed and staged the rehearsal dinner.

Now, on the cusp of fifty consecutive days of sex, we had no interest in the hotel bar or in the bistros and boutiques we could visit arm in arm. This weekend, instead, pivoted on the hotel room—specifically, the bed, where we lay for hour after hour, feasting on treats and watching the Olympics and Food Network. Like the girls, we appreciated cable TV when we could get it; we just didn't want it at home. From experience—we had subscribed to cable in the past—we knew it could wield great power over us, luring Annie and me away from what we believed were more worthwhile pursuits, such as reading books. We feared becoming cable addicts.

In the hotel, we rapidly capitulated to cable television's principal charm—the vast offering of effortless entertainment—and both experienced a total immersion into a consummate state of relaxation. I began to feel almost molten, of a piece with the bed. Given time, I might have congealed into an ingot of flesh and blood and bone.

"Wanna do something, um, energetic?" Annie asked, winking.

I leaned over and reached through her robe to a warm breast.

"Sounds like a plan to me," I said. We grunted and groped for ten minutes and then stopped, neither of us achieving an orgasm on this forty-ninth day. Then we clicked on the television again. It all happened in a blur.

"That wasn't the best, was it?" said Annie as we watched some woman on Food Network stuff grapes.

"Nope."

"I hope this doesn't offend you, but that wasn't so good for me," said Annie.

"Me neither," I said. "I'd sort of fallen under the spell of luxury. I was so relaxed."

"Me too," said Annie.

"But damn, I've loved being here," I said, placing a fresh hunk of Gouda on a slice of baguette.

"The sex fizzled, but this is the best," said Annie. "Love the tune-up."

On the drive from our house to the hotel, we'd received a call from close friends in Baltimore. They, too, were off to a hotel, without the kids, in Washington, D.C. "We do it every season," they said. "We call them 'tune-ups.'"

This time, our tune-up demanded decadent sloth: eating in

bed, drinking in bed, reading in bed, watching TV in bed, having sex in bed. Other tune-up weekends—preferably away and alone—could beg for dinner and drinks, or a movie, or just a long walk. We'd been pretty good about having tune-ups without ever consciously thinking about them in those terms. The year before the sex marathon, for example, my mom had come out while Annie and I tuned up in Aspen for our tenth wedding anniversary, a date we always celebrate. And now we lay in bed on day 49 of our sex adventure. Given the volume of sex we'd experienced, skin-to-skin tumblings didn't hang pinata-like (Yay! Sex candy!) over The Brown Palace retreat. We knew we'd have sex, but it wasn't as though we were getting away so we could corkscrew into a bit of erotic excess. We'd done plenty of that.

"We needed this," said Annie, a glass of red wine in her hand, a small cutting board of cheese and crackers between us. "Even though we have managed to get away a couple times already this year."

"Vegas was work, though," I said. "Wyoming had the easy chair. And the ashram, while awesome, lacked this luxury. I'm digging every minute of The Brown Palace."

We finished the cheese, put the cutting board on a table, and scooted close to each other, with one of Annie's legs draped over one of mine and our shoulders pressed together.

9

The Singing Heart

felt slightly smug, sitting in bed in a posh hotel, waiting for room service to deliver two double cappuccinos. They arrived on a silver platter. The bill for the beverages: $25. Gulp. Annie, our chancellor of the exchequer, surpassed my gulp with an audible gasp when she examined the cappuccino bill.

"The hotel wasn't too bad," she said, referring to the $149 price per night (in addition, we'd gotten bumped up to a better room, free of charge, because Annie asked the front-desk manager; she not only was chancellor of the exchequer but also served as secretary of state). "But this is ridiculous."

We were not wealthy. For about eight years, we had lived entirely on my salary as a journalist; for two of those years, I had supported the family getting paid by the word as a freelance writer. By the time of the marathon, Annie was working part-time and my salary was decent; together, we were making more than ever. But with two kids and the purchase of a house looming (we knew it would happen, we just didn't know where), we had been a bit more "spendy" than we had been in Baltimore, though by no means flamboyant. The marathon, though, was nudging us closer to the flamboyant category. We had spent on lingerie, massage oils, candles, incense, and bath products. Babysitters and a nanny had suddenly entered our world, not in a trickle but, for us, a deluge, costing hundreds. We'd treated my parents to dinner, feasted and drunk in Vegas, spent a night at a yoga ashram, hurried through a week-end in Wyoming, dropped a lot of green on yoga. And now we were sipping $12.50 cappuccinos brought to us by a guy in a tuxedo.

"We're tearing through money," said Annie, wearing a plush white robe and propped up in bed, holding the exorbitant coffee drink.

I, of course, did not have a clear idea of what "tearing through money" meant in specific, balance-sheet terms. I could sense more things were coming our way due to an exchange of cash for goods and services, which led me to believe our pile of dollars was shrink-ing faster than normal, but my brain did not contain a line-item budget, a device containing red flags and warning signals. This was not an ideal situation—I knew Annie would appreciate it if I gained some understanding of our family finances—and I long had vowed to do so. For the next fifty days, though, I could not dive into finan-cial tutorials: Annie said now was no time to rein in the spending.

"This is our big pause," said Annie. "We've been on a treadmill ever since we left New Mexico, ten years ago. We've never doted on ourselves like this. We've not stopped and looked around and just connected. We can afford to keep being a little crazy with the money. We'll just cut back, dramatically, when we finish the marathon."

"It has been awfully nice," I said. "Feels good to spoil our-selves."

"It does," said Annie. "I've learned something. While we can't maintain this pace, I wish we would have budgeted for something like this a long time ago."

"The Brown Palace?"

"Yes, The Brown Palace. And the ashram. And Vegas. And the coffee-shop visits. And the babysitters and the nanny. Not all crammed into one hundred days, necessarily, but looking back, I think we really were deep in a rut. Not just sexwise, but in our life. Everything was day-to-day, so much of what we did revolved around the girls. Our time alone was just the evenings, in our house, sipping beer and hanging out. But no more. I think we should keep using babysitters and even the nanny after this is all over."

"You're not going to get a counterargument from me," I said. I raised my $12.50 cappuccino for a toast. "To us," I said. We clinked mugs.

We remained in bed, both of us swaddled in the fine white robes offered by the hotel, clicking around the television, reading, and eating those bagels I had bought at the deli, with cream cheese. I draped my bagels, too, with smoked salmon. After one of the slowest, most leisurely mornings I'd had in years, Annie and I elected to shoot for the morning delight. Unlike every couple in cinema and television who wake up and then soon have sex, we first brushed our teeth. Then we nearly jumped back onto the big bed, clutching each other and kissing and laughing. As the playfulness grew a bit more serious, I began to feel almost religious about this halfway-point session: Something had clicked inside me, and sex had started to change from this occasional, monumental, pressure-filled evening event to something more natural and easy and relaxed.

At some point in the last forty-nine days, my attentiveness to Annie and her needs had quietly shifted from a pleasurable task that demanded completion before "actual sex" could take place, to an ecstatic end in itself. I consciously understood, now, that this change had taken place, although I couldn't pinpoint a day or a sexual encounter that was the "tipping point." We were having intercourse every night for the sake of the marathon, and I think, fifty days into it, the intercourse helped bring me to this new appreciation. But at this crossroads, I understood sex was much more than the fulfillment of a technical definition ("Once the gold staff is inserted in the satin cleft, the sexual act is complete"). Sex, at least for me, was a full immersion in pleasure—not trading gratifications (I bring Annie to orgasm, and then she brings me to orgasm) but absorption in both Annie and myself, in our flesh. I found pleasuring Annie an end in itself, a pursuit that galvanized every grain of libido I possessed. Foreplay, in other words, wasn't separate from sex. In fact, they were the same thing.

On this, our fiftieth consecutive day, I also realized that sex has something in common with haiku, pitching fastballs, and painting landscapes (stay with me here). With great practice comes comfort and confidence with form. And then comes emancipation from protocol, poise in the face of the unfamiliar and the unprecedented. In broad daylight in downtown Denver with the curtains flung wide on the seventh floor of an old hotel we found nothing but pure pleasure, the fruit of a challenging sexual sojourn that had taken us far.

We requested late checkout. "You know one thing I love about the past fifty days?" asked Annie as we sat in bed. "It's helped me feel sexy again. I haven't felt this sexy since college."

"Seriously?" I said. She nodded her sexy head and shrugged her sexy shoulders, and I was confused. "Any idea why?" I asked.

"It's not like I haven't felt sexy," she said. "When we get dressed up and go out on a date, or when we're having sex, or when you give me a certain kind of caress, then I feel sexy. But I've been feeling this way for fifty days in a row now. It's great."

"And one we need to continue when we're finished with the marathon, because you're very sexy all the time." I stroked her hair and kissed her cheek. "And we need to go on more dates. At this point, how many do you think we have a year? Two?"

"Maybe one," said Annie. "In fact, I can't believe we haven't gone out to dinner yet, just the two of us, during the marathon. That's got to change."

"Something to plan, for sure," I said. "We've got the babysitter now. There's nothing stopping us."

We remained in bed until we absolutely had to leave. When it was time, we shoved all of our stuff into our bags and took off, driving through a gray winter day to our little house, where the girls, this time, greeted us with something more like the "juvenile gaiety" we had hoped for after the ashram visit. Although the girls didn't celebrate our homecoming with banners and song, they did run into our arms, and we kissed 'em all over. After getting the scoop from the nanny—allegedly, no problems—we commenced a day of game playing and dinner making before moving into bed-time land for the girls. Then, quickly thereafter, Annie and I curled up between the sheets, turned off the light, and kissed each other good night.

I ARRIVED late at work the following day because I had a most interesting evening assignment: spending a few hours at a school for strippers. They wore little as they writhed around silver poles. I interviewed a young woman named Brandy, who taught the women their moves and who reported to me that she was "into" her sexuality. As I stood taking notes among the stripper wannabes, I was conscious of my good fortune, career-wise. I could have been getting paid to do many things. Even as a reporter, I easily could have been sitting in a city council meeting listening to talk like this (which I'd heard many times over the years): *City Council President Johnson and the rest of the councillors, the residents of Clarkson Lane and adjacent streets, such as Sparrow Drive and Fox Chase Way, have significant concerns with this builder's intention to construct . . . blah blah blah.* For many journalists, this is about as glamorous as it gets. I'd been there many times. But now I was interviewing a roomful of young women gunning to become strippers. By the time I got home, feeling rather ebullient—nights after city council meetings, on the other hand, usually left me feeling anemic—the girls had long been in bed, and Annie was waiting for me in a cute nightie, sitting in bed and leafing through a magazine, a half-finished India Pale Ale on her bedside table.

"How were the strippers," she asked, bemused. "Hot?"

As I put away my clothes, I told her about the stripper school, pointing out that although some of the young women seemed bent on working in strip clubs, most of the students were young, plain women who just wanted to learn stripteases to entertain their husbands. There were even several grandmothers. This was a closing argument meant to persuade Annie that even though the assignment *sounded* like a guy's dream—an assignment, I must point out, that was happening concurrently with Annie making dinner for the kids, cleaning up, and putting the girls to bed—it was much more pedestrian and less "dreamy" than I had imagined. Which, to be honest, was the case.

"Stripping for their husbands, huh?" said Annie. "Did it seem like a sexy thing? Did it make you want me to strip for you?"

"With some of them, it was pretty sexy," I said. "I'd be *way* behind you if you wanted to take a stripping class. Could be fun."

Annie looked at the clock, which flashed 11:00. "We may want to do a little stripping ourselves pretty soon, however, although not to music."

ANNIE'S BRAZILIAN waxer, whom I was interviewing for a series of stories arguing that pornography had become nearly as mainstream in American society as rock and roll, told me that the big thing on the coasts was "asshole bleaching." Porn stars didn't like their assholes appearing too dark in videos. So they bleached them. My response was something like my reaction to the dungeon: not my sort of thing. The receipt of this surprise nugget of information, though, did make me laugh out loud in the salon.

"Asshole bleaching," I said. "That's hilarious. Or something."

"Here's the deal," said the waxer. "The porn stars bleach their assholes; then non–porn stars who watch porno see these bleached assholes and say, 'I want an asshole like that.' So they then bleach their assholes, too. It's the same thing as the Brazilian waxes. Before porno, you never saw a Brazilian on anybody. Now everybody has a Brazilian, or at least shaves."

Annie was enthusiastic about my meeting with her waxer, and she was eager for details as soon as we had time alone, after the kids were in bed.

"Bleached assholes," I said, after detailing for Annie the arc of the bleached asshole from nonexistent, to a porn presence, to a porn assumption, and then on to the rest of the nation. "Unbelievable."

"I don't think I need to mention that I won't go a step farther than the Brazilian," said Annie.

"You know one thing I thought about while interviewing the waxer? She has spent more time with your vagina than anybody but me since we started dating."

"Even my ob/gyn spends less time—much less," said Annie. "Of course, the waxer is inflicting pain on my vagina, so it's not, you know, like good times when we're hanging out."

Annie walked across the carpet and locked the door. On the way back to the bed, she briefly lifted the hem of her nightie, flashing me that which was Brazilianed.

Good times.

THE FEELING that follows sex—what I like to think of as a "singing heart"—is an extremely desirable sensation. It's free, and if you practice safe sex, it's not physically unhealthy. Why isn't *everybody* a sex addict? It's got to be the work, the dance, the labor behind the invocation of the erotic dream state and its afterglow.

The dream state is a treasure, but it arrives only after emotional, physical, and sometimes even spiritual investments. Some people, though, manage to divorce the act from much of its fraught underpinnings—or at least gloss over them. Like the porn star with whom I set up an interview.

We decided to meet on Friday near the convention center in Denver and enter the "Sex and So Much More" show together, an event celebrating sex and, of course, the many products and services that cater to it. At the end of our first conversation, she said: "I'll see you on Friday. Who knows? Maybe I'll even give you a [static] job." The cell-phone connection fizzed for the word before "job." I had no idea what she'd just said, but I cheerfully responded, "Sounds good to me."

Shortly after hanging up, and after some searching through her website, I discovered the woman was known for her prowess with hand jobs. And then I realized what she had said to me on the phone. The meeting, I realized, could be awkward. Would she try maneuvering me into an alley, her hand slathered in lube?

You ready?

After the girls were in bed, we loaded the *Tantric Lounge* CD Annie had purchased. Annie was wearing cute striped lingerie, drinking seltzer water over ice, and eating fancy dark chocolate I had bought at TJ Maxx. I wore my trusty pajamas and Thurston Howell III robe and radiated the aroma of musk. We massaged each other for a long time. We kissed. And then she, coincidentally, began a hand job (I had forgotten to relay the hand-job story to Annie, although I offered it after we had finished). For whatever reason, this slow, almost melodic affair swept me away like no other hand job: the Seabiscuit of my hand-job universe, a hand-job Rocky, Hand-Job Omnipotent.

"People are coming to me as if I'm some sort of sex expert. A sexpert?" said Annie after Hand-Job Omnipotent. "My friend Amy asked me to create a 'tune-up kit' for her and her husband.

They're going to Hawaii, without the kids. It's a great challenge. I've already sent her a list of 'ingredients.' "

"Ingredients?"

"Silicone lube, pretty lingerie—that sort of thing. I'll probably send her a care package."

This was not a scene I'd imagined just two months earlier: friends coming to Annie for sex advice. I would be a fool if it bothered me, because let's face it, if Annie was becoming a sex expert, it was because she was having sex with one person: me. It was like being married to a massage student, or to a gelato apprentice, or to someone who decides to open a microbrewery that has a menu specializing in fish and chips. Only it was better than those things.

THE NEXT day I stalked the halls of the University of Colorado's Student Union, trolling for students to interview about sex on campus. I'd become lost in sex. It had emerged as the principal topic of my life, the subject of endless conversations and evening journal scribblings. But most people, even college students, don't walk around spouting off about their sex lives, and it occurred to me that when I approached women with my questions about their between-the-sheets habits, they would see not Reporter Man but some pathetic middle-aged degenerate.

"Freak! Security! Security! There's a pervert on the loose!"

So I launched into my questionings with long preludes and preambles, including the presentation of press credentials. I didn't seem to freak out any of the students. As expected, they revealed that sex was almost inescapable on campus. Undergraduates devoted their weekends to hooking up. To please the guys, gals apparently didn't hesitate to kiss each other at parties and bars—not pecks but long, erotic tongue kisses, which were met with hoots, jeers, and high-fives by the guys. One woman said holding hands was much more difficult than just having sex. "Holding hands means something, like you care for each other," she said. "Sex doesn't mean anything."

All of this shocked me at first, although considering my recent schedule—a dungeon with a dominatrix, a porn convention in Vegas, sex shops, a stripper school, and of course asshole bleaching—I can't say it exactly blew me away. The initial shock, I think, was the matter-of-fact delivery by young men and women who in many cases looked like spokespeople for resurgent campus glee clubs: big, white-toothed grins, physics and government textbooks tucked under their arms, jeans and college sweatshirts. Had they been wearing penny loafers and bobby socks, it would not have surprised me. Quickly, though, I considered my own college experience twenty years earlier in Washington, D.C. With the exception of the girl-on-girl kissing craze, not much had changed. Young men and women spent much of their time prowling for sex. Sex didn't always mean much, but holding hands did.

Things on campus may have remained the same, but the quest for sex between Annie and me had changed tremendously. No longer did we hunt for partners. Now, we simply prowled for the sex. This had its advantages—namely, a huge part of the sex equation, the partner, was already accounted for. No need to wade into bars and compete with the rest of the guys for the often perplexing attentions of women. I never was accomplished at this game, but it did generate a certain charge. True, I had no desire to return to the world of exchanged phone numbers scribbled on cocktail napkins and restaurant conversations swirling around the arcs and textures of two lives. But the hunt does have its moments, as most hunts do. Annie and I never could introduce the freshness we frolicked in during our first weeks and months of dating, but that doesn't mean we had to jettison everything we'd learned about the art of attraction and seduction. In fact, we found our odyssey had propelled it back into our relationship, and for the first time in years we consciously worked to allure each other, to look and act sexy.

This evening, for example, I showered and rubbed myself with an essential oil called Sensuous Moment, a variation on a theme of musk but lacking that aroma's more muscular approach to masculinity. Before the onset of the marathon, I'm not sure I would have had a Sensuous Moment moment. I kicked off the marathon forcing myself to try stuff like this, but by now trying it was second nature to me.

It remains unclear whether the Sensuous Moment moment had anything to do with the momentous event that marked this evening's encounter (if it did, I salute you, Sensuous Moment). Either way, shortly after applying the oil to my body, I slipped into bed beside Annie, and soon we were kissing, then petting. Fifteen minutes later we lay beside each other, happy with the consummation of another step in the journey. This is the trajectory to which we had grown accustomed: bed, kissing, foreplay, then blessed consummation, all of it occasionally seasoned with a new twist, like an exercise ball, lube, a new position, and so forth. The time spent doing it varied, given the night, from five-minute quickies to more ambitious twenty-five-minute romps. But here's what made this evening special. We lay beside each other talking, as usual, after the sex. We curled up under the covers and chatted some more, as usual. But then we kissed. We held it and started petting each other. And within minutes, we were doing it again. *A double!* The rare, precious double! We had engaged with doubles before, but the last time had been before kids. So a good decade, at least, had passed since we last corkscrewed ourselves into what the radio djs call a "twofer."

"That was unexpected," whispered Annie when we finished, for the second time. "And wonderful."

MOMENTS AFTER I woke up the next morning, a Friday, my mind raced toward the glories of the double.

"That was wild," I told Annie while we were waking up. "You think we'll do that again?"

She shrugged. "I hope so."

My prework yoga session was a "silent" practice with Vicki—no words from Vicki urging me into this or that position, just me following her lead—and I went straight from yoga to drop off Joni at school. Before hopping into the shower, Annie said, "Howsabout a morning delight?" The idea of a double still lit my brain, and a morning session offered the potential for another kind of double— an excellent variety of the phenomenon involving both morning and evening sex. But upon entering the house I wasn't thinking imminent intercourse. I was thinking: *I'm not in the mood. I've got to get to work. Let's do it later.* So when Annie repeated her question, I said, "Um, maybe."

"Don't get too excited or anything," she said, rolling her eyes. "Contain yourself."

She took Ginger to preschool. I hopped into the shower and then nearly pranced out, straight to the heater, which I turned up to full force. I lit some incense and slipped between the cool sheets, creating what I called my "sleeve of warmth." I still was on a double high, it turned out. Minutes after Annie walked out the door, I was primed for a romp.

"I could smell the incense as soon as I walked in the door," said Annie as she stripped. "It was like a smoke signal."

"What did the signal say?"

"Sex upstairs."

We went at it, breathing hard, feeling comprehensively alive: It was still morning, and we'd already had sex. Erotic energy raced through my veins. We joked around in bed for a while, comfortable with each other, and then . . . back inside. A double! At this point—a pair of doubles in twelve hours—I felt like what I imagine a surfer in New Jersey, known for relatively choppy and short waves, might experience after sailing through two perfect, glassy tubes in a row: This surfer would feel awesome or even "gnar gnar," described in at least one dictionary of surfer lingo as "the pure awesomeness of what is being described."

With yoga and sex under my belt, I nearly floated into the office—a "floating" I thought of as very "gnar gnar"—where I interviewed the CEO of one of the top adult film studios in the country about the industry. He extolled nearly everything about it, including how "wonderful" it was for his "girls" to be able to exercise so much control over their lives and their sexuality. They make great money, they have fun, and they call the shots, he said. I wanted to say: "Sounds great. I'm assuming you're pushing your daughters to become 'adult entertainers.' Right?" But I didn't.

Then I went to meet the local porn star, Hand-Job Extraordinaire, at (heh) a hot-dog stand. She kept calling to say she was stuck in traffic, so I walked from the stand to the show and was greeted by young attractive women handing out leaflets and wearing nothing but body paint.

I immediately felt bad for the organizers. I'd already experienced the Adult Entertainment Expo, that to which all other sex shows aspire. The Denver organizers had persuaded Jenna Jameson and Ron Jeremy to appear and sign books. Troupes from the stripper school were on hand to perform stripteases and pole dancing (we all shared waves). Every sex shop in the area was displaying its wares. In the "lecture" area, I watched a sad, middle-aged flower-power couple talk about the glories of "sacred sex," which involves much eye-gazing, smiling, and even prancing. But despite all the effort, the show felt like a middle-school production of *Our Town*.

Coincidentally, my brother called *again* while I was roaming through a sex show. This time he had no idea where I was; he just wanted to chat.

"Hey, Slug, I'm not, uh, disturbing anything, am I?"

"Yeah, Mike, I'm actually in the middle of having sex right

now, but I always answer the phone when it rings, no exceptions. Hold on, let me just pull out . . ."

"Ha. Got it," said Mike. "What's up?"

"Believe it or not, another sex show. This one is in Denver. I'm covering it for the paper."

"You and the whole sex thing. Unbelievable," he said. "How does it compare to the Vegas show?"

"It doesn't."

We chatted about our respective weekends for a bit, but I had to cut short the conversation to interview Shayla LaVeaux, a veteran porn star who grew up in Denver, moved to L.A. to "make it" in porno, and had recently returned to her hometown. She was tiny, with zeppelin breasts and an unusually broad smile. She was the kind of woman who winks at people a lot, especially when saying things that are slightly "naughty," an altogether different wink-symbolism than that wielded by Winkmeister Annie.

I also spent time with the hand-job star. She had bleached-blonde hair (I'm not sure about her asshole) and, like Shayla, was miniature, but she seemed rougher around the edges. During our interview I glanced over her shoulder, and there stood beautiful Annie, grinning. We spent the rest of the night touring the show together. She roped me into her mission, which was to pocket as many samples of silicone lube as possible.

When we got home, the girls were asleep, and the sitter was leafing through magazines. As soon as we could, Annie and I plunged into bed.

SATURDAY, I had to write a story for the paper about the sex show. I got up early, wrote for a bit, and then took a break to drive the girls to theater camp, giving Annie a few hours' break from child rearing. Then I spent the rest of the day shuttered in the bedroom, working on my newspaper story, and Annie did a bunch of things with the girls. The first order of business for Annie was the delivery of Girl Scout cookies. She returned home tuckered and peturbed. Despite nearly three hours spent driving around our sprawling subdivision, only about half of the "victims" were at home. That meant more Girl Scout deliveries were in our future.

"I've made a unilateral decision that I'm going to purchase $300 worth of cookies myself—it's a tax write-off!—and we're going to keep them in the back of our van and distribute them to anyone we feel needs a box of cookies. A teacher. The mailman. The FedEx guy. A homeless person begging for change at an intersection. Anyone who might need a 'cookie boost.' Even if they aren't the healthiest things in the world."

I had to hand it to her. The approach was ingenious. Simultaneously, she accomplished goals of helping raise money for Girl Scouts, fulfilling Joni's desire for prizes, engaging in charity work, securing a tax break, and opening up valuable time for us.

Later, after I finished an hour-long, libido-boosting run, we lounged again with the bohemians in the coffee shop while a babysitter watched the kids for a few hours. We separated, and I studied Annie as she sat by herself writing and thought *She has remained as cute as the day we met*. I'd have loved to stroll over and swoop in for a big kiss. Such a move would have seemed only mildly inappropriate in the coffee shop—in fact, it might have been applauded—but it was a moot point anyway. The previous night, Ginger had crept into our bedroom and, at some point, slammed Annie in the lip with her elbow, so we couldn't kiss with much force. This played into our evening in bed, later, after the coffee shop and dinner and bedtimes.

Annie's lip had swelled, pressing it caused pain, so kissing was off limits. We both missed it. Kissing is the simplest, the most basic, form of erotic touch, yet we'd found it's also the best at firing the engines. It presses our cheeks—hers downy, mine sandpapery—and foreheads and noses together. We inhale the warmth of each other's breath. Our lips grow wet and slick, and our tongues emerge, exploring, caressing.

Without this jump-start, Annie felt at a loss.

"I read that Viagra can work for women," she said. "Should I try it?"

"Go for it."

She popped a little blue pill and broke out a new toy she had purchased at the hipster sex boutique's stand at the sex show: a battery-operated device looking something like a fat, rounded bullet that vibrates with manic intensity as it is pressed against the clitoris. We kept the bullet pinned between us, and we had sex. For a solid half hour, we slowly rocked together, the warmth of our bodies kneading our hearts, the bullet electrifying everything.

"I think I might have a Viagra buzz," whispered Annie as we made love. "I'm awfully tingly."

"You sure it's not the new tingle machine between your legs?"

"There's something else going on," said Annie. "I can feel the tingle machine. I know what it's doing. I know what you're doing, too. But something else is stirring the pot right now. In a good way."

"What's it feel like?"

"Increased horniness," she reported.

"Ya' gotta' love Viagra."

It ended up being one of our longest sessions—ever. Was it the Viagra?

Either way, it was really good.

10

The Common Good

On day 57, Annie and the girls surprised me with breakfast in bed—homemade berry scones, orange juice, and cappuccino.

"I'm a lucky man," I said to Joni and Ginger, who flitted about the bed like butterflies.

"We made everything!" said Ginger.

"That's amazing, Ginger," I said. "You're so good at cooking."

"Yes, I am."

"Daddy, we're going to go on a hike today," said Joni, her voice freighted with disappointment. "I don't like hikes. Boring."

"Well, maybe we'll see some animals," I responded.

She shrugged and did a cartwheel. After a healthy dose of hanging out, including an intermission in which Annie fell asleep on the bed with a favorite yoga book on her chest, we moseyed to Boulder for a hike, where we instantly encountered a park ranger.

"There's a mountain lion up there," he said, nodding his head along the trail. "People spotted it today."

"Do you seem them much?"

"All the time."

All the time? Mountain lions stalk their prey. They pounce from behind, going straight for the neck with monstrous teeth. I liked them in zoos. I liked them in places where I was not. With my eyes nervously panning the hills and rocks, we pressed forward, accepting Ginger's handpicked-flower "curprises," which in Gingerspeak means "surprises." We played aimlessly, listening at one point to Ginger squeal "I passed gas!" After several thunderous farts, we collected rocks and basked in the sun. And then we evacuated the lions' habitat for something even more alarming—Stapleton's one "fancy" restaurant. Annie had a $50 gift certificate, and we had a motto to honor.

This was the place with an entire wing of the dining room dedicated to kids, where young Jimmy and Caleb could push around trucks and play Spider-Man while the adults did their best to have a smashing good adult time. Don't get me wrong: I am fond of kid-friendly restaurants. But I'm most fond of restaurants where kids are sitting on seats at tables. They need not act like little angels. Let me stipulate, too, that in diners, pubs, and other more informal establishments most of my reservations about freewheeling children melt away.

So we entered Chez Spider-Man for the first time. And just as I had imagined, kids stormed the space, making vehicle noises, bouncing balls, and shrieking while we tried to enjoy our meals. Our children sat at the table and dined. At one point we actually submitted to the whole "when in Rome" thing and urged them over to the busy kids' area, but they didn't quite trust the weirdness. We felt as though we were having dinner in someone's basement rec room; all that was missing was some Ping-Pong, air hockey, and a retro neon Miller Beer sign. We escaped, spending only a few dollars more than our gift certificate, and rushed home in the darkness.

Restaurants, in theory at least, remove two of the obstacles to evening sex: the preparation of dinner and the cleaning up. There is the complicating factor of eating more, and heavier, food than you might consume at home. But on this night, at least, I'd listened to my inner counsel and ordered shrimp over rice and a salad. I didn't feel any more energetic after dinner, however, than if we had just cooked at home and cleaned up.

And then, regardless of where a meal is prepared and consumed, there is the girls' bedtime, a sequence of small efforts that often push me farther into the foggy exhaustion that begins somewhere around 3 p.m. on most days and truly ripens during the hour or so it takes to prepare the children for their descent into slumber. Usually, the scenario is much less regimented on weekends, but sometimes even a Sunday kids' bedtime comes cloaked in lethargy. Tonight, this first day of the ninth week of daily sex, was one of those Sundays. By 9 p.m., the girls were down for the night, and Annie and I were showered. And not feeling remotely horny.

I sat beside Annie for a while and then asked about her magic bullet. "Are you going to use it tonight?"

"Don't you feel it vibrating the bed?"

The very idea of Annie arousing herself as a prelude to a romp turned on a few switches in my brain and groin. Tired, yes, but suddenly capable of, even eager for, consummation. Soon, we both were nude and bending our yoga-stretched bodies this way and that, the electronic device switched off and gleaming on the bedside table.

I HAD jury duty the following Monday morning. Sometimes, juries are sequestered. The jurors don't go home; they sleep in motels until the trial ends. This prospect scared the crap out of me. Nothing, not even my civic duty, could thwart our quest for one hundred days. We were on the fifty-eighth day! Some stranger's crime was not going to cancel the whole thing.

"Good luck, honey!" said Annie as I walked out the door in the morning.

I'd received the summons weeks before, and both of us were worried about where the trial could lead. I went as far as teasing my hair straight up, in the caricatured manner of someone who had just received an electrical shock, and wearing the 1970s freak-show polyester jacket that I modeled on our New Year's Eve card. Attorneys on both sides, I reasoned, would find me too odd for their jury, and they'd dismiss me from the pool of jurors. I sauntered into the big room where hundreds of folks waited to find out if they'd be selected. People stared as I hunted for a seat. I broke out my book for the day, porn-star Jenna Jameson's autobiography (I was, in fact, reading the book for the newspaper sex series I was researching). People looked away.

I look like a total crank, I thought. *I'm home free!*

Eventually, a woman called my name through a loudspeaker along with a bunch of other names. All of us who were called packed into a courtroom and waited for the lawyers and the judge to appear. I plowed through my book, running my fingers through my hair impulsively to lift it ever higher on my scalp. Names were read. Mine was the last called. Everybody else could leave.

OK, I thought. *But now come the lawyers. They'll hate me.*

At one point I had to stand and answer questions from the judge about my occupation, about whether I'd ever been involved in a trial before, and so on. I reported, accurately, that I'd covered many trials as a journalist. I was sure this information alone would compel at least one of the lawyers to strike me from the pool. Unfortunately, I still was picked for the jury, a small case about a guy accused of robbing another guy's house. But this case, I knew immediately, was not going to send the jury to a motel.

"Whew," Annie said that night in bed, after I'd recounted my day in court. "Kinda' nerve-wracking, and kinda' fun."

"Both of those," I replied.

"This is one of the best parts of the whole project," Annie said. "Just sitting with each other and talking and connecting."

"We've talked more during these two months than I expected," I said. "More than in a long time. Who knew that more sex would lead to more talking?"

"Not just more, but better, too," said Annie.

"That has been one thing that has changed since we started, no doubt about it," I said. "Anything else come to mind?"

We stared into space for a few moments. "Well, the sex is better, that's for sure," said Annie. "It feels more natural. Like it's a big part of our lives."

"That's a huge one for me," I said. "It's gone from being some sort of monumental event, something almost staged, to something more regular."

"But regular in a good way. Maybe sex is becoming what it should be," said Annie. "One of the foundations of our life together."

"I like that," I said. "We're getting better at this. Hard to believe it took us fourteen years to make this sexual, uh, investment."

"I like how we twist into positions we never tried before," said Annie. "I like how right we feel when we're making love. I like how all of this is making me feel more . . . sexy . . . every day."

We paused, and I was surprised about what we had gained in only two months.

"There's the overall connection," I offered. "Not just the sex, or the talking, but, I dunno, the zippiness I feel about our relationship, about you."

Annie nodded. "We touch more in general. I feel *closer* to you than I have in years, and that's saying something, because it's not like we exactly drifted away from each other."

"You know, sex isn't just another activity, like playing cards together," I said. "I guess we shouldn't be surprised it's having an effect."

"I love how things are changing for us," said Annie.

We started kissing lightly, which quickly grew to kissing passionately or, if you prefer, "making out." We joined and moved together slowly. Then the heat between us started bringing everything to a boil, and we went at it with more energy.

"Do you want to go to the edge of the bed?" asked Annie as we made love.

I did, but I couldn't stop myself. I was tumbling, falling. She pressed her knees to her chest and became very much like a pretzel. And then the storm thrust me beyond its grip, into a glimmering oasis. Another world entirely, one that knew of nothing but extravagant pleasure, a paradise in the clutches of a sensualist sovereign. Eventually I recovered. We sat in bed and talked for an hour.

THE TRIAL helped telescope this understanding that I had it good.

The defendant clearly was guilty. It was hard to imagine that his life had been anything other than a procession of disappointments. And here we sat in a windowless jury room poised to deliver to him yet another setback. Most of us agreed that, without question, he broke into the dwelling and stole stuff. A few jurors, however, proved difficult. We haggled over the definitions of terms like "building" and "dwelling," the determination of which would influence the severity of his sentence. Then we argued for quite a while about the burglary charge. One juror in particular was captivated by the idea that the defendant had been framed, and she hatched unbelievably complicated and hypothetical scenarios explaining the "setup."

It was surreal. I thought: *Oh my God. How does anybody ever get convicted?*

Another juror resisted as well. It was plain the defendant had robbed the house, but one male juror insisted that somebody other than the defendant could have done the robbery. After more than an hour of circuitous and maddening squabbling, both holdouts finally relented: The defendant, they agreed, did the crime.

None of us knew one another before the trial. We didn't talk like lawyers, because we didn't know how. There was no boss lording over our deliberations, no pressure to defer or impress. Yet charging the discussion was the power we had over the future of one young man. The situation forced us not necessarily to agree but to talk naturally and without the animating force of so many conversations—personal motive. The point of it all was not to score points in a competitive debate, but to work together for the sake of truth and the "common good."

During the sexathon, I'd found that Annie's and my conversations, probably out of necessity, increasingly abandoned the selfish for our own "common good." Want to have sex tonight? Then first we've got to talk our way into it. Fighting? We've got to negotiate a settlement before carnal relations can resume, a diplomacy we already had engaged with when I roasted in self-pity about my estrangement from the East Coast and lashed out at Annie. Apologies and much talking later, we managed.

I returned from the trial to find Annie in an apron (Why is that sexy?), making madeleines with orange rind. The kids sat on high benches before the breakfast bar, trying to help Annie with the cookies. Kisses all around as I walked through the house, then a spaghetti dinner, followed by bedtimes. The usual. Once the kids were down, I pumped iron, and I must say that for the first time since high school I could recognize something described as "definition" in my arms and stomach, my chest and thighs.

"I can't believe it," I said to Annie as she changed into a new piece of lingerie she had bought at Target. "I can actually feel, like, muscles."

"I can see them, too, and it's definitely a turn-on," said Annie. "I've never been a fan of the bodybuilder look, but the hard body? That's a good one."

I showered and lathered (musk), and after about an hour of aimless conversation, we stepped into the amorous zone. But putting a foot into that region is not the same as frolicking in it.

"I'm having some probs with this," said Annie, breaking off a mild kiss. "It's not happening for me."

"What can I do?"

"Nothing right now," she said. "Can we just talk for a bit?"

We chatted about the kids. We explored the subject of our Subaru, which was making a weird belching sound. Yoga? Eastern religion? We covered them. Had the wide-ranging conversation turned to grass-fed cattle, I would not have felt great surprise. But the clock, again, determined where the evening would end: not falling asleep after a back-and-forth about favorite pasta dishes, but making love.

"I can do it now, DJ," she said, with fifteen minutes to spare. We embraced each other sitting upright, letting our long kiss blossom into something more.

WE AWOKE to a pair of milestones. It was day 60. And it was March, so for the next thirty-one days we could answer "next month" when people asked "So, when are you done?"

Nice to have the milestones.

Too bad they coincided with abounding viruses for Joni and me.

Joni curled up on the couch in a blanket and stayed home. I foolishly went to work and dropped Ginger off at preschool on the way. I didn't last at the office. My head felt like a bowling ball. I left early, electing to pick up Ginger on the way home, to surprise her with a 3 p.m. visit from Daddy.

We returned to the house, and Joni was in Annie's and my bed. I climbed in next to her and we chatted, and before I knew it, we both were sound asleep. Annie, meanwhile, had gone out with Ginger. When I awoke, she had purple and white daisies for me, some sort of vitality-enhancing juice drink, a can of chicken noodle soup, and egg noodles, which I always crave when I'm sick.

"I'm fully armed," she said, sweeping into the room with a big grin. "We're kicking the ass of this sickness. I know all about your illnesses, DJ. You get them. They last for a day. They go away. We need to, uh, have relations today, though, and I'm guessing being sick doesn't exactly contribute to horniness. So I'm coming to the rescue."

I've had low libido many times before. I've had it drained, desiccated, and demolished. And whenever that happened—like, for example, every time I've been sick—I did not have sex. I didn't have such a luxury for day 60. After I had taken the Viagra weeks before, I experienced weirdness with my vision—blurring, in particular. I then Googled "Viagra" and found that it can cause all sorts of eye problems. Ditto for the other virility drugs, Cialis and Levitra. I desired the Levitra parked in my bureau, which I had yet to try. I lacked a sex drive. I was sick. But I was scared about, you know, the whole blindness thing. So I took half a Levitra at about 9:30 p.m.

"Hey, half blindness is better than complete vision loss," I reasoned.

Turned out the Levitra was key. Not only was I sick, but Annie and I had another fight, this one borne out of Annie's frustration with trying to juggle the roles of employee, nurse, and mother. She had managed to keep the many things she multitasks up in the air, but not without enormous, and withering, effort. She revealed she was angry with me for bringing Ginger home early, which forced her to step away from work and merge with her role as mother. I failed to empathize with her situation, instead tossing indignation into the mix. ("I'm *sick* for Christ's sake! Give me a break!") Then together we levitated an argument out of ether. Annie stalked out of the room, and I remained in bed, reading. We remained apart until the clock forced us together.

I'd never had sex before while angry.

I didn't caress her. She kept her hands at her sides and her eyes closed. It was purely mechanical, about as erotic as the workings of a clock. It was, without a doubt, the worst sex I'd ever had. Annie agreed. We concluded the round of robotism without orgasms, obviously. By the time it ended, I just wanted her to leave the room.

She didn't. She cried.

"What kind of mother," she asked, "actually gets mad when her child is sick?" She talked about how she couldn't bear to live in the pile-of-nonsense house we were renting any longer. This summer, she said, things must be settled. We must be out of the rental shack, at the very least.

"It doesn't really matter where so much," I said. "East Coast, the West. As long as we escape this place. Nearly anything would be an improvement."

The statement was somewhat of an argument-ending gambit. With Annie's crying and my comforting her, the fight was nearly over, like the tail end of a sizzling batch of popcorn: the emphasis on *anywhere* was like removing the popper completely from the heat. At the same time, though, I increasingly did feel that way. Annie and I had great jobs. The Front Range supported plenty of good schools. Real estate in the area wasn't exorbitant (by East Coast standards). Colorado, physically, is a stunning place. Meanwhile, the newspaper industry had nearly collapsed since we moved to Denver. I was lucky to have a newspaper job to begin with, and the prospect of finding new gigs seemed awfully bleak. I had struggled with place enormously since I moved to Denver, but now, 60 days into the adventure, it felt as though the struggle had exhausted itself.

I WOKE up understanding quickly that I would not go to work. My joints ached. My head felt as if it had swelled with cement. I blew my nose every few minutes. If Joni hadn't had a hundred-degree fever, though, and Annie hadn't been so saddled with child rearing while trying to do her job, I still might have driven to the office. But I felt crappy, Annie needed a break, and poor Joni was desperate for some care. She migrated to our bed, and the two of us, in pajamas and heavy socks, spent hours playing games. We talked nonstop, mostly about how soon we'd have a real house, with a yard and dogs and cats.

"Hamsters too, Daddy?" she said.

"You got it, honey. Hamsters. Turtles. A lizard. Whatever you want."

It was magical time, and I cherished every moment. I knew such episodes were fleeting. Joni had changed since our move from Baltimore two years ago. She loved our big old house in Charm City, she'd visited her grandparents and cousins near Philadelphia routinely, she'd developed a close group of little friends, and then suddenly—just like that—it all went away. Few things in my life had introduced as much guilt as the move. Now, two years later, she was growing up. She still missed Maryland, but she seemed to be adjusting. That night, I read books to Ginger and then played a bunch of games with Joni—Uno, Yahtzee, and Sorry. She won every game. I put her to bed and poured a hot bath and swirled it with Epsom salts. I sat there reading a magazine and hoped the heat would burn away my sickness. I emerged, took a quick shower to wash away the bathwater, and sauntered over to the bed, where Annie sat reading something on her laptop.

"What are you reading, honey?"

"Erotica," she answered. "I'm getting bored with sex."

The news struck like a sucker punch. The little ball of libido I'd been husbanding and nursing to strength deflated.

"Bored?" I croaked.

"I'm lacking desire tonight," she said. "It's like one minute we were just cruising along, we were flying, and then I ran out of gas."

"Damn," I said. "How's the erotica working out?"

"Not so great," she said. "It's not bad, but to be honest, I'd rather be reading my yoga book."

"Any erotica genre in particular you're reading now?"

"Just men and women having sex," she said. "Lots of foreplay. Nothing graphic. You know, the woman meets some hot guy in a bar, they flirt, they bond, they kiss in the bar, and then they're in his apartment. That sort of thing."

"That's what you're reading now?"

"Something like that."

"And it's not working?"

"It never really sends me into the stratosphere. But tonight it's doing nothing."

"Is this it?" I said after a few minutes. "We stop here?"

"Are you crazy?" she responded, her eyebrows lifted high. "We've gone way too far. I'm not stopping now."

"Whew."

We lay beside each other for a long time talking, me resting my chin on her shoulder.

"You know what's almost here?" said Annie.

"Spring?"

"My birthday!" she said, lobbing her first birthday bomb of the year. Many more, I knew, would land between us in coming weeks.

"Very important day," I said.

"I'm already thinking about what I'm going to do. I'm thinking Boulder. Some shopping. Maybe a nice cappuccino. Maybe some yoga."

"Sounds like your kind of day."

"Yes. And so was today," she said. "Thank you so much for staying home today with Joni."

"It was a great day," I said. "I'm so happy I stayed home."

"Me too," she said. "I honestly feared I would lose my mind if I had to give up another day of work."

"I'll bet."

Saying good-bye to professional work had been one of the hardest parts of Annie's approach to motherhood. Until she got the pasta gig, she rarely had time to be alone, to just be herself for a big chunk of time. Yoga had arrived in her life like an angel. It wasn't just the stretching, she said, but the time alone, the extended engagement with her own thoughts, that had contributed mightily to her sense of well-being.

"Office work—at least what I remember of it—was sort of like that, too," she said. "I could just hole up and bear down on my work."

"It's true," I said. "With my gig, sometimes entire days pass and I'm consumed with the work itself, barely speaking to anybody. I like days like that."

Annie looked at the clock. "Speaking of labor, maybe we should get started."

Her boredom scared me. "Why don't you lie back," I said.

"But you're sick!" she said. "That's too much work!"

"But do you like it?"

"I love it," she said.

She smiled and melted into the bed. After about ten minutes she embraced her orgasm, and then she pulled her knees to her chest and I slid inside.

"How was that for you?" I asked after a few minutes.

Annie looked at me, her eyes sparkling, a mischievous smile enlivening her face: "I'm not bored anymore."

A FLOURISHING e-mail jag with my high school friend Shave— the Vegas buddy—transported me to the summer weekend in Maryland along the Chesapeake Bay shore that my friends and I had dubbed "Rowboat Hell" weekend. It was, Shave declared, the funniest trip ever. Most of us were 18. Some of us occasionally consumed various legal and not-so-legal things. The parents of one of us had a small vacation house on the bay where they spent most of their weekends. One weekend we decided to pay them a visit. On the way, we pulled into a field thick with tall stalks of corn, parked our cars, and ate a bunch of magic mushrooms. For some reason, I was alone in my little brown Datsun B210, and I was the last to pull out of the field. Unfortunately, I backed into an irrigation ditch. The nose of the car pointed toward the sky. I looked through the windshield, and all I could see was blue and clouds.

Then the mushrooms kicked in.

It was hot, the sun was brilliant enough to power through the haze, and I was stuck in the middle of a cornfield. I listened to the cicadas hum for a while and wandered around my car on an outrageous mushroom trip. Finally, an old farmer driving a big green tractor appeared. He wagged his head from on high, the sun throbbing behind him, and studied this idiot with the wild eyes who looked as though he was 12 years old.

"You need a tow?"

I finally arrived, to the stolid family and their sturdy friends and a pageant of teenage freaks willowing their way around the property. Shave remained in a hammock for much of the day. My friend Kubi and I captained a rowboat into the bay and drifted onto some rocks. We were tremendously high and couldn't figure out how to use the oars to escape from this Rowboat Hell. We'd work the oars halfheartedly and laugh and then look up and say, "We're still here." Then we'd repeat the scenario. This went on for a long time.

At dinner that night, I was certain the adults would appreciate my Dead Kennedys and Black Flag albums. Guess what? They didn't.

Kubi, a ridiculously long and lanky lad, spent the next day with a daisy behind his ear. When he water-skied, the flower stayed in place. I assured the patriarch of the family that I knew how to sail and took their Sunfish out on the bay. I could sail with the wind behind me, no problemo. But when I tried to return to the dock, which meant sailing into the wind, I flipped the boat, over and over again. The patriarch had to rig up his big sailboat and rescue me. I was all grins. He wasn't.

"Rowboat Hell" weekend had happened more than twenty years ago, yet it remained vivid as Shave and I e-mailed about it. I felt like the same fledgling fool, but now I probably was about the same age as the sailboat-piloting patriarch. We'd played that summer, that short shower of pixie dust bridging the conclusion of one memorable era—high school—with the dawn of something bewildering and novel, something sneaking into adulthood. At some point later, I unwittingly and without ceremony fully merged with the world I previously, and not that long ago, envisioned as an entirely separate place, full of framed family photos on office desks and two-glass-of-wine dinner parties, tax forms and urologists and a studied and sober appreciation of the splendors of Verdi.

So I was e-mailing with Shave, and the usual Haunted Middle Age musings ghosted my brain: Youth is wasted on the young; aging is bittersweet; yada yada yada. Then one pleasant, nonwistful thought drifted through my mind, something divorced entirely from melancholy: I was 40 and having much more sex than I'd ever had before.

So there, puckish youth!

Nyah nyah nyah nyah nyah.

Later in the day, though, I resolved that now was not the time to wallow in irrational exuberance. The night before, Annie had acknowledged boredom. This was not good. I went to Barnes & Noble and bought *The Complete Idiot's Guide to Tantric Sex*. By the time I arrived home, I was feeling much better, but vestiges of sickness lingered, so that night I took a maximum-strength herbal energy pill, one for the good ol' libido. Joni, too, had improved, but her recovery was attributable largely to a comment she had made the previous night. Her fever had been spiking, then settling, then rising again. She was lethargic but not floored with flu symptoms. In an attempt to figure out what was going on, I'd asked, "Joni, does your throat hurt?"

She'd responded: "Only when I swallow, Daddy."

The next day the doctor ran a test, and yep, Joni had strep throat.

Annie and I stayed up late poking around on the Internet. At 11 p.m., we still hadn't even touched each other. When we finally did, Annie looked exhausted, and while my brain was zinging from the pill, my body was shutting down.

"What do you want to do?" asked Annie, stifling a yawn.

"I don't know," I answered. "What do YOU want to do?"

Said Annie: "Are we in seventh grade?"

We talked for a while; then she said: "I like 9:30 sex."

"It's a sexier hour than eleven," I said.

WE BOTH awoke to laughter. Ginger, who along with Joni had crept into our bed in the middle of the night, was giggling in her sleep. What would I have paid to crawl inside her head and seen the sassy pig? The silly princess? The bespectacled octopus?

"Mama, did you know that elephants are not mammals?" said Ginger a few hours later as we drove to a trail near Boulder for a hike (mountain lions be damned).

"Really?" said Annie. "What are they?"

"Elephants, Mama, elephants."

Our resident zoologist brought along her net, which she called her fishing rod. Almost immediately, Joni started climbing big boulders, because that's her favorite thing to do. We pressed ahead. At one point I looked back to see Joni hanging her head.

She "walked," but each step covered no more than two inches of ground. It was well shy of a shuffle. She advanced at the pace of an ant. This was Joni's way of saying: "I'm extremely bored."

"Don't forget, Joni," I shouted to her. "Troll will happen up ahead!"

"Yay," she chirped, switching instantly from ant to cheetah.

Soon we found a grassy area in a pine forest and commenced troll, which ended abruptly when Ginger fell and planted her hand in a prickly-pear cactus. She didn't cry, not even with a hand full of needles.

"You're so brave, Ginger!" I said.

"I know, Daddy."

It was a long day of physical activity and child rearing, and Annie and I could have gone to bed early—"nighty night, hon"—but we knew the frolics would not be over until they turned erotic. So on the drive home, we decided to play one of our favorite games, "daylight savings time," during which Annie rushes around the house moving clocks forward an hour before Ginger notices. A cruel trick, possibly, but we had sex to accomplish, and we were spent. We shepherded the girls into their rooms after a wee bit of book reading and storytelling. We invoked the sex sanctuary, blasting the heater, pumping the incense, and igniting the candles. We showered, sucked down beer and seltzer water, and read for a while, Annie about yoga and me, I had hoped, the new Tantric sex book. But I had spent many, many hours reading books about sex, not for my job but for the marathon. I previously had dug into the Tantric book, and a few things stuck with me, but soon it all started to blur together with the other dozen or more books I already had finished. I stared at it, its daunting textbookness, and couldn't muster the energy to crack the cover. So I leafed through magazines.

Wearing sexy black lingerie, Annie broke out the year-old

massage kit and retrieved a feather and some edible powder. She accidentally spilled powder all over herself, and we both laughed a bit about the sudden storm of sex dust.

"We're like warriors or something," said Annie. "We've got our arsenal."

"Or artisans," I countered. "We've got our tools."

"Lie back, carpenter," said Annie, holding up the feather, as WFMU music filled the room with vibe. I removed Thurston Howell III and my "sexy" pajamas. "I've got a new tool. Although, it's actually an old tool: a birthday present from last year. Which reminds me," and here she singsonged the phrase "My birthday," a style of speech, the singsong, she rarely unleashed, reserving it largely, year after year, for the words "my birthday."

The feather seemed corny, and at first it was, but then the sensation ripened into something nice. It grew sensuous. I closed my eyes and let her surprise me with new feelings, stirrings somewhere between a tickle and a caress.

"Your turn," I said.

Annie held out the feather, then launched herself to the bed. Her fully exposed body, an extravaganza of hot flesh, said: *Bring it on, baby.*

"Much better than expected. Cool," she said after a few minutes of feathering.

Then, after a solid twenty minutes of feathering, we consummated the day's erotic event. Thanks largely, I think, to two months of routinely spending ninety minutes in a sweltering room and stretching, I felt as limber as a 13-year-old Romanian specialist in the uneven bars. Well, OK. More like a middle-aged guy who recently revisited his hamstrings. But still.

"The feather," said Annie after we'd slipped under the covers. "I'm not so sure we would have used it three months ago. We've actually had the feather for a year."

"Without the sex adventure, I think it's safe to assume it still would be in its box."

WEEK 9, I felt, was an important milestone. Play had been bubbling, but we'd finally consciously hugged it. Our blossoming poise with communication, I thought, had brought us closer and helped leaven the sex. When we fought, we didn't stew for long. Good sex depended on many things—mutual attraction, energy, time, and much more—but communication had to be foundational, a broad, strong base for the rest of it. We'd talked our way out of anger and into lovemaking. We'd talked about our bedroom likes and complaints. We'd made each other laugh, we'd voiced and explored our dreams, we'd talked and talked and talked, and then we'd talked some more.

11

The First Move

The days were lengthening. Slowly, the tundra thawed. In the morning, while still in bed, I stared through the window and smiled. I was happy.

"We're now entering the big 10," said Annie. "We're well past the halfway point. I think we're going to do it."

"I feel strong," I said. "Before we started, though, I wasn't so sure."

We'd coupled the sex—a physical workout in itself—with an abundance of exercise: lots of yoga for Annie, weight lifting, yoga, and running for me, and hiking for both of us. I'd long been addicted to jogging, but now I felt the same compulsiveness about yoga. Renewed youth raced through my body. I could bend and maneuver my limbs as I hadn't done for years. I lost a few pounds, too, and Annie shed more. At this point, she was down five pounds from her premarathon weight. Neither of us believed the sex itself had much to do with the weight loss, but our diets hadn't changed much. My dinners might have been slightly less caloric than before, but the difference, I think, was negligible. What siphoned away the weight, without a doubt, was our mutual dedication to our formerly neglected bodies. The sex inspired Annie to introduce yoga into our lives, which strengthened our torsos and limbs and energized us for the daily sex, which prodded us to honor the yoga and eat healthy, and so on. A most lovely cycle.

Now, however, was no time to start coasting. We still had about five weeks to go, which in the context of daily sex did not place us squarely on good ol' easy street. So while Annie took the girls to a neighborhood park on this spectacular day, I stayed home, opened the windows, and not only cracked open the *Idiot's Guide to Tantric Sex* but finished it, hoping to find something fresh to invigorate the evening's romp. Soon Annie called to say they were done playing, so I hopped on my four-foot skateboard and rolled into the park. In the distance, all by herself, was my Joni, her pink helmet bobbling around on her little blonde head, her legs pumping the pedals of her pink bike with the white basket as fast as she could go, her face in the grip of a huge grin.

"I'm all by myself, Daddy!" she exclaimed, working to catch her breath. "Mommy is way back there," and she pointed way back there, where her mommy and Ginger indeed were plugging along.

We played troll, we climbed on playground equipment, we all got on the skateboard at once and rolled down the tundra's tiny hills—a family of vigorous little elves, brimming with youthful zip and fine fettle. We squeezed in as much frolic as we could before Vicki the babysitter arrived.

Then Annie and I motored off to the coffee shop where they played music from my 1980s youth, like "Riding on the Metro" and "Tainted Love." Everything breezed along splendidly. Annie smiled as she wrote in her journal. I felt bouncy. Spring was coming, and I sat in a room full of people smoking their defiant little lungs out. I could have broken out into an aria (although I probably would have started coughing, given the tobacco clouds). I went to the graffiti-covered bathroom to take a leak, and everything changed.

The room began to turn. I placed my hands on the wall to remain upright. I closed my eyes, and when I opened them again everything remained in motion, only the whole room now was sort of cockeyed, too. I worried that I would collapse. Then the spinning slowed like a merry-go-round toward the end of its run. It skidded. It stopped. I stood up straight, looking around for signs of wheeling or tilting. Nothing. The room had righted itself; the ride ended. *That was fucked up,* I thought as I left the bathroom. *Really fucked up.*

I told Annie about it as we drove back to the house.

"That sounds really fucked up," she said.

The incident worried Annie into the evening, and that night she gave me a long, earnest foot massage while wearing a new sexy top I bought her at Target, a purchase that, I think, finally nudged our financial commitment to the Minneapolis corporation out of the realm of mere "loyal customers" to "serious investors" or even "takeover specialists."

That frilly top cinched it for them, said the gravelly voiced chairman of the board when the chief financial officer presented him with evidence of the transaction, first thing in the morning. *Set up a meeting between the board and these Browns from Denver.*

After the massage, Annie hovered above me, just rubbing my arm. I always made the first move, but tonight, she seemed ready to launch the inaugural erotic salvo. The idea that she might kickstart the session tantalized. I waited.

Nothing.

I said, "Are you going to make the first move?"

"Uh, this is embarrassing," said Annie. She sat down. "I've become used to you making the first move. It's like I don't know how to do it."

"Hey, no biggie," I said. "It's never too late to start."

"That's a pretty funny idea isn't it—the 'first move,'" said Annie. "It sounds so teenage."

"And very Seinfeld," I added.

"Why are we still even involved with such a thing?"

"A habit, I guess."

"Well, we've been breaking habits for sixty-four days now, and I get a charge every time one shatters on the floor," she said.

"To many of our old habits, I say bon voyage," I said. "Some habits aren't so bad. Like my habit for fish and chips in pubs."

"Not the healthiest of habits," said Annie, smiling. "But not one worth breaking, either."

"But to return to your point, I can't think of a single sex habit I'm sad to see fade away."

Tentatively, Annie reached over and stroked my chest with her fingers.

"I think you're making the first move," I whispered. She grinned.

"Lie back," she said, pressing me down with her hands. "Let me give this whole 'first move' thing a whirl. I'm awfully rusty."

"So far, so great," I said. She kept pressing me down, then climbed on top and began kissing me, a first move that led to a long, passionate session.

And then it was my turn to be embarrassed. Annie always seemed to respond with great enthusiasm to neck and ear nibbles. Usually, I kept my explorations to the lobe. This time, however, I went from nibbles and gentle breathings to tongue swabbings. After we finished, she put the kibosh on the tongue excavations.

"It really reminds me of awkward teenage gropings," she said. "When you do that, I'm brought back to high school and inexperienced guys in parking lots."

And you know, whenever I tongued her ear I felt similarly. As if I was 16 again. Not in a good way.

The shared chagrin pleases me, in retrospect. Before the sexcapade, I think neither of us would have announced our criticisms; they would have dwelled like demons, somewhere abysmal and dark and malignant. I also believe that before the sex experiment, if Annie had complained about the ear swabbing, or if I had waited for her to make the move, we would have wallowed in embarrassment and recoiled from roaring ahead with sex.

ANNIE SAID it started with me moaning. I just remember lurching up in bed at 5 a.m. and opening my eyes and feeling as if I was back on the merry-go-round, now spinning at a hundred miles per hour, on the deck of a cruise ship in the middle of a storm, with everything in my vision tilted, in double and triple, and appearing in the manner of a Cubist painting. I could not stand up, so I dropped to the floor and crawled to the bathroom. Even that was difficult. I draped myself over the toilet and commenced vomiting. I'd had food poisoning several times before. One time, I became so sick from eating a bum oyster in Florida that I lost fifteen pounds in two days. But this was much worse. I remained clasped over the toilet bowl or curled up on the bathroom floor. I shivered and my teeth chattered, but sweat gushed out of me. The nausea was so intense, so relentless—cruel, really—that I wept. Annie told me later I repeatedly screamed "Make it stop!" She talked with our physician and with a close friend in Florida, an emergency room doctor who had come to our aid many times. He ordered me to the hospital and gave Annie a list of medications they should prescribe for me. Our Colorado doctor, too, urged me to the hospital. Instead, I went back to bed and fell asleep. The very idea of getting into the car, going on a drive, and sitting in a hospital seemed obscene, impossible, absurd.

Meanwhile, Annie did her best to shield the girls from my spooky caterwauling. She called Ginger's preschool and begged the director to admit Ginger for the day—Ginger usually didn't go to school on Mondays. Then she called the mom of one of Joni's friends and took Joni to her house before school. By 8:30 a.m., both girls were away from Abominable Daddy.

A few hours later I was sitting in the emergency room. Talking demanded too much exertion. Only one thing seemed to anchor me, and it wasn't something I sought; it just invaded my brain and decamped for hours:

> *Hare Krishna, Hare Krishna*
> *Krishna Krishna, Hare Hare*
> *Hare Rama, Hare Rama*
> *Rama Rama, Hare Hare*

Namaste, Annie. She had a yoga CD, which she played constantly, including during our drive to the hospital. Prominent was the Hare Krishna mantra.

After hours of sitting while bent at the waist and hearing—in my head—the Hare Krishna chant, I finally saw the doctor. I mentioned that the week before, when I was sick with Joni, I had "self-medicated" with leftover antibiotics.

"Let me ask you something," she said. "What do you do for a living?"

"I'm a reporter," I replied, thinking she'd say, "Wow what an interesting job! Do you have a 'beat'? Have you ever interviewed a mobster? The president?"

Instead: "OK, so you're not a doctor. But you're diagnosing yourself and medicating yourself. What's up?"

Startled, I replied, "Well, there's this thing called the Internet, that comes with this other thing called Google. I combined them and I came up with a plan of attack—"

"Right," she said. "And your bright idea is probably the reason for all of this vertigo and vomiting."

She prescribed three things, and we went home. The girls, who had been exposed to Insane Monster Dad in the morning, seemed relieved that I wasn't sounding like an alternately furious and sad werewolf. We put the girls to bed, and I grabbed a shower and then slid between our sheets. Sex? It seemed repellent. The idea of rocking back and forth terrorized me—what if it sparked a new round of vertigo? And then, of course, there was the whole "I-emptied-my-guts-into-a-toilet-today" thing. I was hoarse from vomiting, weak from vomiting, sore from vomiting. I was dizzy. Sex?

And then I considered the Heisman Trophy.

If I actually have sex tonight, I thought, *then I rule. No guy, ever, has been as sick as this and actually had intercourse. Vertigo sex? Never happened. Ever.*

When Annie came to the bed, I said, "You ready?"

She nodded. "Day 65."

It was one of the quickest quickies on record. I'm not sure the incident offered even a crumb of pleasure to either Annie or me. The session was worthwhile only in the sense that it sealed another day in the procession. Something to repeat someday? No. Something to forget. I already have.

"I'VE RARELY been as scared as I was yesterday," Annie said in the morning. "It really sank in when I noticed the whites of your knuckles as you gripped the toilet seat. That, to me, said you thought you were moving."

"I really felt as though I was on a sinister merry-go-round ride," I said.

"But you managed to have sex."

I beamed. Old Dependable had charged through the vertigo and risen. The office, on the other hand, would have to wait. Vertigo hid while I slept, but I still was dizzy, and I feared driving to work. Driving and vertigo didn't mix. I sat in bed all day with my computer and did not step outside. I wasted far too much time lost in online real-estate porn. The searches weren't in Burlington, Baltimore, or Boston. I was house hunting in Colorado.

"Great kitchen but no yard."

"Lovely yard but busy street."

"Amazing house but too deep in the mountains."

My mom called, worried about my hospital visit.

"I've been so upset," she said. "I want you to get completely checked out. Who knows what's wrong? Maybe it's more than just this vertigo thing. You know, Aunt Barb had that once, and it lasted for a long time. She had to get on medication for a while. She still gets dizzy sometimes. I want you to see a doctor about this."

"I will, Mom."

"Maybe it's this whole sex thing," she said. "Maybe it's just too much for your body. Are you still doing it?"

Again.

"Yes, Mom. Still doing it. I don't think that's got anything to do with it."

"Well, I want you to take care of yourself, honey. Dad and I are worried about you."

Dad picked up the phone from another room.

"You're OK, right?"

"Yeah, Dad. No problemo."

"How's the marathon going?"

At 9:40 that night, I consciously reflected upon how *little* interest I had in sex.

To be specific, I had none.

I wanted to lie under the covers and read, then turn off the light, then go to sleep, in that order. Earlier in the evening I had experienced another bout of vertigo, a round of dizziness mercifully short and mild, but nevertheless it mangled my nerves and wounded my libido.

"You know what I thought about a lot during yoga tonight?" said Annie later after examining a few houses online with me. "This notion I encountered in a Baron Baptiste book. He says that instead of focusing on 'nowhere,' you instead should simply submit to 'now here!' Get it? 'Now here!'"

"Got it," I replied absently, still mired in my "maybe there!" real-estate stupor.

She cocked her head. "Do you notice anything different?" she asked.

"Your hair?"

"My eyebrows!" she exclaimed. "I asked Michelle, my waxer, about them today, and she was so excited she nearly fell over. She was like, 'Yes! I've been so wanting to wax your eyebrows!' Kinda embarrassing, really. Were they that bad?"

"I never noticed anything bad about your eyebrows."

"Anyway, I love my new eyebrows," she said. "I look as if I'm perpetually alert, but that's OK. It makes up for all of the sleep I've been losing."

And then Annie revealed her freshly plucked Brazilian. We played a WFMU show, and she held out, as if on a platter, the silver bullet with its new batteries. The thing had puttered to a stop during an earlier session.

"The return of the bullet," I exclaimed. "Well hello, old friend."

"You know the batteries for that bullet cost $11.57?" Annie said after we'd finished. "But then I thought to myself, 'What's an easy orgasm worth?'"

I CALLED in sick at work the next day, and Annie and I managed a quickie again while the girls were in school. But I made it into the office on day 68 of sexual excess, my first visit to the newsroom since the Demonic Carnival. People seemed concerned. When I explained the scope and depth of the horrors that had visited me, one of my editors urged me to turn around and go home. I stayed put but didn't accomplish much. I was feeling especially gentle.

Later, on the drive home, I talked with my brother and, as usual, his voice boosted my spirits. That voice—like my mom's and dad's—is a chute leading me straight to another place; to a country road lined with high, root-gnarled banks that Dad had dubbed "the spooky place," and where he would stop the car and try to scare Mike and me as we laughed wildly; to Mom bodysurfing with us for hours at the Jersey Shore; to walking with Grandma to the bakery to pick up white, string-tied boxes of Danish pastry, doughnuts, and crumb buns. I've undoubtedly idealized my childhood, and the foundation of so many of my Colorado struggles could lie in the selective memories that, pieced together, constitute my idea of home. But then again, I had Annie and two perfect daughters, a job, enough money to buy a house. Couldn't I just build my own home? Wasn't home simply us?

Increasingly, I was beginning to understand that it was. And I don't think it's out of line to credit the marathon, at least in part, with this blossoming realization. The lovemaking had brought Annie and me together in more ways than one.

As soon as I arrived back at the shed, well before Annie and the girls were to appear, I made tuna casserole for the girls, vacuumed the entire house, straightened up all the rooms, and lit incense all around. For no good reason, we were ten weeks into the marathon, yet we still had not hired a housecleaner—a curious oversight given the high regard in which Annie held housekeepers (you may remember that the word itself, "housecleaner," in Annie's opinion, is the "sexiest word in the world").

You are pleading for details: *Why? All it takes is a phone call and a modest investment. What gives?*

I wish there were some funny story to explain it, some episode involving a babushka-wearing Russian émigré, a bucket of beet juice, and a pet wolf. But the real story is awfully pedestrian.

Although we sometimes remembered that we'd like to hire a housekeeper, our days were so crammed with child rearing, work, planning for trips, having sex, and so on, that we never got around to picking up the phone and making a few calls. (Months after the marathon, though, we finally did and arranged for a housecleaner to come once a month.)

On this particular day I recalled Annie's appetite for professional housecleaning, and I figured that coming home to a clean, orderly home would warm her heart.

It did, and a few hours later we were sitting on the bed, kissing.

"You want to try a basic Tantric position, where I enter you while we're sitting, with our legs wrapped around each other?"

"Something you picked up from your *Idiot's* book?" asked Annie.

"They're awfully fond of it in the book," I said. "It's like the foundation position, or something."

We arranged ourselves into the position, placed our foreheads together, and embraced. Her breath was sweet and warm, gently fogging my cheek as we rocked with me inside, my legs beneath hers, our chests and cheeks together.

"Slow and easy, for sure," I whispered.

"Very."

We sat there doing it extremely slow and easy for five minutes or so.

"So this is Tantric," I whispered.

"I guess."

Another few minutes.

"Maybe I need to read the book more closely," I offered.

"I think it's like yoga, or something," said Annie. "You've got to practice a lot to really get it."

"Wanna stop just practicing?"

ON DAY 69 it would have made sense to honor this raunchiest of numbers, this harlot of a digit. Instead, we dismissed this classic position, one that never did much for us, and made love in the cold, unfinished basement while Ginger sat on our bed upstairs watching *The Wiggles.*

I had taken Joni to school. She'd run up to the school door as always, making the "I love you" sign-language gesture behind her, and when I got home, I cranked up the basement space heater and installed Ginger on the bed for her promised visit with *The Wiggles.* Then Annie and I had descended into the concrete-floored space of must and dust and biting chill despite the heater.

Two years earlier, in Baltimore, we had packed a lot of stuff in cardboard boxes and deposited most of them in the Stapleton basement, where they still sat stacked, piled, jumbled, and scattered. Why unpack, we reasoned, when we'll be moving again soon? Wedged between the boxes was an upholstered daybed that had belonged to Annie's deceased grandmother (the one for whose benefit we'd maintained separate phone numbers while living together in Minneapolis). Covering the daybed were a thin sheet and a skimpy blanket. Annie undressed and slipped under the blanket. I stripped and nestled in beside her, shivering. We embraced and hugged. We caressed each other until heat of a different order warmed us.

Afterward, we laughed as we quickly dressed in the frosty room, surrounded by relics of our Baltimore life and feeling illicit, daring. Younger.

Later in the day, Annie e-mailed me about "intense guilt" she was feeling about several things.

"I had to bail on using Vicki as a babysitter a few times this year, so I asked her to babysit for a bit today, thinking I'd do something constructive. Like work. But instead I drove around the city running errands. ERRANDS! While we pay a babysitter by the hour. Not good. One of them—get this—was to that hipster sex store you went to, with the g-spot things and the toys. You know what? I was underwhelmed. And I think I know why: I'm sexed-out. The place just seemed redundant. Anyway, I hope you don't mind my using the babysitter while I ran ERRANDS! ILYSM!"

I responded: "Of COURSE I don't mind! Don't feel guilty. You're constantly trying to coordinate things, you're constantly organizing. Classic about being 'sexed-out'! ILYSM!" There's that sappy acronym again. (Sorry, hipsters! I apologize, lads!)

EARLY IN the marathon, Annie and I had decided to spend a night alone in a state park about an hour and a half away, if the nanny, who at the time had yet to watch our kids, worked out. We'd booked a yurt, a conical, canvas-sided structure, and because the nanny excelled, we kept the reservation. When we'd stayed in the same yurt, about four thousand feet higher in elevation than Denver, almost exactly one year earlier, we'd woken up to a foot and a half of new snow and a blinding blizzard. The minivan, with the girls in back, almost didn't make it home. This time the weather prophets weren't calling for trouble, but we elected to take the all-wheel-drive Subaru, just in case.

As dusk approached, we arrived at the yurt, opened a bottle of French wine that we'd bought years ago in Baltimore, unwrapped the cheese Annie had purchased for us at a jewel of a cheese shop in Denver, and gorged on Gouda, French bread, and wine. Then we trudged up a snow-covered country road to a place famous for spectacular views of the Continental Divide. We couldn't see the Divide—gray cloaked everything, and it was snowing—but the walk inspired: enormous evergreens with snow-laden boughs; ravens perched on branches caw-caw-cawing; the sky swiftly melting from gray to navy blue to starless black.

Back at the yurt we sat around for a while, drinking and eating. Annie and I then pulled the mattress from the timber-framed bottom bunk onto the floor and clambered into bed.

"Check it out," said Annie. "We've got a lot of time here. With nothing to do, really. Other than have sex."

"We could be like those swinger types," I said. "Do it for hours."

"Even a hundred minutes. That would be cool," said Annie.

We'd never spent an entire night, much less a whole weekend, lost in carnal pleasure. And here we were, alone in a warm yurt on a cold mountain evening, with little more around us than snow and trees, stars and coyotes. There was nothing to disturb an extended erotic junket, no Netflix, bedtimes, or books.

We slipped beneath the covers, pulling the blankets to our necks to stay warm.

"All-night sex?" I whispered.

"Seems silly, I guess, don't you think?" said Annie. "Let's not time what we do. Let's just do."

We pressed our bodies together for heat, more heat, and as our blanket holster warmed, so did everything else.

12

The Reading of the Lists

We woke up staring at snow and fog drifting across the skylight. Another morning somewhere other than in the little house on the plains. I scampered across the yurt's frigid floor to the tin coffeepot, into which I poured cold espresso we had brewed at home. I placed the coffeepot on the stove's hot surface, and we waited twenty minutes for the espresso to heat. Then on went the silk long underwear, winter coats, and boots, and soon we walked outside into a spectacular winter landscape of weightless snow and clearing skies and arresting views of distant mountains caked with powder. We walked for about an hour, talking nonstop, exchanging exclamations about Colorado's wonders and marvels, its richness of wilderness and wildlife.

Back at the yurt we hung our clothes by the heater and slipped under the covers again.

"Ch-, ch-, chilly," chattered Annie, whom I think of as a human furnace; for Annie to complain of cold, it had to be at least verging on Arctic. She embraced me for warmth. As we stared up at the skylight, she asked, "Does it get any better than this?"

I turned to her—what you could describe as "making the first move"—and said, "Yes."

By the time we'd finished, the room—or at least the tiny hollow we'd made for ourselves under the blankets—felt desert hot.

"IT'S LIKE I'm living a cruel joke," said Annie the next day, back at the house. Joni had recovered from strep throat the week before, we thought.

"It can't be strep throat again," said her doctor earlier that morning, in his office. "But what the heck. I'll test her again."

Strep throat.

"Here's my day," wrote Annie in an e-mail. "There was the waiting room full of sick kids with toys they have slobbered and goobered over, where we waited for 40 minutes. Then the visit with the doctor, then the drive to the pharmacy area of the grocery store, only to be told it would take them 45 minutes. We then drove to the office to drop off a laminating machine, then returned to pick up the prescription, only to be told our information 'wasn't in the computer,' even though we'd been there less than 10 days before for the same prescription. So we waited for another 20 minutes. Then we spent nearly 40 minutes driving to deliver our taxes to the accountant. We got lost in the horror of suburban Denver, per usual. Both girls fell asleep in the minivan. On the way home I decided to stop at Target to get Joni a new board game, and we selected Clue. We got home and Joni ascended the stairs to our room, where she curled up in a ball and remained for the duration of the day. When she woke up, I played Clue with her, and she and Ginger watched PBS, or as they call it, 'PBSKIDSDOTORG.'"

Annie's bleak e-mail compelled me to walk across the spring tundra to the yoga studio near my office. I bought her a blue hoodie with Buddha on the front, and a thick bracelet emblazoned with words in Sanskrit. Real Indian incense, too. When I arrived home, Annie was sweating in the kitchen: boiling pasta, stirring a homemade sauce, baking a loaf of Italian bread she'd smeared with fresh garlic, salt, and olive oil. Bottles and jars, dishes and utensils mounded around Annie as she moved through the kitchen's steam. The vacuum cleaner was out—she obviously had run that over the carpet. The girls had scattered the pieces of several puzzles on the floor. Annie looked overwhelmed.

"Hi, darling!" she said when I stepped inside.

The girls ran to me: "Daddy! Daddy! Daddy!"

Holding the bag of surprises, I walked toward Annie.

"Daddy, Daddy, what's in the bag? Something for me?" asked Ginger.

"Yeah, Daddy, what's in there?" said Joni coyly.

"Sorry, girls," I said, dropping the bag on the counter, stepping into the kitchen, embracing Annie, and giving her a kiss. I grabbed the bag and handed it to Annie.

"For me?"

"Yes. You needed presents today."

"But my birthday isn't here yet, although it's close."

"I know all about your birthday, and this has nothing to do with it. Just presents for the heck of it."

I reached into the bag and first bestowed upon her the hoodie, then the rest of the gifts. She hugged me, kissed me, and placed the bracelet on her wrist immediately. Then she stripped off her sweater and slipped into the hoodie. The girls smiled and oohed, but there was a hesitation behind their reaction that nearly screamed: *You're serious? Nothing for us?* It pleased me that I'd successfully applied something I'd learned during the sex journey: Presents, even tiny ones like the Hanky-Panky thong and inexpensive Target lingerie, helped salvage days that otherwise were a wash. And they improved days that already were good.

Buoyed, Annie left for yoga while Ginger nearly vibrated with energy, walking around the house in the jerky manner of a wooden soldier and talking about "poopy in your eye" and "pee

pee" and so on. Joni appeared listless and weak. We read and played games, the girls went to bed, and then I prepared for what was billed as a special night.

At Annie's suggestion weeks earlier, and based on something a magazine had recommended for couples, we agreed to read aloud the things we love about each other. After she was home and showered, we sat side by side on the bed, chatting about our days, our love lists on our laps.

"I love your adventurousness," I told her, once we'd decided to start the Reading of the Lists. "That's number one. You don't shrink from challenges. You leap toward them. I love that."

Tears again glazed her eyes, only this time they came from a reservoir located somewhere other than the one in which sadness dwells. She smiled as she cried.

"I love when your hair goes crazy," she said. "I love that you don't care what people think, and I love how it looks."

I didn't weep, but I suddenly felt awfully warm.

"OK, my next one is related to my first," I said. "I love your courage. You're the bravest person I know. A brave woman, a brave mother, a brave daughter. Brave in so many ways. Courageous."

"I love how you can calm down Ginger," said Annie. "You're the master."

"I love your oven body," I said. "You're never cold!"

"I love your silliness," she said.

And so it went. For nearly half an hour, we regaled each other with compliments. With each bouquet tossed my way, I felt a little bit more confident and light.

"Again, I've got to say it," said Annie. "It's been fourteen years, and we're just now doing this? I can't wait to do it again. I feel so good right now."

I did too. I never had forced my mind for such an extended period of time upon the subject of Annie's abundant sweetnesses. The longer I spent excavating—"Oh yeah, I love her naughty augh," or "I can't forget about her magical childbirths"—the more I said to myself: *I'm a lucky man.*

I went downstairs for a few minutes, and when I returned, Annie was in her chartreuse Victoria's Secret lingerie. We embraced and kissed slowly, luxuriously.

"Hey, you still using the bullet?" I asked, and without hesitating she pivoted to her bedside table, withdrew the bullet, and pressed it to herself—all in one swift balletic move. We let the currents carry us away, and then curled up under the covers and fell toward sleep.

"I want to do that again," mumbled Annie as we kissed good night. "The whole compliment thing? It was one of my favorite things ever."

"YOU MADE it through, right?" asked my doctor a few days later, during a sex-marathon checkup. "You had sex."

"Yup."

She released a dramatic "whew."

"I was so worried that would destroy your quest," she said. "I even called the ER doctor when you were in there and told her to prescribe every last thing you needed to get you healthy fast. I told her you needed to have sex."

Now *that's* a doctor!

She poked the light tool in my ear. "Uh, you aren't going into the mountains, or flying, anytime soon, are you?"

"Nope, although I've been in the mountains since the vertigo."

"You're lucky," she said. "Your eardrum is full of fluid. I can see it bulging. It could have exploded."

Exploded? What sort of damage exactly, I wondered, would an eardrum explosion cause? Would it take my head with it? Flesh shrapnel? I shuffled out of there to my office, where I shambled around all day like a 90-year-old, marking every few minutes with

a generous yawn. When I got home, I examined the three medica
tions I was taking and Googled them. One of them had the sid
effect of "exhaustion."

Goodie, I thought.

Later, Annie put on her orange Hanky-Panky thong and a lin
gerie top.

"Do you know what happens the instant you enter me every
day?" she asked as we danced together under the sheets. "The
image of the number, as written in big Broadway lightbulbs, ap
pears in my head."

"You saw that tonight?" I said, my rocking stilled, poise
above her.

"Yes," she said. "I saw a bright seventy-four."

I INTERVIEWED a professor about "male performance" in the
context of Viagra, how performance and masculinity are closely
linked. Which forced me to consider my year to date—seventy-fou
straight days of performance. In many ways, performance defined
who I had become. Most of my friends, colleagues, and family
members knew about the project, and many of my exchanges with
them continued to verge on the nudge-nudge, wink-wink.

"How's it holding 'up'?"

"Everything still working?"

"You finding it 'hard'?"

I decided to buy Annie a bouquet of flowers—a performance
of a related but much different sort—to mark day 75. I entered
the house, and there she was again, in the kitchen, working hard
with the kids underfoot. I held the flowers aloft, and her whole
face smiled as I approached. She grabbed a vase, filled it with
water, trimmed the stems, and plunged the bouquet into the vase

"I'm such a sucker for flowers. They melt my heart. And it's
not even my birthday. Yet."

How, after fourteen years, had I not yet understood that flowers melt her heart? Her response quickened my spirits. A few hours later I emerged from the shower to find Annie wearing her fancy French lingerie, lying on her stomach, and waiting for a massage. Just beholding the thong framing her backside set off fireworks in my groin. I brought my hands to her flesh, and she moaned.

"Oooh, yeah," she said. "My shoulder. Definitely my shoulder. It's killing me."

I worked it until my hands ached, my gaze fixed on her butt. Then she flopped onto her back, and the lacy bra somehow improved the spectacle of her soft breasts. I finished with a massive foot-massage flourish.

FORTY-EIGHT HOURS and a couple of rounds of sex later, I popped a Cialis and climbed into the shower. We planned to have an afternoon delight in the basement bordello—the cold, cement rectangle sardined with boxes, furniture, and much more—while the kids watched videos. We'd deprived them of all "moving pictures"—our term for television fare—all morning. They were jonesing. With the Cialis coursing through my veins, we planted them before the "moving-picture machine" and trekked downstairs.

"Shivery," said Inferno Annie, wrapping her arms around her body.

"I popped a Cialis about thirty minutes ago," I whispered.

"Thought you'd need a little help?"

"I just wanted to try a full tab. So far, nothing has compared to the Viagra. I swallowed a full serving of that but only halves of the others. I don't want to sell the other ones short."

"What about the whole blindness thing?" asked Annie.

"Hasn't happened yet," I said, looking her up and down—her painted lips, breasts pushing against the long-sleeved patterned top, the swan-white legs descending from a short denim skirt. "Thank God."

I wagged my eyebrows, and she grabbed the hem of her skirt and pulled it up. A thong. Flesh. The rising commenced. Annie collapsed on the daybed, giggly and happy, and I began nibbling her neck. Her perfume held an intoxicating hint of spice and blossom.

"I'm much warmer now," she said. Then she whipped out the bullet. "My Cialis! We'd better hurry. We don't want any little people walking down those steps."

Like the Viagra, the full tablet of Cialis delivered almost reckless erotic energy to my groin. Day 76, done. Day 76, hot.

Blazing sex in a cold basement on a random Saturday, with the kids upstairs watching cartoons and with not much else planned for the day. No swank hotel. No exquisite four-star restaurant. No spa or artisanal chocolates or night at the theater. Just ten minutes of morning sex in a basement.

Simple.

And damn was it good.

As Annie walked up the steps, she singsonged: "My birthday."

13

To Bask on the Island of Our
Own Creation

We'd released an avalanche of flesh pleasures upon our relationship, our small world circumscribed by children and jobs and webbed with meals, hobbies, illnesses, chores, dreams, and much more. Despite fourteen years of sex with each other, Annie and I had begun the marathon as mere acolytes, our catechisms of the flesh conventional, untested, and taken for granted. Twelve weeks into the procession, though, we'd overhauled the manual.

There was a marked improvement.

Exhaustion still haunted us, but no longer did it dictate our erotic lives.

We'd deposed it, stripped it of its powers, handed it a merely ceremonial title. But exiled leaders sometimes return to their homelands, bent upon vengeance and retribution. With eleven weeks down and about three to go, Annie and I knew anything could happen. We remained fixed upon our mission.

IT WAS supposed to snow a foot. We got an inch. But the day was frigid, gray, and windy, and stepping into the 105-degree yoga room was like therapy, mental and physical. Billy kicked my ass.

At one point, he said if anybody had a problem receiving foot massages, raise a hand. I didn't even consider it.

I was glad Joni was awake lying on her bed when I returned. I sat with her for a few moments and tried to close her door on the way out, but she insisted it remain open. Complicating our project a bit, Joni had started demanding that her door remain open at night.

"Are you fading?" I asked Annie after Joni was asleep.

"You want the day's Cliff Notes?" she asked. "I made play dough from scratch, and I made clay from scratch so Ginger could make her own beads. I made two loaves of bread, an Indian cauliflower dish, and braised greens. I packaged up two things to mail, did four loads of laundry, vacuumed once, put toys away four times, and talked to my parents. I tried to do a yoga practice in our bedroom, with a yoga DVD, but Ginger tried to do it with me. At one point, she placed a stuffed animal on my back, then draped a blanket over the stuffed animal, then climbed onto my back. It made me laugh, but needless to say, I didn't get much yoga done."

At Annie's urging, I lay down on my stomach, and she draped her body over mine. This was one of the best feelings I'd had in a long time—Annie's kiln body on my back, her breasts pressing into my shoulder blades. So soft and pliant and warm and wonderfully fleshy.

"Mmmm," said Annie after a while. "I'm so comfortable I could easily drift off right now."

"I could sleep too," I said.

Annie rolled off, alarmed. "It's about that time," she said, glancing at the clock. She ran her fingers along my thigh. I caressed her cheek. I cradled her chin in my palm and brought my lips to hers.

"Let's just do it fast," she said. "A quickie."

"OK," I said, subduing a yawn. We rocked together for about ten minutes. Just gentle rocking, a little kissing. And then we were done.

• • •

WE SHARED an uneventful Tuesday, including the sex part, with one exception. The litany of tasks Annie had mentioned the day before stuck with me. There was nothing especially unusual about that sort of afternoon for her, which was stupefying on the face of it, although I rarely inventoried her days like that. The list reminded me of the power of the hug, at least for Annie. So somewhere around lunchtime I walked from the office to my car, drove the six miles to our little house, walked inside, and gave Annie another of those surprise hugs.

"Now *that* was a gift, DJ," she said when we parted. "Thank you, thank you, thank you."

ON WEDNESDAY I spent part of the gray afternoon at New Frontier Media, a publicly traded corporation in Boulder that distributes much of the pornography found on cable television and in hotels. I was there to interview the company's president and to tour the sprawling facility. I entered the "control room," which looked like that darkened chamber with screens everywhere at NASA headquarters—the theater they always show during a shuttle launch. A different kind of liftoff, however, was playing on the screens at New Frontier. In this room, a pair of guys spent their days watching live feeds to New Frontier's different channels, making sure everything was operating smoothly. (I wondered if these guys had special qualifications for a job that could be accurately described as "watching pornography.") This was day 81 of the marathon. I might as well have been watching Jacques Cousteau swimming with giant tortoises. After sex on eighty-one consecutive days, porno stimulated precisely nothing in my brain. Would the porno have aroused me if I hadn't been immersed in our own sex adventure? I thought so.

After the kids were in bed that night, Annie and I traded massages, and I helped her leap into Orgasmland. When her 'gasm was over, I was limp, which was unusual.

"I can fix that," chirped Annie, bringing her palm to my softness. I rallied, but then it drooped.

"Hmm," said Annie professorially. "Interesting." She revisited His Lameship. Eventually her magic triumphed, and we fused but only briefly.

We heard Ginger's door open. We saw our doorknob turn, but the door was locked. I covered myself and Annie opened the door. Ginger shuffled inside, plopped on the end of the bed, and began shrieking. The lights, Mommy and Daddy's wakefulness, the music—we had been listening to WFMU—the medicine she started taking that day for strep throat (yes, Ginger had picked up the infection): Everything conspired to crumble Ginger's delicate little world.

"Sorry, honey," whispered Annie. "I don't think there's any turning back from this one." Annie put out her arms, and Ginger weaved into them, pressing her head to her mother's cheek as Annie lifted her to the bed and then fixed Ginger beneath our covers, placing her head on a pillow. I rose and blew out the candles.

"Oh well," I whispered as I joined them. "Win some, lose some."

"Don't worry, DJ, even if it didn't end the way we wanted, we still did it. We won," she said.

MORE PLODDING days of work and child rearing passed. Sex continued to accumulate. We were nearly to day 90, and I still looked forward to intercourse. In fact, I found that as time passed I anticipated each day's erotic event with *increasing* enthusiasm, like someone who finds a good break and surfs once, three times, a whole week, and then can't imagine life without paddling into the waves every day. By the time Saturday rolled around, marking

he last day of our twelfth week of daily sex, I found myself, as I
ay in bed in the morning, dreaming of the flesh on which I'd be
avishing my attention in just a few hours.

We'd tantalized the girls all week about a big surprise that we'd
be unveiling on this day, a Saturday. First, Vicki came over to
watch them.

"Where's the surprise?" asked Ginger.

"You'll see."

Annie and I then hastened the minivan north to Boulder,
where we had booked a room in a hotel for the night. That was
he surprise: a hotel, with cable television and a pool. The girls
would join us later. Annie and I had always loved hotels. We glad-
lened to cheap chain motels off freeways, we adored quirky old
out-of-the-way motels run by oddball families, we cherished big
esorts and snooty urban boutique hotels. Give us a hotel, any
hotel, and you'll make our day.

"It's fun to be adults," Annie often says after we check in.

The Boulder hotel targeted corporate types, so the room was a
suite with a balcony. The place was exceptionally neat, up a notch
or two from standard motel fare.

Annie turned up the heat in the frigid room. "Just like the sex
len," she said. "Only different." She winked again. "Let's get
naked and have hotel sex."

The heater hadn't yet boosted the room temperature to tropical levels, so we hurried our nude bodies into bed and pulled the
covers to our chins, building sleeves of warmth. We lay on our
sides, entwined. With the covers draping my back, I lifted myself
above Annie, and we savored each other's lips and tongues. I
pressed her breasts together and marveled at the display.

"I love them," I said. "They're perfect."

We had tentatively planned to keep it short—we couldn't wait
o introduce the girls to their "curprise"—but the pleasure of simply being together beckoned us to prolong everything, to sink

into the languor, to bask on the island of our own creation, and that's exactly what we did. Then, panting and still, Annie and I lay under the covers for a few minutes, just staring silently at the ceiling and catching our breath. When we rose, wobbly knees compromised our ability to walk from the bed to the bathroom. Annie stayed in the room as I drove back to Denver to pick up the girls. Both of them turned manic—literally hopping around on one foot—when I revealed the surprise.

We ordered pizza to the room and then went to the pool and splashed around for a bit, a hotel amenity that we rarely escaped no matter the temperature of the acrid, indoor air or the questionable water.

That night, Joni climbed into bed with Annie, and Ginger crept in beside me. We bought the movie *Chicken Little*. Midway through, Ginger said, "I'm tired," and within ten seconds she was snoring. When Ginger's snores became thunderous, we actually had to increase the volume. Joni, too, fell asleep watching the movie.

"This is one of the first things we've done explicitly for the kids since we started the marathon," whispered Annie, propped up with Joni on the bed beside me. "They deserve this, and more. When we're done, let's do something special for them. I feel we've been neglecting them."

"Neglecting?"

"All of the yoga, for example," said Annie. "They aren't used to one of us being absent from dinner so often. The weekends away from them. Again, that's a new one for the girls. Sometimes I think we rush through the bedtime routine so we can climb into the sack together."

"What's interesting is our lives still revolve around them," I whispered back. "We've had all sorts of adventures without them; we're out of the house a little bit more, but still. They are the center. I agree that we should do something special for them, but I'm not feeling guilty. Are you?"

Annie presented a face that I like to think would be familiar to ministers, who during a lifetime of sermons and proclamations about the meaning of life grow accustomed to a certain glow that occasionally lights the faces of parishioners.

"I was feeling guilty," she admitted through a smile. "But when you put it that way, not so much!"

"We're pulling it off," I said. "We're changing our lives, for the better, and not at the expense of the kids. In other words, we didn't have move to an ashram in India, or something, to 'find ourselves.'"

"Yes!" whispered Annie, her face still radiant.

14

Making Love in the Afternoon

ove happens. Yes, it takes nurturing, heat, and light. It demands commitment. It requires certain chemistries. But for lucky people, for whatever combination of factors, love blossoms. It's unconscious: a force, a fire, a spirit. Romance, by contrast, is alert. It's intentional. It has an intelligence. It's a dance, of sorts. Both people in a relationship must consider what pleases their partner; but surprise—something new—claims an important piece of the romance puzzle. So delivering romance is much more complicated than simply referring to a list of likes, picking one, and going for it. In sum, it's magicians' work.

Consider our second date, in Philadelphia.

"I'll pick you up at your house around noon," I said. "We'll sit in the sun and watch the game and talk. Fun?"

"Sounds great to me," she said.

On the way to her house, I bought a bottle of cold champagne and a pint of raspberries.

"Raspberries!" said Annie. "Did I tell you they're one of my favorite foods?"

We pulled into a parking lot so vast it seemed to capture the horizon—we were going to a Philadelphia Phillies game—and we proceeded to drink the entire bottle of champagne, eat all of the berries, laugh, and talk nonstop, while sitting in the car. By the time we entered the stadium, the first five innings were over. This was the date, we both agree, where we thought to ourselves: *This person could be the one.*

My parents understood this, too. They were at the game, seated on the other side of the stadium. We knew that, but what we didn't find out until later was that they had watched us through binoculars.

"You guys talked and laughed the *whole time!*" said my mom when I returned home. Later, after we moved to Minnesota, she told me she knew, simply from watching us in the ballpark, that we would get married.

It was the romance—the spectacular early-summer weather, the raspberries and champagne, the urban excitement, our quips and jokes. The day became a perfect stage for us to dance with each other, and move to melodies known only to the two of us. We had some chemistry, it turned out.

Fourteen years and many, many bottles of champagne later, we woke up in a Boulder hotel room, now with two kids who can thank a Phillies game—among other things—for their existence. We planned to spend the day shepherding the elves around Boulder, so the day didn't present much in the way of romance. But we knew that at the conclusion of this thirteenth week of sex romance awaited us, a simple night out at a restaurant. Alone. We'd hired a babysitter. We would dress to seduce each other. The place was tiny and cozy and renowned.

We'd eaten out with the girls plenty of times during the previous three months. We'd been to restaurants without the kids, but they were in Las Vegas, where we dined with Shave, with my parents, and later with the *Post*'s restaurant critic. Each restaurant was fun and spiced with romance for Annie and me. But none of them turned on romance.

The winds shaking the hotel in the morning were outdone by

the torrent within room 254—Ginger kicking, screaming, hitting the bed, scratching anything that came near her.

"I've got a theory about this," said Annie. "Ginger watched a bunch of cartoons yesterday, and she also was assaulted with commercials. Doesn't this always happen when she engages with media outside of our little controlled universe? All of the TV screwed with her head, with her little spirit. It's like she's a little bit curdled."

The tantrum continued downstairs in the breakfast area, where we ate stiff eggs, chalky potatoes, saccharine French toast, and bacon like reconstituted dust, all of it displayed on silver chafing dishes. I, the Ginger Whisperer, had to remove Ginger from the room at one point and calm her down in a hallway. Nothing made her happy. We milked our time, never mind the portable hurricane. We swam in the pool and soaked in the hot tub, and despite Annie's sensible theory, we squeezed in a few more cartoons before descending upon downtown Boulder for a day of walking, shopping, and eating. We bought a lavender-laced smelling stick for Ginger at a health-food store. The stick, which Ginger hugged like a dollie and called "smelly stick," was supposed to induce "calm." We plowed through samples at Whole Foods ("Free is best!"). We enjoyed coffees and pastries at an elegant coffeehouse, where the baristas thought of themselves as artisans, for good reason. Their espresso drinks were inspirational.

As we pulled off the highway and headed home, I thought the shopping was over, but just before arriving at our neighborhood Annie spotted a drugstore.

"Pull over," she said. "I've got to get something."

She returned minutes later with a pregnancy test.

"You think you're pregnant?" I asked. "What about the birth control?"

"It doesn't always work," she said. "And I have some of the symptoms."

Fifteen minutes later: "I'm not pregnant." She added, "I was pretty excited about the prospect. But very scared, too."

"My feelings are identical."

TWO DAYS later, after an afternoon delight that featured Annie so shrouded in incense that it took some work to find her grinning on the bed (her gleaming smile cut through the smoke), I was sitting cross-legged (criss-cross applesauce) with the kids on the floor and making something with blocks when Joni broke into song, belting out the Simon and Garfunkel hit "Cecilia." She had learned the tune at theater camp, where the teachers had changed the song title to "Ophelia" and altered the lyrics to fit the Shakespeare play *Hamlet*.

A few days later, Annie bought the real song on iTunes, and Joni spent hours listening to it. Annie and Joni researched "Simon and Garfunkel" via Google, so in the morning, facts about the duo spilled from Joni's lips. She couldn't believe that Paul and Art had been friends, then weren't. The shrinking and thinning of Paul Simon's hair amazed her. Joni always bonded with underdogs, so she preferred Garfunkel to Simon. She memorized the original lyrics to "Cecilia." Including the line "making love in the afternoon, with Cecilia, up in my bedroom."

Joni didn't know what "making love" really meant, at least in the context of the song. But it still jarred. I wondered what kids at school told her about the world: about wealth and poverty, black and white, and of course sex. Was she hearing things? Was she questioning the world we'd parceled out to her? She'd entered elementary school exceedingly innocent, a child nursed on stories about faeries and dragons and hobbits living in hollowed-out pumpkins. She'd never heard a racial epithet, never encountered her parents lusting after a fancy car or a mansion, and never seen us do anything romantic except for kissing and embracing. But now she was leaving the cocoon we spun around her, for hours every day. For how long would pure innocence endure?

In another chapter of growing up, Joni had an obvious crush on her theater teacher, a juggling comedian.

"You should see her around him," said Annie. "She literally bats her eyes and acts coy. She can't pull her eyes away from him. And he gets the biggest kick out of her. The guy, I must say, is absolutely hilarious. Just like her mother, she's going to fall for the boys who can make her laugh and laugh and laugh."

"That will be cool as long as those jokesters also are sweet, devoted, successful, gentle, and doting," I said. "Very doting."

"Doting is key," said Annie. "We've become especially skilled at doting. In fact, I'm about to enter an especially sweet doting zone." She paused and then came the singsong: "My birthday."

She added: "First, though, we've got some doting ahead of us tonight."

"Yes indeed," I said. "We've got session of doting number eighty-eight on tap."

On day 89 I didn't head to the office until late in the day because I was spending the evening going to strip clubs—for my job—with an executive from a national strip-club empire based in Denver. I showered in the morning, after the kids were in school, and sped between the sheets to create my sleeve of warmth, my hot pocket. Annie followed right behind me. We hugged and talked, laughed and kissed. Then kissed some more, and then much more. We embraced our inner 14-year-olds and went crazy with kissing, exploring each other's mouths with our tongues, getting a touch more slobbery than usual, letting our lips smoosh as they hadn't in years.

"I've been so horny this morning," she said.

"Why?" I whispered.

"I'm just horny," she said. "No reason I can think of other than horniness."

"That's a new one, isn't it?" I said. "Just random horniness."

"Absolutely," said Annie. "I had no idea that having so much sex would make me hornier. I suspected, in fact, the reverse would happen."

"Sounds like maybe you're becoming sort of 'guy.'"

"You never know," said Annie. "I like being horny. One good thing about being horny during these hundred days is I know I'll get some satisfaction every day."

"That's a plus," I said, leaning over, kissing her, and eventually entering the palace. I had read the day before in a men's magazine that it's good to lean forward when you're inside, to better stimulate the clitoris. I leaned forward. She seemed to like it. When we'd finished, Annie said: "You know what else is making me horny? The date! Tomorrow!"

After the lean-forward sex, I worked from home for much of the day, then ran by the office before grabbing dinner at a new Whole Foods in a strange new, upscale neighborhood hatched from the middle of a middle-class city between Denver and the foothills. From there the strip-club-empire executive and I visited five properties. We began with a "gentleman's club," a watering hole for lawyers and businessmen who could eat steak in a fine dining room while a stripper danced in a structure resembling a giant birdcage. One of the clubs felt like a frat house. Another was more flush hip-hop style than rich golfer. There was a biker bar with a swingers club upstairs and a small room inside where booze wasn't allowed and the dancers could writhe fully nude. And then there was the all-nude club that 18-year-olds could patronize because it didn't serve alcohol. There, the waitresses were topless, and the dancers had tattoos and piercings and would wrap their thighs around the ball-capped heads of the yahoos and squeeze. I saw breasts everywhere, up close.

Perky ones, stiff ones, bouncing ones, fat udders, more than six hours of them, and poor saps draining their wallets to be in their company. The night at the strip clubs revealed powerful women and male doofuses. That's what men often are in the presence of sexually charged women: total doofuses. I arrived home at 1:30 a.m. and did what I'd wanted to do all night but couldn't because I was working: Like a total doofus, I guzzled a beer.

And of course the next morning I felt rotten. (*What?!* you are shouting. *Again?*) The combination of something I'd eaten the previous day, the inhaling of a lot of secondary cigarette smoke, and the late-night beer conspired, gently I might add, against my constitution. I spent the day at work feeling slightly queasy, eager to get home. For Annie, meanwhile, home was the very kernel of a life revolving around work, from the pasta labor she spent hours attached to every day to the child rearing that took place while I was at the office. She rarely escaped reminders of toil—she enjoyed no oasis away from her work's uncomfortable pressures. That evening when I arrived home, Ginger was in full freak-out mode, and a drained Annie whispered, "Date. We're going on a date."

She made pancakes for dinner because of my unsettled stomach. (She dotes! I love her!) Then she went to her Brazilian waxer for a third treatment while I took care of the girls. Ginger remained upset, and I put her to bed while she was crying.

"Date," Annie whispered again when she got home. "Date. Date."

"Yes," I whispered back. "Grown-ups. A drink. Dinner. Candlelight. Date."

"Date," she chanted, smiling. "Date."

Vicki arrived, and I showered and stood before my closet, staring at its contents. What look, I thought, would Annie find most appealing? I didn't have much of a wardrobe, so the ensemble possibilities were not what you might describe as "dizzying." I went with clean blue jeans and boots and a pink-checked dress shirt, and I mussed my hair into something chaotic. This seemed to be a popular look with the young people—maybe even a fashion approach the very young New York writer would have applauded, although I don't want to get ahead of myself.

"I love your hair," said Annie when I came down the stairs. "You look delicious."

Annie wore a black top with a plunging neckline, beneath which I could see the tantalizing edges of her Huit bra. I almost felt vertiginous again.

"My God, woman," I said as we pulled out of the garage in the minivan, her spicy perfume dabbing the air. "I could devour you."

The hostess led us across weathered wood floors to the perfect little table, right beside the front window overlooking the sidewalk. The lights were dim. Silverware and porcelain clattered; a murmur of low voices dabbed the air. Romance steeped everything. Martinis appeared before us, throwing off copper glints in the low firelight. The waiter decorated our table with several courses of tapas: rosemary, olives, and almonds, shrimp in a garlic and paprika sauce, fried artichokes, fennel and tomato gratin. Stiff-crusted bread and olive oil. Another martini for Annie.

"I feel almost sparkly," said Annie as we talked and ate. "I feel sexual. Like we're a sexual couple. I have this intuition that people are gazing at us and something inside them says, 'That couple has fantastic sex.' We're glowing."

Since Joni had been born, seven years before, we'd been depending for the most part on one paycheck. We'd moved so often we didn't have a stable of babysitters we could tap. They arrived this year in January, of course, but we'd used them for hotels, coffee-shop visits, a dinner with the food critic, a yurt, and an ashram. Now we finally were leveraging a babysitter for the event that probably gave birth to the species in the first place: the romantic date. We had neglected the species babysitter, in large part, because of finances. But we never truly had embraced the romantic date, even when we didn't have kids. Finances, again, told the tale. We were poor in Minneapolis, and for the first year in New Mexico. In Florida? Pregnancy, infancy, and poverty. In D.C.? Poverty and toddlerhood. In Baltimore? Pregnancy, toddlerhood, infancy, and poverty. We also owned a big old house that sapped most of our "disposable" income. Our dates? For most of our life together, a rented movie, some beer or wine. But something happened during our dinner this night. Annie said we should go out more often, and it wasn't an offhand comment. We both were feeling the same thing. The daily sex unquestionably had buttressed and added muscle to our relationship. This night on the town was especially honeyed with romance, not just an escape from the house with a little dose of romance thrown in.

It was magical. Possibly our best date ever.

"I could sit here for hours," said Annie. "Just sit here at this table talking."

We held hands across the small table. "This is exactly what I wanted, what I dreamed about," I said. "It was worth the wait."

"Absolutely," said Annie. "It's fun to be an adult sometimes, isn't it?"

BEFORE THE marathon, chances are we'd have opted for sleep instead of sex after a late-night out. We didn't have the luxury tonight, although by now I didn't associate *not* having sex with "luxury." The act had merged with my life. I didn't contemplate evening sex with trepidation, worried about whether I'd be energetic enough; I relished the thought. Shortly after we both were naked and kissing in the sex den, Annie invited me inside, and I RSVP'd the offer. The date had lubricated the carnal machinery; Annie had radiated sexuality all night. I was hungry for her. I stayed inside, barely moving, while she used some sort of magic muscles to squeeze me. Back and forth, slowly, gently.

"What a perfect night," said Annie as we rocked. "Perfect. I'm so happy."

"Loved whatever you were doing there," I said. "The squeezing."

"Oh, Kegels!" said Annie.

We wrapped our arms around each other and smiled as we talked, and then we stopped, blew out the candles, and fell asleep.

15

That's Sexcellent

And so began the final push, a shortened day because the clock sprang forward an hour while we slept. We'd plowed through fights and illnesses, menacing easy chairs, haunting depression, and vertigo, although let's face it: By "we" I mean *I* suffered through illnesses, menacing easy chairs, haunting depression, and vertigo—and Annie helped me out. None of these conditions plagued Annie, not for one second, since the sexpedition started. I'd been with Annie for fourteen years at the time. How many times had she been sick? Maybe six? For me, on the other hand, half a dozen approached my annual average. In terms of the fights, I clearly started one of them; the other, I would argue, was more of a joint effort.

All of this is my way of saying that I'd lugged to the party a bunch of things that were as unwelcome as presents of a gold cross, a year's subscription to "bacon of the month," and the unabridged writings of Mahmoud Ahmadinejad would have been at a bat mitzvah. Wise Annie showed up with a respectable check. Despite my myriad "issues," though, we'd managed. We'd had sex despite taxing days at work, exhausting child rearing, and late-night dinners. We'd done it in a basement, a Las Vegas casino, a classy hotel, a cheap motel, a Victorian bed-and-breakfast, and a yurt. We'd had early-morning sex, late-afternoon sex, and lots of evening sex.

Ninety-one days down, nine to go.

We hired Vicki for the afternoon to watch the girls while we visited the coffee bar for some reading and writing. It was a spectacular day, however, brilliant and warm, and the idea of bagging the smoky coffeehouse for a hike in the foothills came to me in the form of a "vision." Annie immediately endorsed the notion. We entered the wilderness, following a narrow path around a few low peaks near the city of Golden. This was the first time, we noted midway through, that we'd been on a solo hike in the close-in mountains since we'd moved to Colorado, a realization you could compare to living in New Mexico for a few years and one day saying, "Hey, let's try this green chile stuff."

As we trekked to the top of Mount Galbraith, we pledged to, from this day forward, exploit babysitters to take advantage of our proximity to mountain wilderness. We'd exploited our proximity to wilderness (not to mention green chile) nearly every weekend during our five-year sojourn in New Mexico, but we didn't need babysitters back then.

Annie and I walked alone along a ridge. One side offered views of the Continental Divide; the other, Denver's downtown in the distance. Huge boulders lay about, with smatterings of evergreens and yucca. We paused and looked at each other, and Annie gave me the raised eyebrow. The same idea had graffitied my brain moments before. I was strategizing the right time and place for the delivery of the "look" when Annie preempted me.

Outdoor sex was relatively rare in our history together, but it claimed a brilliant, you could even say gaudy, trophy among the thousand or so sexual encounters we'd had. On one of our first dates, we spent a weekend in Jim Thorpe, Pennsylvania, in a red tent Annie had given me for my birthday. We hiked those rocky Pennsylvania trails, and we played along the edges of a wide stream. Eventually, we removed our clothes and waded into the river. At one point, I carried Annie upstream and plonked her into a deep pool. We splashed around in the cistern, which led, of course, to sex in the caramel-colored water, with the sun thumping overhead and diamond-bright rapids shushing over nearby rocks. It was not the best sex we'd ever had, not even close. But it was outdoor sex, it was stirring, and thus, the ornate trophy. It never will be forgotten.

Nor will we forget the sex we had on the side of a cliff during our "training" period just prior to the kickoff of the marathon. And now we were poised to do it again in the great outdoors. We left the trail and began wandering around on the ridge, looking for somewhere private and comfortable. We found a pile of boulders with soft pine needles matted between them. We stripped, and I drank in the staggering views. I felt the wind whip me and the sun warm my butt and legs and face.

We laid Annie's jacket on the dirt, and went at it in the sunlight, facing east, on top of the mountain, hearing nothing but wind and creaking trees.

"That was thrilling! I actually said, to myself, 'Hi Denver!' while we were doing it," Annie said as we got dressed.

She reminded me of a magazine article we had read years earlier that featured a house in the woods somewhere with big glass doors opening from the bedroom onto a deck. The bed was on rollers, and whenever the couple wanted to sleep outside—or presumably, have sex under the stars—they just slid the bed onto the deck.

"A house like that would be a dream come true," said Annie.

RECOLLECTIONS OF the Mountain Mount stirred my brain as I woke up the next morning. Annie's flesh always intoxicated me, but the vision of it beneath the blue sky, with the breeze tossing her hair and the magpies staring down from their swaying perches and the smell of pine and dirt and sagebrush perfuming the bright mountaintop—well . . . Many of the previous months' individual erotic encounters might be forgotten, but I was certain a catalogue of images of mountain sex would remain forever. It was a bit early for the solemn presentation of a trophy, but I felt confident that Sex Among the Boulders one day would receive trophy consecration and join the Sex in the Caramel Waters and the Sex on the Cliff trophies on a mantel.

We'd traveled far. We knew we'd come back to our lives removed from the adventure's rigors soon, but it seemed likely that things would be different, *had* to be different. We'd seen and felt and tasted so much. Adequacy no longer was acceptable: We demanded panting flesh, ravishment. We'd grown spoiled.

I TOOK Ginger to preschool, dropped her off in the lunch room, then hung up her little pink coat in her empty classroom. I stood in the quiet for a few minutes and gulped the atmosphere—the perfume of glue and Magic Marker and gerbil bedding; the yarn and the tape, the little wooden cubbies with each child's name emblazoned across the top, the pile of stuffed animals around a low couch; the Popsicle sticks and tins of crayons and waxed-paper cups and little blankets for chilly children. I often envied Ginger's preschool teacher, Johnny, just as I had envied Joni's preschool teachers in Baltimore. I could spend the day swaddled in toddler innocence and be happy, I fantasized, and not for the first time. I have reported this daydream to Annie several times over the years, and she usually lets loose an ironic snort.

"Tell you what, DJ," she has said. "Stay home with the kids for a few months, and then see if you still want to work in a preschool."

Hours later, on the way home from work, I stopped off at a too-precious gift shop and bought Annie an Indian-style shirt and a card for—sing along here—"her birthday." Soon I was in our bedroom, my computer on my lap, writing, wobbly with happy energy because I wasn't at my desk. I was at home, Annie was downstairs, and the girls soon would fill the house with their out-sized personalities. Later, while Annie squeezed in a quick yoga hit, I took the girls to their favorite restaurant, a diner where the waitstaff dress as though they're from the 1950s and the music on the jukebox ranges from Chubby Checker to Elvis to Patsy Cline. The girls were obsessed with the glass-walled machine that for a quarter uses a crane to retrieve candy from a great pile of the sweet stuff. We sat right behind the machine, and one of them mentioned it about every five minutes.

"We're going to get dessert *and* the candy machine, Daddy?" asked Ginger repeatedly.

We devoured corn dogs and grilled cheese, French fries and a burger, and two little ice cream sundaes. The girls took turns with the candy crane, and then we were off, back home for bedtime. I put both girls to bed, taking my time with their stories and our conversations. I brushed their hair away from their eyes. I caressed their cheeks with the backs of my hands, and I kissed their sweet foreheads.

"I love you, Ginger. Have a good sleep."

"I love you, Daddy."

"Good night, Joni. You're the best in the world. I love you."

"You're the best, Daddy. I love you."

Annie, who had returned home, performed roughly the same rite with the girls. I traveled downstairs, and fixed Annie and my-self some hot peppermint tea, and climbed back up the steps, to the bedroom. I clicked into an FMU show and lifted weights for probably the thirtieth time in the past ninety-something days while Annie read a magazine. Then I flopped in bed beside Annie. We chatted for about twenty minutes before I shot Annie the look, along with a similarly evocative shrug, and she nodded in assent.

. . .

It was day 94, it was nearly eighty degrees outside, and it was Annie's thirty-ninth birthday. The previous day, I had stopped off at a market and bought French bread, feta cheese, and an assortment of Greek, Italian, and French olives. Ever since we started dating, Annie occasionally would drift into a dreamlike state and talk about the best breakfast she's ever had, in Turkey: French bread, olives, and feta cheese.

The girls and I crept down the steps while she slept. I warmed bread in the oven, sliced the feta, placed the olives in a little bowl. I made a cappuccino, poured a glass of orange juice, and placed a square of exquisite English butter on a small plate. I arranged all of it on a breakfast-in-bed tray and carried it up the steps, with the girls giddy behind me, bursting to sing the Happy Birthday song, which we launched into at the landing.

Annie now was up and dressed and beaming. She sat and ate, singsonging "my birthday" several times. Ginger handed her three colored plastic Easter eggs for a gift. I gave her the card and the shirt, and she seemed intensely happy.

I took Joni to school, and Annie delivered Ginger to her preschool. Then, alone (I had to work, unfortunately), Annie fled Denver for Boulder, one of her favorite towns, a place she sometimes refers to as "my nirvana." She took a yoga class at the studio of, as she called him, "yoga celebrity" Richard Freeman. She bumped into him in the shabby studio and reported later she was startled.

Oh my God, that's Richard Freeman!

She window-shopped along Boulder's pleasant pedestrian walkway and then headed to a grand park called Chautauqua, with paths leading deep into the foothills. She hiked, she grabbed a post-jaunt cappuccino, and she bought herself a pair of sexy, sparkly earrings. All afternoon I imagined her in her nirvana, and for me there was something almost impossibly cute about the daydream's particulars: Annie by herself in a new yoga studio, traipsing through stores, hiking in the Flatirons, a slight smile fixed on her face.

I wonder what she's doing right now? I thought as I worked from home, extremely disappointed that I couldn't be there for her big day because of work deadlines.

She returned beaming, effervescent with good cheer, recounting the details of her day for me, and relishing random ingredients: the lemony sunlight, the spectacular cappuccino, the utilitarian yoga studio.

"It's not over yet," I said. "Your special day continues!"

Earlier in the day, I'd "created" a radio station through an online service called Pandora that lets you determine what sorts of music the station plays based on a band, or even a favorite song. I hinged Annie's station on the Simple Minds song "Don't You (Forget About Me)," because the tune was huge in 1985, the year Annie graduated from high school. The station played as I put the girls to bed and Annie readied herself in the den.

She looked hot in her Huit lingerie and red-painted toenails.

"Time for a birthday foot massage," I announced.

I lingered over her soles and toes as never before, pushing into her arches with my knuckles, pulling each toe, interlacing my fingers with the spaces between her toes, and stroking. I rubbed the back of her heels, petted the tops of her feet, and kneaded her soles. Annie lay back with her eyes closed, listening to the music.

"How was that?" I asked, placing her feet back on the bed.

"Orgasmic."

"Speaking of orgasms . . ." I said.

"I love my birthday," said Annie in an extended singsong.

DENVER FINALLY was thawing. I took pink-helmeted Joni to school on my gigantic skateboard. She perched on the board's prow, and I captained the ship from behind. We did this whenever we had time and the weather was cooperating, and for Joni it stood as a big adventure. Kids would gather around us whenever we rolled onto the playground, pointing at the sight of dad and daughter together on the same skateboard. "Wow! That's awesome!" the big kids would shout, and Joni beamed at all of the attention.

Annie, meanwhile, went to the office for her usual Wednesday afternoon meeting, her one regular commute and face-to-face confab with her boss. It was the penultimate week of the marathon, and Annie still hadn't told anybody at the office about it. But for reasons she couldn't quite understand—"It just happened," she said—she dropped the bomb.

"So that's the story," she said in her peroration. "My husband and I are almost done with one hundred consecutive days of sex. It's been crazy. And it was all my idea."

Whenever Annie is embarrassed, she turns lobster red, and by the conclusion of her report, she said, she felt as if she had claws for hands and a serrated, meaty tail.

"I actually used the word 'penetration' in front of my boss," she told me that afternoon while the kids were still in school, her face flushing at the memory. "Being a lawyer, he quickly became obsessed with the rules of the whole thing. His first question? What, exactly, constituted sex during the marathon? So, penetration."

"Wow," I said, laughing at the thought. "That's some conversation."

"Oh, it didn't stop there," she said. "He cross-examined me. He couldn't stop himself. And with every question, I grew a brighter shade of red."

"That must have been quite the scene," I said, laughing some more.

"The office manager had a good line about it all," said Annie. "When I finished revealing the marathon, the first thing she said was, 'That's sexcellent.'

"The classic part came at the end, when the plant manager

walked into the room and, after being hit with the details of the marathon, the two men launched into an extended session of yukking it up. They were particularly taken with the idea of convincing their wives to take part in a hundred-day sex marathon, entering the fact that our marathon had been *my* idea as Exhibit A. I was so embarrassed," said Annie. "But they did crack me up. Total clowns."

"Excuse me," I said to the guy behind the huge display case of expensive fishing reels in the Bass Pro Shops. "I need a fishing rod for myself, one for my three-year-old daughter, and a bunch of lures and whatnot. I haven't fished in years. I have no idea what I'm doing. I can't even put line on a reel. Can you help me?"

The guy with the gold tooth took over, pleased with my complete submission to his authority. He walked around the fishing section, grabbing stuff and talking about how this lure is great for trout because of its color and another one is perfect for shallow streams because of its shape, and so on. Nearly a hundred days earlier I'd stepped with caution into Bass Pro Shops, worried that my version of masculinity wouldn't jibe with the store's. Now I was blithe. Daily sex had fortified my sense of manliness, and this time I didn't wonder if I should wear my machismo prominently on my sleeve. I was a sexual male, not a shuffling, middle-aged cream puff who had left behind the vigorous and demanding pleasures of sex for the effortless, bland amusements of hobbies and interests.

"Thanks, man," I said.

"No problem. Good luck."

I spent the rest of the day at home, working out of our smoke-smudged bedroom.

Annie and I talked a lot that night: housing prices; the fledgling synagogue started by friends of ours; Annie's love for helping people start their own pasta-selling businesses; schools; the delights of hot springs; the kinds of dogs we wanted (me, border collie or mutt; Annie, labradoodle or mutt). This stood as one of the premier triumphs of the sex marathon: The daily physical connection had led to stronger connections elsewhere in our relationship. We had recognized this early in the marathon, but things didn't stall after the epiphany; they got better. We'd always chatted easily, but during the previous one hundred days the evening chats had grown increasingly engaging and wide-ranging.

She lay on her stomach and I climbed on her back and we lay like that awhile, just breathing together, barely talking.

"I'm ready," she said eventually. We talked while we had sex. We laughed. This was new, for us one of the treasures we'd unearthed during this long adventure.

WE ENTERED the final weekend with the rare Denver day of rain. But when you don't see, smell, feel, or hear rain for months, it's not a deflating event. It's romantic. On my way home from work my mom called.

"So back to the cabin tomorrow, right, honey?" she asked.

"That's right! Can't wait."

"Only a few days to go. I'm so proud of you. Such an achievement."

"Uh, thanks, Mom. It's pretty cool, for sure."

"You guys be careful down there. You're bringing the girls, right?"

"You got it. We're going to have a blast. It's so beautiful."

"Dad and I will have to go there with you guys sometime. Sounds like a fun place. Anyway, good luck, honey! I'll talk to you when you get back, and after you've finished the marathon!"

That night, Annie gave me new underwear for yoga, a high-tech pair of boxers. "I noticed that after yoga, your underwear is sopping wet," she said. "This underwear is supposed to wick away sweat."

Another small star in a galaxy of thoughtful Annie gestures. We sat in bed, talking for a while. In the morning we'd head to the cabin that we'd nearly sanctified as a holy site during the "training" period, the scene of a frenzy of carnal interludes during a long weekend. This time, though, we'd have the kids with us. Would they go to sleep easily? Would the cabin help vanquish my weariness, or would the whole child-rearing-dense trip sap our strength?

The highway climbed and climbed, then leveled off for a while, then rose some more, through pine forests and between cliffs. A big valley sprawled below us, and we plunged down into it, a spectacular plain of grass and snow hemmed in by white-capped mountains. Finally, we arrived at the cabin where Annie and I had celebrated our anniversary just months before. The girls were so excited they hyperventilated. They played, I got the fishing gear ready, and then we walked down to Chalk Creek. I saw trout darting across the shallows and in the pools. I pointed them out to the girls, who both underwent an instantaneous conversion from fishing agnostics to angling apostles: *Behold! Witness the swarming of the fish!* We didn't catch anything at the creek behind the house, but later we drove up to a nearby lake, and on my first cast I caught a trout. The girls yelped and touched its belly before I released it.

Later, after a good deal of lounging in the spectacular hot-spring pool, we started a fire in the spacious stone hearth and ate spaghetti at the big dining room table. We roasted marshmallows in the fireplace and made s'mores. As bedtime approached, Joni persuaded us to let her stay up a bit later, so she could sit in the hot-spring pool with us in the night chill. After Ginger went to bed on the bottom bunk ("The top bunk is scary, right, Daddy?"), Joni, Annie, and I slipped into the pool. For the next forty minutes, Joni talked nonstop about the planets, the sun, how stars are ormed, how scientists had recently discovered a new planet, although they weren't sure it was an actual planet. Her lecture amazed us (the words "astronomy scholarship" zipped through my brain, although I kept the phrase to myself). We'd never heard her so engaged with academics. She showed us different planets in the sky. She saw a shooting star and exclaimed.

After we put Joni to bed, we began gearing up for session number 98. We had fantasized about doing it in the hot tub or before the fire, but we were far too tired for either. So we straggled into the bedroom, yawning. We had the closest thing to "sleep sex" I've ever experienced.

On this last day of double digits, day 99, we began the morning with pancakes cooked in a huge cast-iron skillet, and then we spent hours, literally, just lazing around the hot springs. We played games. The girls went inside for a while and colored, and Annie and I remained in the tub. The possibility of sunburn occurred to us, but we dismissed it. Winter had been long. We wanted sun.

Things were different in the evening, after the girls were in bed. Rejuvenated after spending an entire day just hanging out, we stripped and slipped into the hot-spring pool and listened to the coyotes and the river, watched the stars, and talked for a long time.

"You want to do it in front of the fire?" asked Annie.

But of course.

Our cell-phone alarm clocks started beeping at 6 a.m., awaking us to the very precipice of our goal: just one more step.

"This is it," I said as we roused ourselves in bed.

"The big day," Annie said. "I can't believe it. I'm also a little bit nervous."

"Nervous?"

"Can you imagine if for whatever reason we just couldn't swing it today? Maybe we get a flat tire and we're stuck. Never more than a few inches from the girls for the day. Nowhere to do it."

"Jeez," I said. "Scary thought."

"We've got to get home and into bed."

I flashed my eyebrows.

"You know, we are in bed now," I said.

We had talked about completing the trek in the cabin, waking up in the morning, and just doing it. But given how much time we had spent in our bedroom, we felt we sort of owed it to the sex den to finish up there. Now I wasn't so sure.

"I thought about that last night, and again this morning, before the alarm went off," Annie said. "And I still like our original idea—to nail number one hundred in the sex den. It's only right."

After a moment's hesitation, I agreed. I prepared bagels for everyone, and cappuccinos for me and Annie—we had carted our espresso maker to the cabin. We packed our stuff into the van, took out the trash, straightened up, woke up the girls, fixed them in their car seats, and got on the road just before 7 a.m. We passed herds of elk, antelope, and mule deer, and we saw several coyotes out for morning hunts and a few bighorn sheep. The girls slept, and we absorbed the passing scene, something you can take for granted when you live nearby, but never should.

I wanted to mark the day somehow, with something other than sex. For the past few years Annie had complained about how she hated to shop, how she seized up at the thought of walking into a store and buying a pair of jeans. She didn't think anything looked good on her. She didn't want to spend much money. Stores intimidated her. "I need a personal shopper," she had said just a few weeks before.

So later on day 100, I shopped. I walked from my office to a Banana Republic, and within a minute out they popped from the display: a pair of blue jeans cuffed at the calves, like capri pants.

They were artfully distressed and felt like butter. Hours later I put Ginger to bed, and Annie, Joni, and I gathered in our bedroom. Annie exclaimed as I held the pants aloft, snatching them in her hands and immediately pinning the waistband to her hips.

"Oh my God!" she said. She stripped off the black pants she'd been wearing and plunged her legs into the jeans, yanking them to her waist, buttoning them, and twirling around for us.

"Awesome," I said. "Perfect."

She stepped into the bathroom to see for herself in the mirror. I watched her turn in the mirror, pursing her lips as she always did whenever she examined an outfit in a mirror. I'd always loved the lip-pursing thing.

"DJ, I can say without a doubt that these are the best jeans I've ever had," she said. "Ever. I am absolutely, positively smitten with them. I don't even know what to say, other than I love you."

"That's saying a lot," I responded.

Then, after Joni was in bed, I popped a bottle of inexpensive French champagne and lit candles and incense, and we talked for a long time. Annie did not remove her new jeans.

"I feel sexy in these," she said. "I'm not obsessed with my ass. I'm not worried they look too 'mom.' I actually feel cool."

"It's nice when fashion corresponds with reality," I said. "They do look especially saucy on you, though."

"You just like saying 'saucy,' " she said.

"True," I answered. "Good word."

We changed into robes and looked at pictures from the cabin weekend and laughed. Beneath her robe Annie wore the Huit bra and my parents' gift, those black panties emblazoned with "100 Days" in rhinestones across the ass, which she had worn only once before, on day 1. We lay next to each other. We kissed, we petted, and we purred. She kept talking about our weekend, though, and so I stopped moving toward the final destination, instead sitting up and trading observations with Annie about the weekend, about the girls, about Colorado's spectacular nature. Of course, we talked about where to live, as if what we were doing at that moment wasn't living.

"It's getting closer," I said at 11 p.m. "What do you think? You going to be able to manage tonight?"

"Maybe we should just skip it," she offered.

"That's probably the right idea," I said. "My machinery is spent. It needs a break."

"Same here."

"We're not having sex tonight," I said as I traveled down her legs again.

"Nope," she whispered. "No sex."

I'd been here many, many times in recent months, and I knew my way around.

I took my time, losing myself for the umpteenth time to pure pleasure, to the here-and-nowness of our erotic storm.

At 11:28, we aligned our torsos again.

"Yes!" shouted Annie. "We did it!"

Epilogue

And then the next day, we did it again.

At some point during the marathon, the *Post*'s gossip columnist had said, "Douggie, you can't just stop at one hundred days. You know that, right? You've got to do one more. For good luck."

I'd immediately dismissed the idea with a blithe wave of the hand, but the suggestion stuck with me.

"Guess what, honey?" I said to Annie that night as the kids ran around and Annie worked her pots and pans and magic for the evening's dinner. I leaned in close and whispered: "We've got to go for 101 days."

She lifted one eyebrow in a certain way that stands as the universal gesture for "Explain this, please," but by the end of my presentation, she agreed. So just minutes before midnight on day 101, we formally ended the sex marathon with a bit less excitement than we had felt the night before. The hundredth erotic encounter had seemed like a party, but number 101 felt like a stray commitment agreed to long ago and half forgotten—some evening presentation by a friend of a friend, a tax attorney who was giving a talk about estate planning over Maxwell House and Chips Ahoy.

Oh God. I forgot. Do we have to? Oy.

We didn't do it again for a few weeks, a conscious decision to give our bodies and our libidos a break. For months Annie and I shared an enthusiasm for the marathon's end. In the evenings, Annie had the option of tucking into a good book and seamlessly merging this activity with sleep. I could inhale a large plate of fish and chips, suck down three pints, and wrap up the feast with a brownie at 9:30 p.m., all without some nagging inner counsel whispering about how the meal could "negatively impact" the evening, and how he would "welcome the opportunity" to "endeavor to facilitate" the "termination" of my "ill-advised pursuits."

But one August Wednesday four months after our sex epic, we were quietly sitting in bed and reading after putting the girls in bed for the night, and Annie said: "I miss the marathon."

I turned to her, placing my book on my lap. "I know what you mean," I said. "Having sex for one hundred straight days, it turns out, was *fun*."

"The sex was key," Annie said. "But what I miss is everything else the sex brought to the shindig."

"The connection," I offered.

"We *really* bonded for those hundred days."

By then, Annie and I had decided to stay in Colorado. Months later, we bought a ranch house in Annie's nirvana, Boulder, and the last remaining home demons haunting my Colorado sojourn—most of which had fled by the middle of the marathon—flapped their wings, whipped their forked tails, and took off. We both loved our new house and community. The kids had excellent schools, and they quickly gathered friends around them. Our jobs were humming along, and things were looking up. The sex had improved markedly, from a predictable arithmetic of pettings and "moves" to something more like a night of improvisational theater, including a fluid range of positions and the occasional use of props. Annie never again used Two Fingers and a Thumb or the magic bullet, although lube routinely made an appearance. The

JUST *DO IT*   303

only prop I used during the sexpedition, which I shrink from articulating in the first person (and which, when pronounced, appears in my brain as if scrawled in flames), remains in a drawer somewhere, never to be touched again. To those who embrace the device that shall not be named, no offense. Like the dungeon and asshole bleaching, it's just not me.

But back to Annie's line, "I miss the marathon." Both of us said it from time to time as weeks and months passed, as the marathon receded like some spectacular sabbatical involving a castle, wildflower meadows, and a path leading to a private beach, the sort of memory for which the word "wistful" was coined.

SHORTLY AFTER moving into the new house, we bought a hammock that really was more like a seat than a stretcher and hung it from a big tree in our backyard. The next morning, we sprang for another hammock and dangled it from the same limb—the girls had fought so fiercely and incessantly about the hammock that we quickly decided we needed one for each of them. During summer evenings, after the elves were in bed, Annie and I always brought beers to the garden-thick yard, and during what we called "hammock time" we would swing and talk. By now, the marathon had been over for more than a year, but we still occasionally asked each other what the whole thing had been about, usually while swaying in our hammocks. Would we ever try it again? Had the marathon really introduced long-term changes into our relationship? Had it engendered anything entirely novel and concrete?

"The knitting," I said one warm night. "I think we can find a direct link between the marathon and the knitting."

"Makes sense," said Annie.

The year after the marathon, Annie turned 40. Needless to say, a biggie. I invested a lot of time and thought in her exit from her 30s, but none of the gifts that crossed my mind seemed worthy.

Jewelry? A long weekend somewhere? It finally occurred to me that Annie would treasure something handmade, because that's just Annie—very Annie. I toyed with taking pottery classes, on the sly, and throwing a few pots for her. Or, if I learned some basic woodworking skills, I reasoned, maybe I could make a table for our new house. And then it hit me: Annie loved to knit.

I'd never betrayed even a tuft of interest in understanding how to make clothing out of sticks and string. If I secretly figured out how to knit and made her something, she would treasure it forever and cherish her fortieth birthday. So I took knitting lessons from the owner of a yarn shop.

I spent a few nights a week using fancy yarn to knit a long, broad scarf, sitting with groups of women who gravitated to the store in the evenings to sip tea (and sometimes booze) and to, as they called it, "stitch and bitch." Sometimes I felt like Norm on *Cheers* when I stepped into the store. The women, in unison, would yell "Doug!" The owner would then command me to tell people I hadn't yet met what she called my "aww" story. I'd then report what I was doing there, and they would, without exception, say: "Aww."

Annie knew I was doing something in the evenings that related to her birthday, but she assumed it was something more, shall we say, masculine.

The scarf achieved its objective. Annie barely took it off for days. In addition, the girls and I spent evenings in the basement for weeks, making things for Annie: wooden boxes and canvases that we painted, clay that we shaped into cups and bowls, a pair of stepping-stones for the garden, and so on. Annie cried as we presented the gifts, and she repeatedly said, almost in the manner of a chant: "This is my best birthday ever."

ONCE SEX swooped back into our life after the brief hiatus, Annie and I did it with more passion, virtuosity, and volume than we had displayed before the marathon. What had been three times a month, if we were lucky, progressed to about six times a month: two weeks a month with just one fling between the sheets, and two weeks with a pair of romps. The improvements in our sex life percolated into other aspects of our life together. We touched more. Our conversations seemed easier and more lit with honesty. I felt I understood Annie's interior world better than ever, and she felt the same about me.

Just one hundred days of daily sex had accomplished something important in our relationship that had escaped us during the previous fourteen years of making love, moving around the country, and raising children. For the first time in our marriage, I think, we *really* began to fit together. Not only on dates, not only during great vacations or during incandescent (but brief) moments that sometimes occurred during lovemaking. But also while cooking, in the middle of a Saturday spent pursuing species within the genus "child activity," even while I toiled at the office in Denver and Annie worked at home in Boulder. And every time we made love.

Annie and I never had drifted too far from each other, but to the extent that our lives had veered in separate directions and our union had wavered, the marathon succeeded, as Annie put it early in the adventure, in screwing us back together again. A year later, the bond still seemed fresh and strong. Yet from time to time we still voiced regret about the marathon's ending.

We longed for the intensity we'd experienced during those one hundred days. It was as if we were decent weekend sailors who one summer decided to let the wind carry us from Florida to Trinidad to Dakar to the Cape Verde Islands to Lisbon. A year later, our sailing abilities were of a different order, and our trips much more ambitious. But still we dreamed of returning to that dreamy, stirring summer on the sea; we missed the atmospheric ferment of it all.

Here's the beauty part. Where revisiting a sailing trip would have required large periods of time away from work and home, and substantial financial investments, repeating the sex adventure demanded only that Annie and I have sex. So at some point we stopped invoking the marathon, because we understood that having sex for one hundred consecutive days, though sometimes quite a gas, was entirely unnecessary. Just making love for a month would do wonders, we thought. Or for two weeks. Or for even ten days or one week.

Just do it.

Just Doing It

You read the book, you loved the story, and you still are celebrating the message that having sex with your partner—more sex—is good for you and for your relationship.

Time to get started, right?

You could just hop in the sack right now and begin your own sex trek—a long weekend, a week, a month, whatever. But then you would miss an element of our sexathon that we found powerful and lively: the planning part.

We took months to prepare for the sexpedition: reading, getting in shape, talking about sex. This was out of necessity— when Annie came up with the idea for the sexathon, we had several holiday commitments that would have interfered with having sex every day for 101 days. No couple needs to set aside months, but I think dedicating at least a week to planning is smart.

As Annie and I got ready for our entrée into a season of sexual excess, the anticipation of the journey—all of that sex, for all of those days—ripened our desire for each other. We talked about sex more than ever before, a development alone that was worth the wait. We thought about sex, read about sex, dreamed about sex—and then, finally, we began actually having daily sex.

It was most excellent.

So if you can wait for a spell, even just a few days, do it. Plan your sexpedition down to the massage oils and the incense, the new pajamas and the *Kama Sutra* guide, and the fresh flowers for the bedroom.

At its heart, the sexathon is ridiculously simple: have sex every day for as many days as you can. But there was nothing easy about doing it for 101 consecutive days. Yes, many romps were thrilling. Sure, making love with each other every day brought us closer together than ever, which—in a splendid circle—made the sexual appointments increasingly easier. Nevertheless, there was a lot of exhaustion to overcome. There were bouts of empty desire. There was boredom, yearnings to just melt into TV rather than have sex, and hectic schedules: kids, schools, commutes, careers, dinners, cleaning up, bedtimes, and so on.

Annie and I managed, despite the scattered roadblocks, the occasional detours, and the surprise land mines. We learned a lot. And we recommend a sexathon (although 101 days is a bit excessive) for any couple—especially those who aren't doing it as often as they would like.

Before you start, though, we would like to offer some pointers. Let us help you understand what to expect, how to get past the obstacles, and how to make your week, month, or (gasp) 101-day sexpedition successful.

Exploit Anticipation

This gets back to the recommendation that you plan the sexpedition before you begin the march. Dangle the block of lovemaking before yourselves for a week or more. Talk about it, think about it, prepare for it. When the big day finally arrives, your libidos will be fully charged. This should be exciting. Revving and tuning the engines before you start helps shape the adventure, removes the very idea of it from the humdrum, and makes it exotic and thrilling.

Create Your Sex Den

That portrait of Granny in an ornate oval frame hanging above your bed? Move it. The *Dora the Explorer* dolls in a corner? Get rid of 'em. The laundry on the floor, the pile of magazines on the bedside table, the clutter swamping the top of the bureau? Clean. It. Up. You probably could have sex every day for a month within the nucleus of a clutter fest, but that would sort of be like drinking glorious, expensive wine every night out of a styrofoam cup.

Your bedroom should be an adult sanctuary. By "adult," we not only mean a space free of kid stuff but also a space "conducive to adult, carnal pursuits," which suggests you remove the collage of aunts and sisters, parents, great-uncles, and nieces from the walls. Rid the room of work—that pile of briefs, the computer, the briefcase bulging with client data. If the bedroom is the only place suitable for performing office drudgery in the house—we're skeptical—then find a way to quickly hide it in the evening, when the two of you are finally finished with the customers and the bosses and you can focus on each other.

Work, granny, kid stuff (and clutter, of course)—all of it distracts from your intimate life, which should be entirely divorced from *SpongeBob,* that family trip you took to Disney a few years back, the irritating mess of books scattered across the floor, and the mess of e-mails in your inbox.

Respect your love life. Create your sex den. When, finally, it's time to head to the room with the big bed, you'll want to hang out with each other, talk, unwind. And maybe, you'll get in the mood.

Something New

For seven years, the two of you have had sex in the evening under the covers of the bed you share. It always begins with him making the "first move," which involves some petting and kissing. Clothes are shed. Bodies are flung together. Sex happens. Approximately nine minutes later, you're getting dressed again and returning to the TV, the book, or the fridge for another beer.

There's nothing wrong with your sex formula. Sex can be a ritual, with a set pattern of rites and incantations. And this is okay. But sometimes it's refreshing and illuminating to yank yourself out of the rut, to think of sex as something open-ended and freeform, instead of a trusty formula. During the preparation phase for your sexathon, talk about things you might like to try. Maybe he would like her to wear a pair of sexy thigh-high stockings. Maybe she would like to explore porn together. Maybe you find out that both of you have long been curious about role-playing. Decide upon something new that you will try, sexwise.

And then during the sexpedition, give the things you agreed upon a whirl. But wing it, too. Go for a session in the kitchen—just watch out for that paring knife. Push that exercise ball against the side of the bed and try doing the deed while using the exercise ball for. . .bounce (she's sitting on the edge of the ball, and you're standing up; you'll figure it out). Do it outdoors.

This adds a measure of spontaneity to the sexathon. Since you are doing it every day, there's nothing spontaneous about doing it each night—in fact, it's planned. But that doesn't mean the sex itself must fit into some formula. The kids are down, the two of you are in the basement trying to find something, and suddenly, you are undressing each other. A session starts out on the bed, but then she decides—Surprise!—to move the festivities into the shower.

Here's one thing that was new to us when we began our

sexathon, and now is always around: lube. If you haven't tried the stuff, visit a sex shop (they have the best selection) and grab some. If it doesn't work as well as you dreamed, buy a different type. Annie and I tried several lubes; we liked about a third of them.

Lube or not, even a week of doing it different will change your sex life, for the better.

Date Again

Nearly a decade ago, you met. The first date was a blizzard of sparks. For the next year, you saw each other on dates, three or four a week by the end. Your lives spun around each other. You lingered over dinner at restaurants, trading stories about each other's lives. You held hands and went on long walks in the park. And you had sex. A lot of sex. Just doing it, in fact, dwelled somewhere near the center of your life together.

You moved in together, then got married. Maybe you had kids. And somewhere along the line, the effervescence that once arrived at the mere thought of your mate went a bit flat. Now, you—the couple—no longer occupies the heart of your life. Your careers have commandeered increasingly more of your attention and maybe even passion. Your kids, understandably, snagged a big chunk of your heart, and much of your life now hinges on their wants and needs.

You must recapture your romantic life. The sexpedition is a perfect place to begin. If you have kids, hire a babysitter and do something alone, and preferably not the usual routine. Instead of hitting the neighborhood bistro where you always go for dinner-dates, hire a babysitter for the afternoon and go on a pleasant hike in the mountains (and maybe, do it beneath a pine tree). Or, skip the movie and take a salsa class together, grab a drink afterwards, and hit a dance floor somewhere. Check in to a cheap motel and have a wild romp in the neon light.

The idea is to invite a certain freshness back into your union.

A twist to the tried and true date: Take lessons in something you want to do together. You've spent years driving past tennis courts and observing the couples whacking the yellow ball back and forth. You've envied their playful adult time together and fantasized about sitting down in your whites and downing a gin and tonic after a vigorous back-and-forth. Now is the time to take that tennis lesson together. Unless one or both of you is a competitive freak or a miserable sport, you'll have fun—and there's a good chance you'll get hot for each other.

Yak It Up

It's Tuesday. It began rudely at about 6 a.m., when Junior started making noises about breakfast. There was the groggy cereal pouring and coffee sipping, the hurried shower, the too-long commute, the interminable day at the office (four meetings, lunch inhaled at the desk, a massive headache about 2 p.m., Ibuprofen), the gridlock on the way home, the dinner. There was help with homework and doing the dishes, there was cleaning up the house and kids' bedtimes.

Sex?

Howsabout TV?

Chances are, after a typical—that is, long—day, the physically and emotionally demanding act of sex doesn't always leap to the top of the "to do" list. But during the sexathon, you're going to have sex regardless of where sex lives in your mental list of things you want to accomplish at 9:30 on Tuesday night.

You can't always pivot immediately from the kids' bedtimes— or if you don't have kids, dinner and cleaning up—to sex. Which means you need to bag the TV. You must jettison the magazine, put aside the book, and stay far away from that laptop. During those precious hours you have together and alone every night, you need to dedicate as many minutes to each other—as opposed to your parallel but separate media universes (*SportsCenter, Mad Men*)—as possible.

What you need to do is shower—it will help wake you up—and put on something decent: maybe some nice lingerie for her, possibly some clean pajamas or a robe for him. Sex is enormously powerful and important, and it needs to be treated with respect. If you want to go for a round of lovemaking with fetid breath . . . well . . . we feel for your partner. Enthrone sex. Revere it. At the very least, take five minutes to prep for it—a quick shower, maybe something that smells good splashed on the body, some sexy evening wear. First you need to sit on top of your bed and talk to each other. At some point, one of you will stroke the other's arm or thigh. Soon, you will move in closer together, and you will kiss. And then you're doing it.

Just ninety minutes earlier, you thought sex was impossible. But you cleaned up for each other, and you talked. You got in the mood.

Now, you're swanning around in your post-sex high, and you're reading that great book, too.

Little Surprises

Your sex marathon should not be a code phrase for "costing us a fortune." That said, we do recommend small investments. There's that babysitter, if you have kids. There are those tennis lessons, that night of drinks and salsa dancing. But importantly, there also should be little presents.

A nice bouquet. A cool (but inexpensive) bracelet. An on-sale rugby shirt, a book you know he would love, a bottle of champagne.

During our own sexathon, we discovered that little surprises like this helped usher back into our lives the bubbly feeling of dating again. When you dated, you traded petite presents, you thrilled to the little surprises you could spring on each other—showing up at her door with the kind of wine she mentioned was her favorite, watching his eyes when he opens the envelope and out drops a pair of tickets to the movie he really wants to catch.

For many of us, the volume of these little surprises wanes and drifts until presents no longer are surprises, they are things to be delivered on birthdays, the holidays, and anniversaries.

Bring 'em back to the rest of your life! Just don't think you've got to go nuts with wallet-thinning. Keep it simple.

Gifts are physical manifestations of thoughts—when a smiling Annie hands me the book I mentioned I wanted to read, I understand immediately that she had been thinking about me; that she not only had remembered that I wanted the book, but went out and bought it and wrapped it and could not wait to hand it over and watch my reaction.

This does wonders for the heart.

The List

It was Annie's idea. One night she said, why don't we make lists of the things we love about each other, and read them aloud?

Sure, I replied.

On the appointed day, I sat down with a yellow legal pad and a pen and started dwelling upon the subject of Annie and her manifold endowments.

Her sense of humor. Her lust for adventure. Her warm body. And so on.

Meanwhile, Annie was composing a similar list about me.

We sat in our candlelit bedroom and began trading entries. Quickly, Annie's eyes filled with tears. The praise exchange didn't coax droplets down my cheeks, but it did warm my heart. By the end of the exercise, we were hugging, our limbs entangled. And then our lips met, and so on. I'm not suggesting the trading of the lists is something to pursue for the sake of sex, although in our case it did lead to lovemaking (of course, in our case, the lovemaking was a given). Instead, create this ceremony for the sake of your bond. The lists ended up being powerful documents; the reading of them, a potent occasion. We will keep making lists, every year or so, and reading them to each other in a candlelit bedroom. You should get started.

Division of Labor

She picks up the kids from day care. She makes their lunches. She makes dinner, does the dishes, and cleans the house.

She works as a corporate marketing executive, too.

This isn't fair.

For the sake of the sexathon, not to mention the health of the relationship in general, scenarios like this need to change. If you're wondering why she's not in the mood, maybe it's because she's charged with scrubbing the dishes while you watch *SportsCenter.* Or if the roles are flipped, maybe he's not feeling feisty because he has to put the kids to bed while you read *Vanity Fair.*

This is pretty basic: Make your relationship, rather than yourself, the center of your universe. If it's a problem, talk about it before the sexathon and establish guidelines for who will do what as you try to dispatch the day's unpleasantries and hardships and slide into sex's many pleasures. We're hoping that the new rules don't die the moment you stop having sex on a daily basis.

With both parties in the couple showering each other with respect and care, the march from housework to lovemaking is a little less arduous—you are sharing the work—and also less fraught with tensions and resentments.

You will launch your own sexathon and discover things that helped, activities that chipped away at the libido, day-to-day routines that got in the way of making love (and routes around those roadblocks). Every sexathon, of course, will be different.

Think of this guide as part of your planning stage. Pick and choose from our sprinklings of advice, take them all, ignore the whole thing and just get started—whatever. The important thing is your agreement to launch into your own sexathon.

Will it be successful? Whether you pull it off for five days or five weeks, it doesn't really matter, although we do think sexathons of a week or more have the best chance to deliver the most benefits. Either way, as far as we're concerned, you have succeeded merely by doing it with each other for a bunch of days in a row.

Acknowledgments

First, thanks Annie! Thank you for having the idea. Thank you for following through. Thank you for, you know, doing it, day after day after day. I can't thank you enough.

Thanks in advance, kids, for understanding why good ol' mommy and daddy not only did it for 101 consecutive days, but then wrote a book about it. You don't know about any of this now, but one day you will.

Thanks to our families for putting up with our . . . unusual . . . pursuit and its day-by-day account in this book.

The book would not have happened if not for my excellent agent Dan Lazar, to whom I owe much gratitude. The editors I worked with at Crown helped enormously, so thank you Allison McCabe, Lindsey Moore, and Suzanne O'Neill. Our friend Will Lippincott was a treasure.

Thank you to all of our far-flung (and nearby) friends and colleagues, most notably to one John C. Hill (Hellooo), who really is part of the family. Thank you, to our peeps in New Mexico and Florida, in Pennsylvania, New York (that includes you, Andrew the Esq.), and Michigan, in Maryland, Washington, D.C., Alaska, Hawaii, Colorado, South Carolina, Iowa, Nebraska, California, New Hampshire, Massachusetts, and more. Thanks for your ideas (you know who you are). Thanks for your e-mails. Thanks for just being our peeps.

In addition, thank you lube manufacturers (and thank you, Doc, for urging us to give the stuff a whirl!). Thanks, exercise-ball makers! Many thanks, pharmaceutical companies, for giving us Viagra, Levitra, and Cialis. To those who make sexy women's lingerie, including those thigh-high stockings, I salute you. I'm grateful to all of the companies out there that helped turn our bedroom into the "sex den": the incense people, the candle folks, those who sell "massage kits" (with feathers!) and nice-smelling stuff, including products that smell "musky." Beer—particularly, India Pale Ale—was instrumental in our success. I bless you Twisted Pine Brewing Company, Avery Brewing Company, Boulder Beer Company, Breckenridge Brewery, Great Divide Brewing Company, Flying Dog Brewery, and all of you hop-happy places I'm forgetting. Namaste, Billy and all of you yoga teachers who, unwittingly, made our quest a little easier. Finally, thank you WFMU. You rock.

Book Group Discussion Questions

for Just Do It

1. Do you think Annie and Doug had a decent marriage before they began? Do you think that their apparent "lack of sex" (three times a month) is typical for long-married couples?

2. In the book, Doug talks about his "performance anxiety." Do you think this is typical? Do you think women suffer from the same plight?

3. Annie sometimes talks about her body image. She said at one point that she thinks her "butt is too big," but Doug disagrees. Do you think men perceive women's bodies differently than women do? Why would that be? And, if so, why doesn't the message—that a few extra pounds just isn't a deal breaker for most men—get out there?

4. Annie and Doug planned for months before beginning the 101 days of sex. Do you think this was necessary or should it have been spontaneous? Adding to that, sex experts often tell couples that they have to "plan" for sex or make a date for sex. Do you think this takes away from the spontaneity?

5. Annie talked about the emotional intimacy that was created during the 101 days. Do you think it's possible to achieve the same without the Herculean effort of having sex for 101 days? And, for men, do you think emotional intimacy is really what they are after or is it just physical?

6. Pornography was one topic that not only was discussed, but also explored during the sexathon. Annie's verdict: She ultimately found it degrading to women, but could understand the appeal. What is your opinion of pornography? Do you think it can help or hurt a long-term relationship? And do you think pornography debases women and sex or do you think it can be healthy for all (from the actors to the viewers) involved?

7. Annie and Doug went to some extreme measures during the sexathon to achieve their goal (like hiring a babysitter so they could go on a hike and have sex on top of a mountain!). What are some suggestions you might have to achieve sex with your mate if you are battling lack of time, lack of desire, etc.?

8. Why do you think children impact a couple's sex life? Can couples get around the child-sponsored roadblocks to lovemaking? Do you think everyone is challenged by children? The author heard from couples around the world who told him they were in long-term relationships with children and manage to have sex every day. What do you think of this? Is this prevalent or just an anomaly?

9. There seems to be a constant drumbeat in the media that women try to avoid sex at all costs and that men are rabid animals wanting only sex at any cost. Can you comment on this—is this reality or fiction?

10. Annie holds that the sexiest word in the English language is "housecleaner." Is this true for you? If not, what would your word or phrase be? For example, "he even put away the laundry after he folded it." What would the sexiest word/phrase for a man be?

11. Doug and Annie discovered lube after eleven years of marriage. Annie reported later that she thought it was just for post-menopausal women or prostitutes. Do you think as a society we try to hide sexual aids from general consumption and conversation? What are your thoughts about the topic? Do you think Annie was just a little slow on the take and that—DUH?!—she should've known about the magic of lube a long time ago?

12. What about you? Do you think a similar experience would help your marriage? What about Doug and Annie's suggestion for not doing it 101 days, but just devoting a week or a long weekend to having sex every single day, no matter what?

About the Author

DOUGLAS BROWN is a feature writer at the
Denver Post.